Straight Talk on
INVESTING
What You Need to Know

Straight Talk on
INVESTING
What You Need to Know

Jack Brennan

with

Marta McCave

John Wiley & Sons, Inc.

For general information on our other products and services, or technical support, please contact our Customer Care Department within the United States at 800-762-2974, outside the United States at 317-572-3993 or fax 317-572-4002.

Wiley also publishes its books in a variety of electronic formats. Some content that appears in print may not be available in electronic books.

ISBN 0-471-26579-9

Printed in the United States of America

10 9 8 7 6 5 4 3 2 1

To Cathy and the kids. The best family anyone could ever ask for.
And to my dad, a straight talker who has been a continual inspiration to me.

The author's proceeds are being donated to charity.

CONTENTS

PART 3: Manage Your Investments with Focus and Discipline   133

Once you assemble a well-constructed portfolio, you don't have to spend every waking moment tending to it—in fact, you'll be better off if you don't.

PART 4: Stay on Course   173

A look at the things that can cause investors to come unglued.

PREFACE

The last five years have been extraordinary in the history of investing. We saw a record bull market swell into one of the biggest speculative bubbles in history. Then we saw the bursting of that bubble and the onset of a prolonged bear market, the worst one that the U.S. stock market has experienced since World War II. If many investors seem shaken and unsure of what to do, no wonder. Within half a decade, we have been presented with a lifetime's worth of lessons about investing.

Experience may be a good teacher, but it is also a hard one. Ironically, one of the reasons that investors have found the events of the last five years so confounding is the very abundance of financial information available to them today. An explosion of news reports, data, and analysis has developed in response to the enormous growth of interest in personal finance and investing over the last two decades. Bookstores are bursting with financial how-to books, and the media blanket the airwaves, the newsstands, and the Internet with coverage of the markets and investing topics.

Yet amid this profusion of information and advice, there has been little sensible, truly *useful* information stated in ways that ordinary people can understand. In fact, some of what passes for investment advice is downright *dangerous to your wealth*. And much more is simply irrelevant to "real people"—my term for the many millions who don't earn a living managing money. Nonetheless, far too many people remain glued to the TV day after day, following the ups and downs of the financial markets in the confused belief that they have to do so in order to manage their investments effectively.

Several times through the years, people who have heard me discuss successful investing for real people have suggested that I write a book. My answer had always been an emphatic *no* until recently, when I began to fully realize how much damage the information gap was causing. Then came a second catalyst for this book: the approach of a personal milestone, the completion of my twentieth year at Vanguard in July 2002. Anniversaries *do* have a tendency to make you reflective, and as I thought about how much our clients and my coworkers have taught me about investing in good markets and bad markets over two decades, I realized that perhaps those lessons should be shared.

In truth, the lessons of the past five years are not new ones. And therein lies the final impetus for this book: Having reached middle age, I am seeing my own children (as well as nephews and nieces and the kids I've coached in community sports programs) move into adulthood, and I know they can definitely use the sort of timeless, down-to-earth advice we share here.

So I decided to put my thoughts on paper. And rather than taking an academic approach, I decided to try creating something as close in tone as possible to the hundreds of investment discussions I've had with clients, coworkers, and friends over the past 20 years. This book is based on a series of conversations with my collaborator, Marta McCave, about topics that we think are very important for our readers to understand. I hope my experience and Marta's skill at fine-tuning my words make this an enjoyable read for you.

At root, this book is derived not from what I learned at Harvard Business School but from the wisdom of thousands of ordinary people who have successfully accomplished their own personal financial objectives, largely as do-it-yourself investors. Much of what I have to say may seem obvious, but it bears repeating today because of the barrage of "noise"—the chatter of contradictory opinions, information, and facts that focus almost exclusively on short-term events. Most of this noise will do nothing to help an individual accumulate wealth over the long run. Indeed, it too often has the opposite effect—prompting action that reduces the chance of success.

Make no mistake. Acquiring some basic knowledge about investing *is* very important for tens of millions of Americans. Not that long ago, investing in the stock market was something that only wealthy people did. But today, thanks to the democratization of Wall Street, anyone can be an investor. That's a great thing. More people should be investors, because sensible long-term investing is an effective way to achieve financial security. As a society we've removed many barriers that once kept the average person from investing—obstacles such as high costs, regulatory hurdles, and a lack of accessible information. And we've created wonderful incentives for long-term investors through changes in tax codes and retirement legislation. But the easy access to the markets has a downside, and it's that there are many more opportunities for individual investors to go astray.

So, what are the goals for this book? Only three.

First, it's intended to be the type of book that parents give their children when they strike out on their own. Like many of my contemporaries, I wish I had had such a book.

Second, I want this book to serve as a useful refresher about the basics of sound financial planning and prudent investing. No matter what one's age, sophistication or experience, a back-to-basics course is always helpful—particularly during difficult times, when conflicting advice typically abounds.

Finally, this book is aimed at helping people to think about their *serious money*—the dollars that they set aside for long-term goals such as retirement or the education of their children. Frankly, this book won't do much good for those who are seeking guidance about managing their household budget or tips on how to "play the market."

The fact is, making your wealth grow is not that difficult. It's really quite simple. I hope *Straight Talk on Investing* conveys that message of simplicity in a way that real people will easily understand and want to put into practice. In today's challenging market, that message is needed more than ever.

> *Jack Brennan*
> *Valley Forge, Pennsylvania*
> *July 31, 2002*

ACKNOWLEDGMENTS

Many people have had a hand in crafting this book. However, my first acknowledgment goes to the investors at Vanguard, with whom it has been my pleasure to be associated for 20 years. The knowledge and the experiences—good and bad—that clients have shared with me through the years have provided me with inspiration and many invaluable lessons. In turn, many of those lessons have served as the basis for *Straight Talk on Investing*. Real people invest their hard-earned money with Vanguard, and we take our responsibilities to those clients very seriously. If you are an investor with us, you are part of the Vanguard family. This book would not have happened without those family members' contributions.

A second acknowledgment goes to my two predecessors as chairmen of our funds, Jack Bogle and the late Walter Morgan. As a young man at Vanguard, I had the advantage of receiving a great tutorial on the history of the markets and our business from two giants of our industry. No question of mine was too naive; they (especially Jack) always took the time to teach. I'm ever grateful for the experience and knowledge they shared with me—valuable source material for this book.

Obviously, it takes an awful lot of assistance to turn a series of conversations into a full-fledged book. I previously mentioned my collaborator, Marta McCave, with whom I've worked closely for several years and without whom this book would not have been possible. Several members of our extraordinary team of writers and editors at Vanguard—particularly Craig Stock and Mary Lowe Kennedy—have been vital to ensuring that the content of this book is as clear and comprehensive as it could possibly be.

Numerous other members of the Vanguard team have provided assistance. Recognizing that I won't be able to name all of them, I mention a few here—Meg Shearer, Ker Moua, and Kimberlee Crater, along with Lynne Brady, Joan Carlson, Mike Hernan, Andy Clarke, Jeanene Boggs, Fran Kinniry, Colleen Jaconetti, and Matt Walker. I thank them for their hard work in the background to ensure that we produced a high-quality book that will provide good value to our readers.

Many Vanguard officers provided counsel and comments throughout this project. John Woerth, Tim Buckley, Bill McNabb, Jim Gately, Heidi Stam, Jeff Molitor, Kathy Gubanich, and Mike Miller, especially, gave their time and energy (and constructive feedback) to bring the project to completion.

Of course, none of this happens without a great support team: Gail Mellon and Vickie Leinhauser have helped Marta and me through every phase of this project to, again, turn conversations into a book. Their assistance is always valued, but never more so than on this project.

Finally, our editor at Wiley, Pamela van Giessen, has been a constant source of support to us as we took a concept to reality. I'm grateful for her efforts.

P.S. It's my view that successful investing represents a journey without a destination, in that the investor never "arrives" at a point where no more wisdom or knowledge can be attained. Although it's probably a bit odd to do so at the beginning of one's own book, I'd be remiss if I didn't offer a suggestion for next steps on your path to knowledge. Through the years, the two books that I have most often recommended to people who want to move beyond the basics of investing are *Winning the Loser's Game*, by Charles Ellis, and *A Random Walk Down Wall Street*, by Burton Malkiel. Both Charley and Burt serve as members of Vanguard's board of directors, and I can tell you that our investors benefit from their wisdom regularly. You can, too, if you would like to continue your intellectual journey.

Notes

In this book I use several examples from the Vanguard funds to illustrate principles of investing. I cite Vanguard funds in part because I know them better than any other funds, but mostly on the merits of the lessons provided by the data. One of the primary lessons I hope you'll get from this book is to never make investment decisions based on incomplete information, so if you become interested in one of the funds I mention (or in any other funds, for that matter!), consult the fund's current prospectus before taking any action.

We've relied on a number of data sources for this book, including Morningstar, Lipper Inc., Lehman Brothers, Standard & Poor's, Salomon Smith Barney, Frank Russell Company, Wilshire Associates, and Crandall, Pierce & Company. Our thanks to all of them.

S&P 500® is a trademark of The McGraw-Hill Companies, Inc.

PART ONE
Master the Basics

chapter one
SUCCESSFUL INVESTING IS EASIER THAN YOU THINK

Successful investing is not that difficult. It's just intimidating. Some people assume that you have to be rich or possess an important-sounding degree to accumulate wealth as an investor. They think you have to be able to understand all the topics covered in *The Wall Street Journal*—the ups and downs of the stock market, the interest-rate decisions of the Federal Reserve Board, corporate earnings announcements and dividend policies, economic indicators, and so forth. It's true that all of those things have meaning, but you don't have to follow them closely to invest well. Investing really is easier than most people think.

The purpose of this book is to give you the understanding you need to accomplish your financial goals through investing. Over the past 20 years, I've talked to tens of thousands of successful investors. They come from all backgrounds and all stages of life. Some are young; others are old. Some are experienced; others are beginners. Some have advanced degrees, while others never went to college.

Despite their differences, all the successful investors I've met share several traits, beginning with a very important one: They invest with confidence. Confident investors are people who make decisions based on their own personal financial situations, goals, and ability and willingness to take risks. They don't spend their lives haunted by the thought that somewhere out there is a get-rich scheme or investment gimmick that will lead them to a pot of gold.

The Environmental Forces Are with You

This is a great time in history to be an individual investor. There are a wide variety of investment vehicles, including thousands of mutual funds and thousands of individual securities. Educational material has never been more accessible, which means you'll have no trouble learning about the subject. If you have a computer, the Internet makes it easy to manage your investments at any time of day, no matter where you are. Finally, legislative changes have provided many attractive tax incentives for investors. Thanks to individual retirement accounts, 401(k) plans, and other tax-deferred savings vehicles, Americans get extra rewards when they put away money for their future.

Given all these factors, it's no wonder that millions of people have begun to invest for themselves in the last two decades. The explosion of awareness about investing among ordinary people is the most impressive thing I've witnessed in my 20 years in the business. The interest and knowledge are evident in the caliber of questions that Vanguard investors ask when they call our toll-free lines, in the letters I receive from shareholders, and in the questions people ask while making small talk with me at children's soccer games.

So today's environment offers great advantages—but investors must also steel themselves against two environmental challenges. The first one comes from the news media and all the others who make a living sharing their market wisdom with us. They all pay far too much attention to short-term events in the financial markets. In fact, news stories about the markets read a lot like the articles in the sports section. Who's ahead today? Who are the hot players with the golden touch? Who's going to have the best season? What's the best mutual fund this quarter? With so much excited commentary about every market move, it's no wonder that ordinary people sometimes feel intimidated or overwhelmed.

The second challenge comes from my own industry, sad to say. Remember, it's in the interest of many financial services companies to make you think that investing is difficult. They make money by selling investment products and advice. As you've no doubt noticed, there's no shortage of brokers, investment advisers, and financial planners eager to sign you on as a client and charge you for their services. There are financial professionals who want to make you think you can't make your own investment decisions. Don't believe them.

Your task is to recognize those environmental challenges and not to let them stop you from taking charge of your financial life. The reality is, you can succeed at accumulating wealth without spending every moment of your spare time trying to keep up with events. When you feel intimidated by the so-called experts, remember that they *don't necessarily know more than you do*. Indeed, we've all seen the headlines about financial hotshots who have lost millions and even billions of dollars through complicated trading schemes. What you don't see in the news are the countless stories of individual investors who are quietly and prudently amassing wealth through sensible and disciplined investment programs. They follow the four priorities of confident investors:

1. Do your homework.
2. Develop good habits.
3. Be skeptical of fads.
4. Keep learning about investing.

Do Your Homework

Building your confidence as an investor begins with developing some knowledge. Yes, you must be willing to put a little time into understanding the fundamentals of investing. But not much time! I'm talking about knowledge at a very basic level.

There's no need to read thick treatises on financial theory. You don't have to research any company's financial statements. You don't need to watch the nightly business news for the latest insights on why the markets did whatever they did, nor do you have to start each day knowing what happened in the Asian markets or in the Chicago futures pits in overnight trading. None of that is essential homework for individual investors.

But before you put your dollars anywhere, you do need some very fundamental knowledge. Right now I'm going to tell you *what* you need to know, but I will save the details for later.

You need to know a little about three different **kinds of investments**. You've heard of them: They are *stocks*, *bonds*, and *cash*. (*Cash* means not just money in your wallet, but ready stashes for it, like a bank savings account or a money market mutual fund.)

You need to know a little about some of the **places to invest**, including banks, mutual funds, and brokerage accounts. In this book, I'll focus on mutual funds because they are the best long-term investment vehicle for the bulk of your serious money.

You need to know **what risk means**. And here's a case where a lot of people think they already know all about it. But as we'll see, in investing the obvious risk isn't always the most dangerous one.

You need to know **yourself as an investor**. You can make all kinds of wise investments, with the very soundest long-term strategies, and still find yourself unable to sleep at night for worry when the markets are down. Life is too short for that! But there are many ways for you to invest at a level of risk you can live with, and I'll be discussing them later on in Chapter 11.

There Is No Free Lunch

The single question I've heard most from investors over the years is this one: "What should I invest in if I want to make a lot of money but I don't want to take a lot of risk?" There is no investment that fits that description. I always reply this way: "If you don't want to take risk, put your money in the bank. You cannot invest in the markets without taking on risk."

There is a risk/reward trade-off in every investment choice. If you want to reach for bigger returns, you must accept greater risks. Conversely, if you want to minimize your risk, you must plan for smaller returns. Think of it in terms of the old saying, "There is no free lunch." You must give up something to get something. What's important is to *understand* the risk you're taking on so you won't be surprised.

We're going to be discussing the risks of different types of investments, and I'll give you tips for checking out specific opportunities that come your way.

Develop Good Habits

The second key characteristic of successful investors is that they adopt good habits. You can start out with the very best investment plan possible and still end up disappointed if your own behavior undermines your plan. And the first, absolutely most important habit to develop is saving money. You simply cannot spend every penny you earn if you hope to accumulate wealth. The sooner you start saving, the better.

Because this topic is so important—and because saving money is difficult for so many people—I'm devoting Chapter 4 to it. In what follows in *this* chapter, we'll look at other good habits you'll need for managing your investments. But as you read them, keep in mind that your first priority is a disciplined saving program. Believe me—there is nothing that will put you on a sounder footing for success.

In managing your investments, what matters most is how much buying and selling you do. The choice is pretty simple: Either you are a buy-and-hold investor, or you are a trader. If you are a buy-and-hold investor, then once you have done your homework and set up an investment program, you just live your life. Yes, you'll want to monitor your investments on a regular basis, but you won't be inclined to make drastic changes unless something major happens to alter your circumstances, such as a marriage, a divorce, parenthood, or retirement.

Traders—even those who think they're being cautious—are risk takers. They believe they can turn quick profits or avoid big losses by pouncing on fleeting opportunities in the markets, buying and selling rapidly to stay just ahead of everybody else. So they pay a great deal of attention to deciding when to get into some investment and when to get out. They aim to invest when stock or bond prices are about to rise, and sell out when they think prices are about to fall. This approach is known as *market-timing*. Some people succeed at it in the short run, but it's extremely rare to hear of anyone winning at it over a period of years. Indeed, I've never heard of such a genius.

What makes the odds for market-timers so bad is something that few seem to think much about: the costs. You have to pay to trade, and then you have to pay taxes on any profit you make. Even if you are smart enough to beat the market, trading costs and taxes are likely to eat up your earnings over time. Many studies have shown that holding investments for the long term works far better than trying to time the market.

I'm a buy-and-hold investor myself, and so are all of the successful investors I know. I firmly believe that a buy-and-hold strategy is the best path to success. We'll come back to this topic later, but I want to be clear about my bias up front. Trading is really all about speculating, not investing. If you are a trader, this book isn't for you. Sell it to someone else—or better yet, set it aside. One day you will be ready to read it when you've found out for yourself that frequent trading doesn't work. Traders spend lots of time and effort on investments, but get back less than the buy-and-hold investor who simply goes about living life.

Another habit to cultivate is to resist keeping score too often. We're all susceptible to the temptation to check how our investments are doing at frequent intervals. Compulsive monitoring isn't worth the effort. *It doesn't matter* how your portfolio is doing from day to day or from week to week. Look at your balance every quarter if you must—once a year is often enough, in my view—but you shouldn't need to plan on more frequent checks. The danger in looking at your portfolio too often is that the short-term fluctuations will make you think that you have to take action when, in fact, almost always your best course is to sit tight.

We'll discuss other good investment habits later in this book, but these are the three most important ones:

- Save money.
- Be a buy-and-hold investor.
- Don't keep score too often.

Be Skeptical of Fads

Many businesses have an interest in getting you to make changes in your investment program—brokerages, fund firms seeking to get you to switch, gurus selling newsletters, books, and so on. If you are susceptible to the cold call from the stockbroker with a hot tip, pitches about the latest tax shelter, or the hype over last quarter's high-performing stock market sector, you can do a great deal of damage to your financial health.

I can't overemphasize the importance of avoiding fads. I've known many investors who have gone to great lengths to do their homework and learn what they need to do to be successful. And, sadly, I've seen a few who did all the right things for a time, only to turn around and make one major mistake. Fads can lead you into great errors, the kind that can wipe out gains achieved through years of patient investing. Successful investors understand that doing the right things is not the only key to success—you also have to avoid big mistakes.

The dot-com bubble is fresh in our minds today, but there are lots of examples. In the late 1960s and early 1970s, there was a lot of hoopla over the so-called *Nifty Fifty*—one-decision stocks that you could supposedly buy and safely hold forever. At the time, the 10 largest publicly traded U.S. companies were IBM, AT&T, General Motors, Eastman Kodak, Esso, Sears, Texaco, Xerox, General Electric, and Gulf. They were seen as one-decision stocks because they were world leaders with sustainable business advantages that seemingly would always dominate the market. I remember my parents giving me a single share of Eastman Kodak stock for my sixteenth birthday in July 1970 and telling me I would be able to hold it forever.

The Nifty Fifty fad lasted until the 1973–1974 bear market dragged the one-decision stocks down with all the rest. Today, only three of those former market titans rank among the largest-capitalization stocks in the United States. From July 1970 through 2001, 7 of the 10 companies underperformed the broad U.S. stock market. As for Kodak, it produced gains averaging 4.5% a year from 1970 to 2001. The diversified S&P 500 Index's return for that period averaged 12.8% a year, nearly three times more. The flaw in the Nifty Fifty fad lay in thinking that it was safe to pin all of one's hopes on any single stock or small group of stocks.

Keep Learning about Investing

Successful investors need to keep absorbing new information. This is just common sense. In any endeavor, whether it's parenting, a profession, or athletics, you must keep learning to stay up to speed. It's the same way with investing.

Your efforts don't need to be time-consuming. Devote a little bit of regular attention (or a regular bit of a little attention) to the markets and to your own investments. Look at the reports that you get on your investments. Pay periodic attention to magazines or local newspapers or national publications that cover business and investing news. I say periodic attention because it's misleading— and downright hazardous—to slavishly follow the movements of the markets or the fortunes of particular segments or companies on a daily, weekly, monthly, or even annual basis.

What you want to accomplish is threefold:

1. To deepen your understanding of what happens to your investments.
2. To protect yourself in case of developments that threaten your investments.
3. To keep abreast of new opportunities.

New investment opportunities will surface from time to time. You can distinguish the significant ones from the fads by taking a close look at the trade-offs. Should you be willing—as some investors were in the 1990s—to give up the diversification of a broadly based mutual fund in order to seek a higher return by sinking all of your money into one hot-performing stock? No way, and I'll explain why in Chapter 6. Should you be willing to give up the safety of a passbook savings account at the bank for a higher-yielding money market fund that invests in high-quality short-term commercial debt—as many investors have done in the last few decades? Sure.

Missing valuable new investment opportunities can hurt you—sometimes a little, sometimes a lot. The rise of money market instruments in the late 1970s is a perfect case in point. Money market funds revolutionized the financial industry because they offered market interest rates on very liquid high-quality securities. Investors who continued to keep their short-term savings in non-interest-bearing checking accounts after money market instruments became available missed an important opportunity to create more wealth for themselves.

Another example is index mutual funds, which weren't readily available to the public until 1976. Indexing is an investment strategy in which a fund seeks to mimic the behavior of a market index by holding all the securities in the index or a carefully chosen sample of them. That may sound less than exciting until you realize that index funds have a tremendous cost advantage that can mean greater profits for their investors. The trade-off is that, with an index fund, you will never "beat the market." It took decades for the news about index funds to sink in, but now millions of investors have realized that the *certainty* of keeping up with the market is a very worthwhile trade-off for the *possibility* of beating it. Investors who have ignored the opportunity to invest in index funds have done so to their detriment. We'll discuss indexing later in this book.

So there you have it. The four priorities of confident investors are: Do your homework, establish good habits, be skeptical about fads, and keep learning. By now, I hope you're thinking that this stuff isn't so difficult after all. Let's get on with the rest of the basics.

Basic Information

Every investor needs to know certain terms. Some of them are so basic that you're prob-ably already familiar with them. Others may *sound* familiar, but in the financial world they take on a different meaning than the one you're used to. We've tried to avoid using investment industry jargon in this book, but there will be some terminology that gives you pause.

I don't want to interrupt the text to explain things you may already know. But it's important to be sure that you get the information you need. So I'll include Basic Infor-mation sidebars like this one along the way to make sure the terms we're using are clear. If you're already familiar with the terms, just skip these sidebars. At the end of the book, I've also included "Some Industry Jargon," an explanation of investment terms that you're likely to hear from investment providers.

This Basic Information sidebar will be the most basic. For starters, you should un-derstand something about the risks and rewards of three fundamental asset classes—stocks, bonds, and cash investments. We'll discuss the asset classes in more detail further on in this book, but for now, an introduction is sufficient.

Asset Classes

Just to take care of this musty-sounding but essential term: An *asset*, as you know, is simply something of monetary value. In finance, the *asset classes* are types of invest-ments that offer different combinations of risks and rewards.

Stocks

Stocks represent ownership. If you own a share of General Motors stock, then you are a part-owner of General Motors. That gives you the right to vote on certain policy issues, and it means that you share in the company's business results. If the company does well, you can benefit in two ways: (1) The value of your stock rises, so you could sell it at a profit if you wanted to, and (2) the company may decide to pass along profits to you and the other owners in the form of a dividend. On the other hand, if the company does poorly, your stock can fall in value and dividends can cease to flow. In the worst case, the company could go bankrupt and leave your stock utterly worthless.

What makes a company do well or poorly? There are many variables. A company with prudent management, a sound business strategy, and high-quality products or services that steadily sell is likely to do well. But other, external forces will also affect a company's prospects. These forces include interest rates and other economic factors, new technologies, competition, government regulation and legislation, and customer preferences. In addition to all those pragmatic influences, a company's stock can rise or fall due to investor sentiment—which is as changeable and as difficult to forecast as the weather. Add to that the fact that even the smartest company managers can make mistakes, and you'll see why many people view stocks as the riskiest investment.

Stocks *are* risky. As traders constantly second-guess each other about market trends and all the rest, stock prices jump around from day to day and month to month. Over long periods, though, stocks as a group have rewarded investors more than any other investment. Since 1926, stocks have provided average annual returns of 10.7% a year.

A final note: Stocks are often called *equities*.

Bonds

A bond is essentially an IOU. When you buy a bond, you are lending your money to the issuer, typically a company or a government agency. The issuer is promising to pay you a stated amount of interest on the loan and to return the money at a certain time (the maturity date). When you buy a typical bond, you know in advance how much money you are going to receive in interest and when it is going to come; that's why bonds are called fixed income investments. (You'll often hear a bond's interest rate called the *coupon*— a term dating to when investors actually clipped coupons from paper bonds and presented them to get their interest.)

Though bondholders are creditors, rather than owners, they care about the soundness of the company or agency that issued the bond because that affects the prospects for payment. U.S. Treasury bonds are considered the safest investment in the world because they are backed by the full faith and credit of the United States government. Most established companies can be counted on to pay the interest on their bonds and repay the principal at maturity, no matter how their stock prices are faring.

Retirees who need a steady source of income tend to favor bond investments because of the periodic interest payments they provide. But you don't have to be a retiree to appreciate the stabilizing force that bonds can provide in an investment portfolio. As I'll explain later, many stock investors also hold bonds to help smooth out the inevitable fluctuations in the value of their overall investment portfolios.

But bonds do indeed have risks. The worst-case scenario is default: The bond issuer runs into trouble and can't pay you the promised interest or return your principal. Fortunately, defaults are relatively uncommon. A much more immediate risk involves bond prices. Existing bonds are constantly being traded on the market, and their value changes along with market interest rates. That's no problem for you if you don't need to sell your bond before its maturity date, but for those who do need to sell, the changing prices can result in losses. Also, if you invest in a bond mutual fund, your share price and the interest payments you receive will fluctuate along with the overall market and the fund's holdings.

Finally, there is the invisible risk of inflation. There have been periods when the interest paid on bonds did not keep up with rising prices, so that bond investors were steadily losing purchasing power.

Cash Investments

You may think of *cash* as the bills and change in your wallet, but it's something a little different in investing. Cash investments are very short-term IOUs issued by governments, corporations, banks, or other financial institutions. Money market mutual funds are one of the most popular forms of cash investments. Cash investments have been the least volatile of the three major asset classes historically, which means they are a safer choice than stocks or bonds if your biggest priority is not losing money. But they have also provided the lowest returns. Cash investments are said to have good *liquidity* because it's generally possible to withdraw one's cash immediately and without penalty, but their disadvantage is that they will provide a return that keeps you just about in line with or maybe slightly above inflation. While cash investments are a useful vehicle for emergency funds or money that will be needed just around the corner, they generally shouldn't serve as a large part of your long-term retirement account.

As you can see, there are trade-offs with each of the asset classes, so you'll always need to know what your objectives are before deciding how to invest. If you want to reach for the greater potential returns that are offered by stocks, you must be willing to accept their increased risk. If you want to opt for the greater safety of cash instruments, you must be willing to accept the lower returns they tend to provide.

In a Nutshell

You can invest successfully and confidently if you establish four priorities:

1. **Do your homework.** Develop an understanding of investment basics, such as the notion of the risk/reward trade-off.

2. **Develop good habits.** Become a disciplined saver. Be a buy-and-hold investor. Resist the temptation to keep score too often.

3. **Be skeptical of fads.** If you abandon good habits in order to embrace fads, you can wipe out the gains of many years of patient investing.

4. **Keep learning about investing.** Keep abreast of new opportunities and protect yourself from developments that threaten your investments.

chapter two
YOU'VE GOTTA HAVE TRUST

It all starts with trust. To succeed as an investor, you first must trust yourself to make sound decisions. Second, you must trust the economy and the financial markets to be your partners in building wealth over the long term. Third, you must trust in the power of compounding—the way that "money makes money." Finally, you must do business with firms that you can trust. I know you may be leery of any financial sermons about trust these days. The broad issue of investor confidence has never been more topical nor more visible than in the summer of 2002, as I write this book. Revelations about misdeeds at companies including Enron, Tyco, WorldCom, Global Crossing, Xerox, and Qwest have resulted in huge investor losses. All or nearly all of the stock market value of these once-admired companies was wiped away when the market learned that management had misled investors through deceptive or fraudulent financial statements.

Employees, investors, and the general public have all been injured in the devastation caused by these high-profile breaches of trust. Nevertheless, there is good news in these stories: They show that the system does work. Corporate managers who violate trust by misleading their investors or manipulating their financial statements *are* eventually caught and brought to justice. Moreover, the abuses that have come to light are already leading to improvements in corporate governance and regulatory systems that will support renewed trust in our market system.

That system probably will always experience shocks, but it remains fundamentally sound. The reality is that most companies and most corporate managers behave with ethics and integrity. The reality is that the markets ultimately reward honesty and punish untrustworthy behavior. Veteran investors understand those realities. They also recognize that the financial markets, our market structure, and our corporations are continually challenged in various ways—more severely sometimes than at others.

Yet another reality is that the act of investing is fundamentally a matter of trust. After the current corporate scandals have faded into history, this truth will remain. So let's now look at the role that trust should play in your thinking about investing.

Trust Yourself

Trusting yourself *sounds* easy, but it's hard for many people to believe they can trust their own judgment about investing. So I'm going to emphasize this point: Investing takes common sense and it takes self-knowledge, and you've got both of those already. Trust yourself to know your current financial situation, your future objectives, and your tolerance for risk better than anyone else. You know your own strengths and weaknesses: Is it going to be easy for you to develop disciplined savings habits, or will you need to find ways to motivate yourself to save? Will you be able to maintain a long-term focus, or will you be losing sleep every time the Dow has a down day? You'll want to tailor your investment program accordingly. You are the expert about you.

If you trust yourself, you'll be able to develop a little knowledge about investing and then make sound decisions based on factors that you thoroughly understand. As a result, you'll be less apt to second-guess yourself every time you see or hear something about a particular investment. You'll be better equipped to tune out misinformation and bad advice. You won't be swayed by ego and emotion. Having faith in yourself doesn't mean you'll never need expert advice. But if you should decide at some point that you do want help, you'll seek out a credible source instead of being vulnerable to a smooth-talking salesperson who cares little for your interests. (Think of it as being the hunter instead of the hunted.)

Suppose your brother-in-law brags about the killing he made on some obscure stock. It's human nature to grind your teeth and think, "Yeesh—if I were playing the market, I'd be a winner, too." But if you have faith in your own ability to make investment decisions, the envy will quickly pass. You'll know that your brother-in-law's investment decisions are not relevant to your life, because you have your own set of objectives and a road map for getting to them. Your risk tolerance and time horizon are unlikely to be the same as someone else's.

Having faith in your own ability to manage your financial affairs should make it easier to avoid the pitfalls that you'll encounter as an investor. I'll be discussing quite a few of those pitfalls in this book, but here are some obvious ones for a starter:

- **Don't pay attention to hot tips.** Whether the tip is from a friend or from a knowledgeable-sounding "insider" in an online chat room, be very leery. Your friend may know plenty, but who's to say he knows the whole story about that stock or mutual fund? If it's the online insider who has the tip, you have even more reason to be suspicious. There have been many cases in which unscrupulous people used online forums to deceive gullible investors and drive up the price of a worthless stock.

- **Don't take calls at dinnertime from salespeople pushing investments.** In the first place, you should *never* divulge personal financial information to a stranger who calls you, no matter what the reason. Also, if you think about it, anyone truly capable of picking winning investments would not need to get business by cold-calling strangers. I occasionally get these calls, and I sometimes ask the callers a basic investing question to test their knowledge. I have yet to find one who really knows much about investing.

- **Disregard sage-sounding aphorisms about the markets.** I mean sayings like "Buy on the dips" or "The trend is your friend." Buying during a market "dip" would be a splendid strategy if you could ever be sure it was really a brief dip and not a plunge in the making. As for the friendly trend, the idea is that if you find out about a rising stock or a hot industry, you should jump on the bandwagon. In fact, the trend is not your friend. By the time a market trend is noticeable at all, chances are that the bandwagon is already overloaded, the smart money has jumped out, and you're arriving just in time for the end of the parade.

You're sure to be faced with situations like these during your years as an investor. You won't be susceptible once you know that you truly can trust your own abilities.

Trust the Financial Markets

The second dimension of trust is having confidence that growth will occur in financial markets over time. A growing economy generally means more jobs, higher incomes, and increased opportunities for businesses to earn profits. And increased profits will ultimately raise stock prices, producing gains for investors. Personally, I do believe that the U.S. economy will continue to grow over the long run, as it has in the past. Although any economy will have ups and downs, the U.S. economy is the envy of the world because of its resilience and its ability to adapt and grow over the years. Over the long term, economic growth has averaged more than 3% a year, over and above inflation.

As shown in Figure 2.1, there have been many peaks and valleys in the growth of the stock market, but the general direction has been upward, as measured by

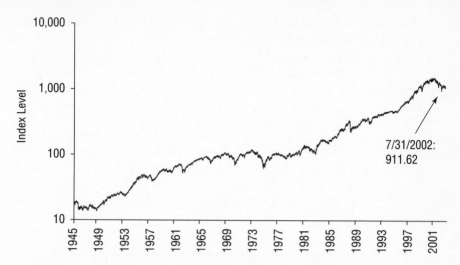

FIGURE 2.1   S&P 500 Index, Without Dividends Reinvested

the Standard & Poor's 500 Index. A $1 investment in the S&P 500 stocks on May 31, 1946, would have been worth $47.53 as of July 31, 2002, according to Crandall, Pierce & Company. If dividends had been reinvested, the $1 would have grown to $405.92. (The S&P 500 Index, which will be cited again and again in this book, is a benchmark for large-company stocks and is often used as a reasonable barometer for the overall stock market because its data go back to the 1920s. An even better benchmark for stocks is the Wilshire 5000 Total Market Index, which tracks every actively traded stock in the U.S. markets, but the Wilshire data date only to the 1970s.)

People tend to forget about that long-term trajectory when the market has one of its periodic downturns. Conversely, when the market spends a year or two doing notably better than its historical average, people tend to become euphoric and forget that a downturn is sure to come sometime. That's just human nature.

The historical trends suggest that you'll be rewarded if you invest in the stock market. But there is no guarantee, of course. You shouldn't put your money in stocks if you don't share the belief that the economy will continue to grow over the coming decades. Without growth in the products and services produced by our economy, there will not be good returns on stocks, and even corporate bonds will prove risky. Instead, put your money in the bank and collect a guaranteed return, or buy U.S. Treasury bills, the safest debt instrument in the world. Recognize that you'll have to be content with very modest returns that may not keep ahead of inflation. Remember the trade-off: Low-risk investments cannot be expected to reward you as well as riskier ones.

Trust in Time

If you believe that the economy will grow over the long term, time will be your greatest friend in accumulating wealth. That's because of the power of compounding. *Compounding* is what happens when you invest a sum of money and then reinvest the earnings instead of withdrawing them. Your nest egg grows much faster because those prudently reinvested interest payments, dividends, or capital gains are all generating further earnings. Compounding is the single most important force in the success of your investment program.

The longer you invest, the more astonishing the effects of compounding are. Consider the simple example shown in Figure 2.2: Suppose you invest $3,000 in a tax-deferred account at the start of each year for 10 years and then contribute nothing more. Next, suppose that the account earns 8% a year after expenses, and that you have all of your earnings reinvested in the account. After 25 years, you would have nearly $149,000, of which only $30,000 came from your pocket. And

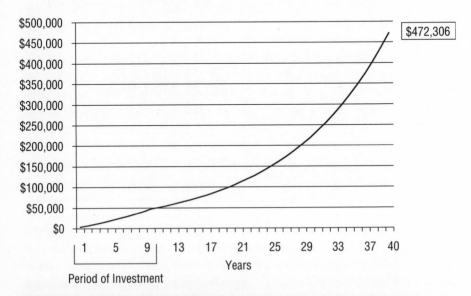

FIGURE 2.2   Growth of a Hypothetical $30,000 Investment over 40 Years

This chart assumes that a person invested $3,000 at the start of each year for 10 years and then contributed nothing more. Investment returns are assumed to be 8% a year after expenses.

after 40 years, that sum would have grown to more than $472,000. The power of compounding is absolutely amazing.

Here's a point that requires special emphasis. If you're going to make the most of the power of compounding, you must reinvest all the income and dividends that you earn on your investments instead of taking them in cash. You must also keep your hands off the money in your accounts. If you repeatedly dip into your long-term accounts to pay for living expenses or big splurges, your wealth won't grow as efficiently as it could otherwise. Like a cook who keeps sampling the food while it's cooking, you're apt to end up with a lot less in the pot than you planned.

Find a Financial Provider You Can Trust

For your safety and peace of mind, you need to establish relationships with financial services providers that you can trust. A trustworthy firm will serve you with integrity and help you accomplish your financial goals. And it won't push products and services that meet the company's quarterly marketing goals but do little for you. Fortunately, there are a number of good investment companies that provide sound products and services.

Picking a trustworthy provider is important to your success in more ways than one. If you do business with a firm that you trust, you will be better able to endure the misgivings that come when your portfolio has a bad year. Believe me, sooner or later, that will happen. It's one of the facts of life in investing. If you trust your investment provider, you'll realize that a stock or a mutual fund with a strong long-term track record is still a good investment even after it's had a bad year.

How can you be sure you are dealing with a firm that deserves to be trusted? There are several factors to look at, but it's not a bad idea to start by collecting referrals from friends or family members. Word-of-mouth is fine, if you trust the person giving you the recommendation and know that he or she has experience and good judgment. Although I warned earlier about believing stock tips from family members and friends, referrals are a different matter. If your sister, to whom you're willing to entrust your children if you die, says, "*I* trust this organization," that should carry a lot of weight with you.

The firm's own experience is an additional consideration. An institution that has been in the business for many years will have a track record for serving clients effectively through up and down markets. The three largest mutual fund companies have roots in the business that go back for 55 years or more. There are plenty of newer firms with talent and ambition, but they must overcome the formidable advantage of experience and credibility accumulated by established firms. It's very tough to earn marketplace acceptance in the absence of long-standing relationships with business partners and clients and a record of good service over the long term.

Experience also counts in the people who manage money. There's a reason that sophisticated institutions look for gray hair (figuratively speaking!) when they hire money managers. Those who have endured bad markets along with the good have the wisdom of experience. Some things simply are better learned by living through them than by reading about them in a textbook. The performance records of tenured money managers are much more meaningful than those of managers with limited experience. A young money manager with a good track record for four or five years isn't necessarily a great stock-picker; he or she may have simply floated up with a rising market. Even in a falling market, a money manager can look better than the competition—for a while—by sitting out the market and holding a lot of cash.

For these reasons, I always want to know how a money manager has performed relative to the competition over the full economic cycle—in bull markets and bear markets. An added advantage of experience is that it teaches humility: Money managers who have been through up and down cycles tend to avoid overconfidence and boastfulness and be cognizant of risks. Anyone who's been in the financial business awhile does not take lightly the unpredictability of the markets.

So experience is important—but don't let it be decisive by itself. Being the oldest doesn't make a firm the best one, nor should you rule out a young firm purely because of its limited experience. Experience is not a litmus test—it's just a factor to be weighed. Still, if you're thinking of dealing with a small organization that you know little about, it makes sense to seek references from others who have done business with the company.

Any trustworthy provider of financial services should be able to provide the following information upon request:

- A clear and complete explanation of the fees you'll be charged.
- A record of the company's past investment performance.
- An explanation of how the performance of your own investments will be reported to you.
- A clear understanding of how the company will respond to any questions you have.

These are the things that we ask about when seeking to hire an investment adviser for one of our mutual funds. Whether you're looking for a mutual fund company, a brokerage firm, or a financial planner, these questions are as relevant for you as they are for a big company like Vanguard. Do as much (or as little) checking as you feel comfortable with, but at the very least, make sure that you are dealing with a reputable firm and that you know what you'll be paying.

Once you've selected a trustworthy provider, stay alert for changes in the ownership or leadership of the firm. Rapid turnover of fund managers should trigger some concern. So should a change of tone in the provider's communications with you. If you ever have doubts about whether your company is being candid with you, it's time to switch. Firms deserve to have your money only as long as they deserve your trust.

Get in the Game

If you trust in yourself, in the markets, in time, and in your investment provider, you still have to do something else to accumulate investment wealth. You must invest. This seems obvious, but believe me, some would-be investors get stuck in the ready . . . aim . . . aim . . . aim . . . mode. They never "fire" because they are always waiting for the right moment to begin investing. They feel considerable envy of those who have invested successfully. But they never take steps to get in the game themselves.

There's a story about a man who prayed night after night, "Dear God, let me win the lottery." But the man despaired every evening when the winning numbers were announced and he was not a winner. This went on for many months until one night, as the man was praying for the hundredth time, the heavens opened up and a deep voice boomed: "Meet me halfway. Buy a ticket."

Trust should give you the courage to take the plunge, secure in the knowledge that you are investing with intelligence and discipline.

In a Nutshell

Your success as an investor is dependent on knowing whom to trust (and whom not to trust):

- **Trust yourself to make sound decisions.** Don't trust hot tips and sales pitches.
- **Trust the financial markets to be your partner in accumulating wealth.** Despite the short-term ups and downs of the stock market, the strength and resilience of the U.S. economy suggest that long-term investors will continue to be rewarded.
- **Trust in time.** Start early and put the power of compounding to work for you.
- **Find a financial provider you can trust.** A trustworthy provider will serve you with integrity and help you accomplish your financial goals.

chapter three
A MAP TO SUCCESS: HMMM, SOUNDS LIKE A PLAN

Yogi Berra once said, "You got to be very careful if you don't know where you're going, because you might not get there." Although Yogi-isms are overused, this one is right on target with respect to personal finance. Having a plan will help to make your financial life easier and, I hope, more gratifying.

Making a financial plan need not be complex. It is all about looking ahead and assessing where and when your needs for money will occur. Then you decide how you're going to meet those needs. It's essentially a three-step process:

1. Determine how much money you'll need to have.
2. Figure out which kinds of investments should provide you with the money.
3. Calculate how much you need to set aside in order to make those investments.

If you're like most people, you have more than one investment objective. For almost everyone, a secure retirement is the biggest goal in terms of the money needed. But other needs may be more immediately pressing: a down payment on a house, for example, or a child's college education. In addition, no matter what else our goals may be, we all need to have a plan for meeting rainy-day needs— the unexpected financial hurdles that life has a way of presenting.

In this chapter, I'll share some financial-planning tips based on lessons I learned through my own experience and that of the thousands of successful investors I've talked to over the years. We'll talk about how to manage both the asset side and the debt side of your personal balance sheet.

The Single Most Important Thing to Do

When people ask me how to go about setting up a financial plan, I usually offer them four words of advice: "Live below your means." It sounds so simple, but it is so powerful.

Living below your means is the ultimate financial strategy. Actually, it's more than that—it's advice for life. If you want to be able to invest and accumulate wealth to help yourself or others in the future, you simply cannot spend everything you earn. Becoming a saver—living beneath your means—is so critical to your financial success that we'll talk about it here and again in the next chapter. And we'll talk about some tools and techniques to help you do it.

Effective saving isn't just tucking away as much money as you can—it's also knowing where to put that money so that it will earn a reasonable rate of return and be there when you need it.

You will see the logic of this if you think of your personal financial situation as what accountants call an *income statement*. In business, that's a summary of how much profit (or loss) a company had during a certain period of time. For you, it's the same thing. Your personal income statement would list your *revenues*— your pay, plus any investment income or gifts you receive—and then subtract your *costs*. The costs would include your fixed expenses (taxes, mortgage, insurance premiums, car payments, and the like) and your variable expenses (food, clothing, entertainment, and other discretionary items). If there is money left over after expenses are subtracted from revenues, that is your *net profit*, which is available to invest. If you have no net profit, and in fact are borrowing to maintain your lifestyle, you are operating at a loss.

Living below your means is tough in a materialistic culture where advertisements constantly play with our egos and television provides endless images of "the good life." But the unsung benefits of being a saver are priceless. You'll have enviable peace of mind, because you won't have to worry about making ends meet. You won't feel wistful about your goals, because you'll know you're traveling steadily toward them. And you'll know that, if need be, you're in position to withstand unexpected expenses. Let's face it: Unexpected financial needs occur in everyone's lifetime. People get laid off from their jobs, they incur extraordinary medical expenses, or they need to help family members financially. If you're a saver following a plan, you can weather those challenges far better than people who spend every penny they earn.

But what about the "good life"? Don't savers miss out? No, they don't—they simply gain control. Living the good life isn't just about material possessions. It's also about having financial flexibility; about widening your options, about having things to look forward to, and about having the means to help others. Accumulating capital is the reward if you choose saving in the saving/spending trade-off.

If you are earning money, the most fundamental financial planning question is this: Are you going to spend it all on current needs and wants, or will you set your living standards below what you can afford so you can save some of what you earn? Even if you can afford many things, the reality is that you cannot afford *all* of them. Before you decide how you'll spend your paycheck, decide how much you want to be setting aside for saving and investing.

Two additional thoughts on saving:

1. It's never too late to become disciplined about saving, but the sooner you develop the saving habit, the easier it will be to achieve your goals.

2. It's a good idea to reevaluate your savings habits from time to time, particularly when going through major transitions in life.

Think of Your Financial Needs as Imaginary Buckets

One of the most useful concepts in financial planning is to think of your financial needs as "buckets" to be filled with the money you earn. The idea is to discover how your savings need to be divided among the buckets, and then be very disciplined about putting them there. These are some buckets typical of most people:

- **Current expenses.** This is what you live on—the money you use for your mortgage or rent payments, food, clothing, car payments, and other essentials.

- **Emergency fund.** Experts recommend that you have six months' worth of take-home pay available to meet unexpected difficulties, such as a short-term layoff from your job.

- **College.** The cost of a college education keeps climbing, and though you can take out loans, you'll come out ahead if you can pay for as much of it as possible out of savings.

- **Retirement.** Many Americans today spend a quarter-century or more in retirement. Don't count on Social Security payments as your sole support for all those years. Most people will need to draw on their own savings to survive comfortably while they continue to pay for taxes, medical insurance, and all the rest.

- **Other goals.** Add as many buckets as you want for other savings needs, like replacing your car, buying a second home, taking care of elderly parents, or anything else you deem truly necessary.

A note on those "other goals": Without getting too preachy, I want to encourage you to include charitable giving somewhere in your financial plan. In my view, anyone who has accumulated money to invest should be willing to give

something back to society. You don't have to be a multimillionaire to support your church or synagogue, your college, or other organizations that serve your community and the wider world. Even small contributions can make a difference when they are combined with those of other givers. And they will make a difference in your own life, too. As my wife and I have increased our giving over the years, we've found it deeply satisfying to be supporting programs that help others.

Once you have designated targets for each of the buckets in your financial plan, you need to think about where you will keep the money. The idea is, first, to get a return on each bucket of money, and, second, to seek the greatest return possible within the dictates of your time horizon and risk tolerance. Because of the varying issues in each situation, different buckets will call for different approaches.

Short-Term Needs

You need immediate access to the money that's needed to meet current expenses, so you would eliminate investment vehicles like stocks and long-term bonds from consideration. A rule of thumb in investing is that you should not invest money in stocks or stock funds that you will need in less than five years. Most people use a checking account for the money that's needed to meet current expenses. That's typically an account that pays little or no interest, so the trade-off for the convenience of the account is that you are earning little or no return.

Your rainy-day fund is a slightly different issue. Since this is money that you don't plan to touch except in an emergency, leaving it sitting in an interest-free bank account makes no sense whatsoever. A better choice would be to invest it in money market funds or short-term CDs, which offer some return while still being relatively liquid, or readily available, should an emergency arise. Such a choice will permit you to make your money work as hard for you as possible. If interest rates are low, you might wonder what's the fuss over a return of 2 or 3 percent. But ask yourself a simple question: Would you rather have the 2 or 3 percent in your pocket, or let the bank have it? Small amounts of interest eventually add up to impressive sums. Suppose you put $10,000 in a savings account that pays 3% a year, and it sits there untouched for 20 years. It will turn into more than $18,000.

Saving for College

You'll face a different set of considerations with mid-term financial goals. College is one of the most interesting investment planning issues because of the special considerations involved. We can all hope that our children will receive full scholarships, but realistically most of us need to plan on paying for college either out of savings or with loans. And it makes more financial sense to be able to pay for it out of savings than for either you or your child to take on a lot of debt. Start saving early, and time can help you foot the bill. College will be a more manageable expense if you finance it with savings that have compounded over the years (particularly if they compounded in a tax-free account) than if you take on debt and pay off the loans and the interest with out-of-pocket money. When you save, compounding works for you. When you borrow, it works for the lender.

Your college-savings bucket will require more active monitoring and management than the others for two reasons. First, you can already figure out when you're going to need the money and roughly how much you may need. If your child is 5, it's reasonable to assume that college bills will start arriving in 13 or 14 years. You can look at tuition data now and forecast what your costs could be for a private or public college. Tuition data are available from a number of sources, including the College Board's website at www.collegeboard.com. Given this information, you'll want to keep an eye on your college-savings bucket as time goes by to make sure it is moving you toward your goal.

The second reason for actively monitoring your progress in saving for college is the relatively short time frame. Suppose you begin saving on the day your child is born. You'll probably want to start out with stock investments because they are likely to offer more growth. But that growth includes a lot of ups and downs—and you don't want to have to cash out during a down period. So, as your child enters her teens and college approaches, you'll shift into more conservative investments that emphasize preservation of capital.

College-Savings Vehicles

There are a variety of ways to save for college, and the investment vehicle that's best for friends or relatives may not be the best one for you. The trade-offs involve costs, investment choices, and the impact that the plans have on eligibility for financial aid. Here is a look at the most popular ways to save for college.

- **529 College Savings Plans** are a relatively new tax-exempt means of accumulating money to pay for college or graduate school. These plans, named for a section of the tax code, are usually sponsored by states. The earnings of 529 accounts are exempt from federal income and capital gains taxes so long as the money goes for qualified college expenses. Most states give their own residents a special tax break in their plans, but out-of-staters generally can contribute as well. And there are no income limits to be eligible to use the plans. The main drawbacks of 529 plans are a lack of investment flexibility, and, in some cases, high costs. The sponsoring state selects the investment manager and investment options—you just work with what's there. In addition, some 529 plans layer steep administrative fees on top of the fees charged by the underlying mutual funds. Before investing, it pays to comparison shop. The effect of 529 College Savings Plan assets on eligibility for financial aid depends on who the owner of the account is. A 529 account held in a parent's name will cut into financial-aid eligibility far less than will an account held in the student's name.

- **Education Savings Accounts** (ESAs; formerly known as Education IRAs) are another tax-exempt investment vehicle. You can contribute up to $2,000 a year on behalf of a beneficiary under age 18, assuming that you meet income limits. The funds can be withdrawn tax-free to pay for qualified educational expenses at primary schools, secondary schools, colleges, and universities. With ESAs, the main drawback is the low maximum contribution. An ESA alone may not enable you to save enough to cover four years of college. In addition, assets in an ESA count heavily against a child's eligibility for financial aid. In college financial-aid calculations, ESA assets are considered to be the student's property—so financial-aid providers will expect that up to 25% (for college aid) or 35% (for federal aid) of the ESA's value will be spent for college each year.

- **UGMA** and **UTMA accounts** are custodial accounts for children established under the Uniform Gifts to Minors Act or Uniform Transfers to Minors Act (hence the ugly acronyms). These accounts have been around for a long time. They offer fewer tax benefits than the other savings programs. Also, when the beneficiary reaches the age of majority, he or she takes control of the assets—whether to pay for college or become a surfer. That said, these accounts allow you to invest as much as you like, where and how you wish. For children under 14, the first $750 of annual investment income is tax-free; the next $750 is taxed at the child's tax rate; income above $1,500 is taxed at the parents' rate. All income for children 14 or older is taxed at the child's rate. In college financial-aid calculations, UGMA/UTMA accounts are considered the property of the student, so aid providers will expect up to 25% (for college aid) or 35% (for federal aid) of the assets to be used for college each year.

Saving for Retirement

Personal finance experts have a rough rule of thumb about how much retirement money you'll need. It states that to live comfortably, you'll need annual income that's at least 70% to 80% of what you were earning just before you retired. This money will have to come from a combination of Social Security, any pensions you have, and personal investments.

People often underestimate how much they'll need in retirement savings. The retirement phase of your life could last decades, and although your investments will continue to produce returns during that time, you are likely to be drawing down your principal at the same time. Suppose, for example, that you plan to draw on your retirement savings for 30 years and that you expect to take a little more out each year so that your spending can keep up with inflation. To be able to ride out periods when the financial markets turn sour or inflation runs high, you probably should not spend more than 4% (5% tops!) of your retirement savings in the first year. A little math shows that you'll need an initial nest egg of $200,000 to $250,000 if you want to be able to spend $10,000 in the first year, and to increase that amount by the rate of inflation in the ensuing years.

Fortunately, there are many ways to accumulate a nest egg for retirement. And today's savers have some advantages their great-grandparents would have envied. Employer retirement plans and individual retirement accounts (IRAs) shelter your investment earnings from current taxes, which makes it much easier to accumulate wealth. With a company retirement plan, your employer might even add to the savings you put in, in effect giving you a pay raise to be enjoyed later in life. The most common ones are 401(k) plans, 403(b)(7) plans, and 457 plans, which are named for sections of the tax code that established them. You can also invest for your retirement by setting up an IRA with an investment provider, in addition to participating in an employer's plan.

Your retirement-savings bucket might be the biggest bucket you need to fill, but it is the easiest of the buckets to manage, as long as you get an early enough start. If you start young enough, building a retirement nest egg is more a matter of saving than investing. Compounding will be a bigger factor in your success than your investment choices.

Here's a piece of advice: If you have a 401(k) or other retirement plan at work that lets you have savings automatically withheld from your paycheck, go for it.

Contribute as much as the plan allows. If you can't make the maximum contribution, at least contribute enough to receive the full matching amount that your employer contributes, assuming that your employer offers a match. Then, make it your goal to get to the maximum contribution as quickly as you can. One of my colleagues used this strategy successfully: When she began working at Vanguard 15 years ago, she contributed to the 401(k) just enough to receive the company's matching contribution. Then, she gradually increased her savings rate by funneling half of every annual raise into her 401(k) until she reached the maximum allowable contribution level. By continuing to pump money into her retirement plan at that level, my colleague has accumulated an impressive sum of money in 15 years.

There are two great advantages to saving through an employer plan. One, your contributions will accumulate on a tax-deferred basis until you withdraw your money. Two, the process keeps you saving without any effort of your own. You don't have to make yourself write any checks, and you won't be tempted to spend the money before "paying yourself" first.

Plenty of ordinary people are saving an unbelievable amount of money through employer-sponsored retirement plans. In the 401(k) plans managed by Vanguard, we have more than 4,000 individuals who have already become millionaires. And thousands of other ordinary people are on the way to amassing extraordinary wealth. One of most impressive plans we manage is sponsored by an oil company. It has average account balances among the highest we've ever seen in a 401(k) plan. Many of the participants are rig workers who live in modest homes in working-class communities. But making the maximum contributions to their company's savings plan is paying off for them in big ways. They're looking forward to enjoyable, comfortable retirements.

You can also contribute up to $3,000 a year ($4,000 a year, beginning in 2005) to a traditional IRA, a Roth IRA, or a combination of the two. Both types of IRA provide significant tax benefits that are well worth checking out. For most people, though, the Roth IRA is the better bet because of the tax-free withdrawals at the end.

- Traditional IRAs let you invest on a tax-deferred basis. Depending on your income, you may be able to deduct some or all of your contribution from your current income taxes. Once you start taking withdrawals, they are taxed as regular income.

- Roth IRA contributions are never deductible—but your withdrawals in retirement will be completely tax-free.

Both kinds of account come with a set of rules, and you can lose money if you break the rules—by withdrawing money too early, for example.

Your Debt Plan

So far, I've been discussing how to manage the assets on your personal balance sheet. Now let's think about liabilities—the debts you owe in the form of credit-card bills, car payments, mortgage debt, and so on. Part of developing a financial plan includes developing a philosophy on debt. My philosophy can be summed up with that old proverb: "Loans and debts make worry and frets."

I've long had a strong aversion to debt. My wife and I started married life with big graduate school loans. I hated writing those loan payment checks every month throughout the 1980s, especially because of the relatively high interest rates that existed at the time. Because of that experience, my wife and I resolved to avoid debt whenever possible. Not everyone feels as strongly about debt as I do, but even if you don't, you should give serious consideration to several debt issues.

In managing debt, here's a rule of thumb I recommend: Try to borrow only for long-lived assets. An education serves you throughout your life, so college loans are okay. A home will last a long time, so mortgage loans are sensible (though watch out for home-equity loans and other second-mortgage borrowing). And cars also are long-lived assets, so car loans make sense if the length of the loan is less than the length of time you expect to own the car. But borrowing for consumables—clothes, dining out, groceries, entertainment, and travel—can land you in debt trouble and is likely to get in the way of investment goals.

Indebtedness is both an economic issue and a peace-of-mind issue, so here are some other important debt considerations to weigh.

1. Are You Mortgaged to the Hilt?

For most people, the single biggest debt obligation is a mortgage. The question here is not *whether* to have a mortgage—few people could buy a house without one—but how to minimize the weight of that debt. Lots of people view their home as their biggest investment, hoping that it will appreciate in value and help to finance their retirement.

But the debt issues of home ownership sometimes get overlooked. Taking out a big mortgage in order to buy an expensive house could create a debt burden that you'll regret later.

You can measure your mortgage burden by calculating your *loan-to-value ratio*. Think of the loan-to-value ratio as the percentage of your house that belongs to the mortgage company instead of to you. Suppose that at age 30 you buy a $250,000 home. You make a $25,000 down payment and take out a 30-year mortgage for $225,000. Your loan-to-value ratio is 225/250, or 90%, because you've paid for only 10% of the house's value. As you make payments over the years, you will steadily build up equity in your home, and your loan-to-value ratio will decline. If your home also grows in value over the years, the ratio will shrink faster. Suppose you still own that house when you're 50, and you still owe $125,247 on the mortgage, but the house is now worth $350,000. Your loan-to-value ratio is just 36%.

Most homeowners don't worry much about their mortgage debt because they count on the house continuing to rise in value. (That may or may not occur!) If you are in a high-risk profession, subject to industry downturns and periodic lay-offs, it is sensible to avoid a heavy mortgage burden, because you don't want the fixed cost of a big monthly mortgage payment if you are out of work for a time. But if you have some reasonable level of job security—for instance, if you are a tenured university professor—you may not be overly concerned about the size of your mortgage. The point is that you should think about your personal situation before taking on a mortgage or other major debt.

2. Are You Carrying Credit Card Debt?

If you have credit card debt, you should pay it off before you begin investing. Some people think it makes sense to start investing even though they are carrying balances on their credit cards. They hope to come out ahead by earning returns on their investment that exceed the interest they are paying on their debt. But you'll see the danger in this approach if you think about it.

Most credit cards charge interest rates of 15% to 18% or higher. To earn more than that as an investor, you'd have to be investing in stocks, and you'd have to be picking investments that beat the average annual gains of 9% to 11% that stocks have earned over the long run. The odds of that aren't very good.

There's an additional danger in thinking that you can get ahead as an investor in spite of credit card debt. When you do this, you are hoping that the short-term returns on your investment—a big uncertainty—will offset debt payments that are a certainty. No matter what the market does, you will still have to make those credit card payments.

I can think of just one situation in which it would make sense to start investing before you have paid off credit debt. If your employer matches contributions to your 401(k) plan, you should get started in the plan right away, while of course paying down your debts as soon as possible.

3. Are You Investing with Borrowed Money?

For the same reason that credit card debt and investing don't go well together, it's never wise to invest with borrowed money. It's a certainty that you'll have to repay the money you borrowed. It's never certain that you'll receive the investment returns you're hoping to receive.

In the day-trading frenzy of the 1990s, many investors began buying stocks with borrowed money. The practice, which is called *buying on margin*, is very risky because it magnifies the impact of gains and losses. If the margin investor's holdings suddenly drop in value, he is often forced to sell the stocks that serve as collateral to pay off the loans immediately.

Here's what happened to one experienced investor who should have known better. According to news accounts, the man bought blocks of Internet company stocks on margin, using his holdings in his own company's stock as collateral. Unfortunately, in late 2000, his company's stock tumbled from a split-adjusted high of $98 to below $5, and he was forced to sell most of his holdings—once worth $1 billion on paper—at a depressed price to make good on his margin loan. It's a tragic tale.

The following example illustrates the risk of margin investing. Suppose two investors invest $20,000 in the same security. One investor purchases the stock on margin, putting up $10,000 cash and borrowing $10,000 from a broker. The other investor pays the entire $20,000 in cash up front. As shown in Table 3.1, the potential for loss is as significant as the potential for gain. Don't let the hope of big gains tempt you to invest on margin unless you are prepared to accept the risk of great loss.

TABLE 3.1   You Can Win Big—or Lose Big—by Investing with Borrowed Money

Two investors buy the same stock . . .

	Margin investor	*Cash investor*
Purchase price	$20,000	$20,000
Investor's cash outlay	$10,000	$20,000
Margin loan from broker	$10,000	$0

If the stock rises, the margin investor enjoys a higher percentage gain . . .

	Margin investor	*Cash investor*
Sale proceeds	$25,000 ($5,000 gain)	$25,000 ($5,000 gain)
Investment return*	+50%	+25%
	($5,000 received on a $10,000 cash outlay)	($5,000 received on a $20,000 cash outlay)

If the stock drops, the margin investor sustains a greater percentage loss . . .

	Margin investor	*Cash investor*
Sale proceeds	$15,000 ($5,000 loss)	$15,000 ($5,000 loss)
Investment return*	–50%	–25%
	($5,000 lost on $10,000 cash outlay)	($5,000 lost on $20,000 cash outlay)

*Investment return does not take into account any fees, commissions, or interest charges paid by the investors.

4. Are You Counting Your Chickens Before They Hatch?

Suppose you've watched the property values climb in your neighborhood, and you're considering refinancing your mortgage to take advantage of that appreciation and get some extra cash. Or perhaps you've accumulated a tidy nest egg in your 401(k) account and now would like to borrow on it. Be very careful.

It's true that sometimes these decisions make good financial sense. But keep in mind that borrowing against your house or against your 401(k) carries a risk. The appreciation in a house or a 401(k) is just a paper gain, not money in your pocket. You won't have real money in your pocket until you sell the house or redeem your 401(k) investments. The risk is that property values or the financial markets will fall, and you'll be left owing money. If you have the misfortune to be laid off from your job, and you have borrowed against your 401(k), you will have to keep repaying the loan or face added taxes and penalties.

Know What You Don't Know

The final point about planning is this: Know what you don't know. Yes, there is much that you can do on your own in setting up a financial plan and beginning an investment program, but it's also important to have some humility about other elements of your financial needs. I'll just make a few comments here because so much depends on your personal situation.

Insurance planning is one area in which professional advice is often worth the money, depending on the variables in your personal life. The same is true of estate planning. Unless you're an estate attorney, you don't know how to write a will. Although there are books that purport to show nonlawyers how to write their own wills, I think that anyone who expects to accumulate significant wealth should be willing to spend the money to make sure his or her will is done properly.

In a Nutshell

Developing a financial plan is a three-step process:

1. **Set a goal.** Determine how much money you'll need for your financial objectives.
2. **Assess your investment options.** Figure out which kinds of investments are appropriate.
3. **Determine how much money you'll need to invest.** Calculate how much money you need to set aside in order to reach your goals.

As you develop a plan to accumulate wealth, remember that managing debt wisely is also key to your success.

chapter four

SAVE MORE—WITHOUT FEELING THE PINCH

My father was a banker, and he taught me about the importance of saving money early on. As a boy, I contributed some of my lunch money to a savings program at school, and when I earned a few dollars here and there by doing chores, I put that money into the bank, where it earned interest. This was my viewpoint on the discipline of saving when I entered the investment-management business in 1982.

I soon had a great revelation. One day, an older acquaintance who had a sizable account at Vanguard called to ask for help with a transaction. He wanted to move some money from his daughter's account to the bank so she could buy a home. When I looked up her account, I was dumbfounded to see that this woman who was my age—under 30—had a six-figure balance. When I commented on it, her father explained matter-of-factly that he'd been investing $50 a month on her behalf in one of Vanguard's stock funds ever since she was born.

It was amazing to see how a modest amount of money, invested with discipline and in an effective vehicle, could grow to such a large sum in less than 30 years. It was a powerful, tangible manifestation of the rewards for disciplined saving and investing. I tell this story regularly to young people who are just beginning their careers or starting families, in hopes that it will inspire them as it did me.

In this chapter, I'll discuss how to transform yourself into a disciplined saver and how to make intelligent, focused decisions on where to invest your savings.

Developing the Discipline of Saving

The authors of the 1996 book *The Millionaire Next Door* conducted a study of wealthy Americans and found that frugality was the most common per-

sonality trait among them. Authors Thomas J. Stanley and William D. Danko wrote:

> How do you become wealthy? . . . It is seldom luck or inheritance or advanced degrees or even intelligence that enables people to amass fortunes. Wealth is more often the result of a lifestyle of hard work, perseverance, planning, and most of all, self-discipline.[1]

At Vanguard, we've noticed that people from all occupations are represented among the Flagship clients who have $1 million or more invested with us. In addition to the highly paid celebrities, business executives, and professionals you'd expect to find in such a group, our millionaire investors include many people of modest income, such as teachers, office workers, oil rig workers, telephone line repair people. Quite simply, they have been very disciplined savers and investors.

You're likely to earn an impressive amount of money in your lifetime, and you don't have to be an NBA star to do it. Just for example: Over a 45-year career, an annual income of $50,000 amounts to something like $2.25 million. The thought of earning more than $2 million and spending every cent of it seems monumentally wasteful, doesn't it? True, much of that sum will be eaten up by taxes and

---

[1]Thomas J. Stanley and William D. Danko, *The Millionaire Next Door: The Surprising Secrets of America's Wealthy* (Atlanta: Longstreet Press, 1996), pp. 1–2.

bills, but there will be plenty left for you to spend or save. With a plan for saving, you can keep your hands on a good chunk of that $2-million-plus you earned. And if you invest that chunk, with time you can turn it into much more.

Most people feel a strong temptation to spend any money that's in their pockets. To defeat that urge, try not to let it get into your pocket—save it before you see it. If your employer has a retirement savings plan, sign up as soon as you can. Have the money subtracted from your paycheck—then you won't even notice that you're saving it. Do this with the "extras," too: If you inherit some money, or you get a raise, or the government sends you a tax refund, add at least some of the cash to your nest egg. If you really want to accumulate wealth, live by this aphorism: "When in doubt, save it."

A friend of mine whose firm is one of Vanguard's large corporate clients puts this idea very well. He says, "When I'm talking to our employees about the importance of saving and investing, I urge them to think of themselves as 'Personal Financial Entrepreneurs.' We're all Personal Financial Entrepreneurs, running our own financial operations, first in our working years and later in retirement."

Need help developing good savings habits? If so, you'll want to take advantage of programs that force you to save. Automatic investment programs allow you to funnel a portion of every paycheck into your investment account or make regular transfers from your bank account. They are a great boon because they offer a painless, systematic way to invest. I have always relied on the convenience of payroll deductions; money from my paycheck goes right into my investment accounts.

Tax-deferred vehicles offer additional incentives to save, along with penalties for taking the money out prematurely. With 401(k) plans and other employer-sponsored retirement plans, your contributions come out of your pay before taxes are taken out. The power of the tax break is astounding, as shown in Figure 4.1. Over 45 years, a $3,000 annual contribution to a Roth IRA earning an average annual return of 8% becomes more than $1.2 million. Contributing the same amount to a taxable account would get you just $894,945 after 45 years, assuming that half of the 8% annual investment earnings would be subject to tax each year at a 27% rate.

The disincentives for pulling money out of tax-deferred or tax-free accounts are also valuable. If you invest money in an IRA or a 401(k) or a 529 plan, there are generally penalties for making premature withdrawals except in special circumstances. It sounds crazy to think that grownups need to have a lock on their piggy banks, but the fact of the matter is that most of us do.

The Magic of Dollar-Cost Averaging

There's another advantage to automatic investment programs. When you invest a set amount in the markets on a regular basis, you are using a strategy known

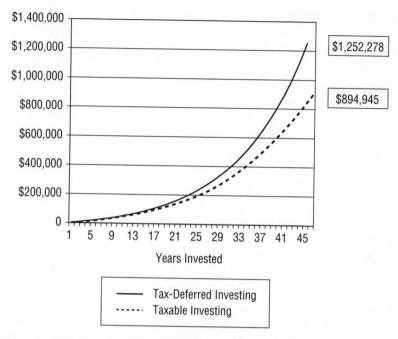

FIGURE 4.1 Tax-Deferred versus Taxable Investing of $3,000 a Year

This chart compares the final values of two hypothetical accounts, one tax-free Roth IRA and one taxable. In both accounts, the investors contributed $3,000 annually for 45 years and earned annual returns of 8% after expenses. One-half of the earnings of the taxable account were taxed annually at 27% before reinvestment.

as *dollar-cost averaging*. This has two great advantages: (1) It takes the emotion out of investing because you don't spend time agonizing over the "right" moment to act, and (2) because the amount you invest is fixed, you buy more stock shares or mutual fund shares when the price is lower and fewer when the price is high.

To reap the advantages of dollar-cost averaging, you must make regular purchases through thick and thin. It's easy to do that when the markets are climbing, but it can be very hard to keep on buying when the markets are heading down. Of course, dollar-cost averaging is no guarantee of wealth. It does not eliminate all of the risks of investing. It does not ensure that you'll make gains, nor does it protect you against a loss in declining markets. But if you patiently invest those fixed amounts in regular installments, you'll avoid the financial loss and the emotional pain of making a large investment at some point, only to see a sharp drop in the market immediately afterward.

A Set of Super Savings Tips

Savings Trick #1: Setting Aside Salary Increases

Saving money doesn't have to be painful. You might feel a bit of a twinge when you start, but you will quickly adjust your lifestyle, and you have to do it only once. Table 4.1 illustrates a scenario that I like to share when people tell me they just can't get started saving money. This basic approach is something that anyone should be able to do.

Suppose you're earning an annual salary of $50,000, and you're spending it all. Your income in Year 1 is $50,000 and you have $50,000 in expenses, which we'll define as $30,000 in fixed expenses (mortgage, taxes, Social Security withholding, and so on) and $20,000 in variable expenses (food, clothing, entertainment, etc.). With $50,000 in income and $50,000 in expenses, your net "profit" (to save or invest) is zero in Year 1.

In Year 2, suppose you get a 5% raise. That takes your income to $52,500. Your fixed expenses have not changed, and neither have your discretionary expenses, as yet. With your raise, your personal income statement has just gone from break-even to a $2,500 profit. Will you choose to spend it or save it?

Let's say you are fortunate enough to have a retirement savings program at work—a 401(k) plan, perhaps. And let's say you decide to take your $2,500 raise and contribute it to your 401(k). Your income statement (available cash) shows you are back to break-even, after savings. But you don't really have a profit of zero. At the end of the year, you still have $2,500 in savings. (We're ignoring taxes and whatever return those savings are earning, to keep things simple here.)

In Year 3, suppose you get another 5% raise. That raise, applied to $52,500 salary, takes you to $55,100. Since your salary has grown, you raise your contribution to $2,750 a year—5% of your salary. You're saving $250 out of your second raise of $2,600. After a 4%, or $800, increase in your variable expenses, you would have $1,550 available to spend or invest as you wish.

TABLE 4.1 A Personal Cash Flow Statement

Year	Income	Fixed Expenses	Variable Expenses	Added to Retirement Savings	Available Cash
1	$50,000	$30,000	$20,000	$0	$0
2	$52,500	$30,000	$20,000	$2,500	$0
3	$55,100	$30,000	$20,800	$2,750	$1,550
4	$57,900	$30,000	$21,600	$2,900	$3,400
5	$60,800	$30,000	$22,500	$3,050	$5,250

Let's assume that the raises continue, and you continue to invest 5% of your salary in your retirement plan. At the end of five years, you'll have saved $11,200. If your 401(k) investment earns an average of 8% a year during that time, your nest egg will have grown to more than $13,000.

As my illustration shows, once you establish a saving routine, you'll hardly notice the portion of future salary increases going into your savings plan. The lesson: Adjust your lifestyle *once* and you will never have to change it again in order to save reasonable amounts of money.

By the way, the same approach can be used to pay down debt. Suppose you have a target date for when you would like to be debt-free. You would use your available cash (the money left over after you pay your expenses) to pay off credit cards or to prepay your mortgage.

Suppose, for example, that your various credit card balances have ballooned to $20,000. At a fairly typical 1.5% monthly interest rate, you're being charged $300 a month in interest alone. The card companies may require you to pay only a total of $500 or $600 each month, because they're in no hurry to have you reduce your debt burden. But now let's say that you get a raise of, say, $120 a month. That might push up your take-home pay by $80 or so, after taxes and retirement plan contributions. If you apply that $80 to your credit card payments—perhaps using automatic bill-paying to make sure you do so—you'll have cut the balance by an *extra* $960 in 12 months. As a bonus for paying down that extra $960, your monthly interest charges will drop by nearly $15—more than $170 a year. If you keep paying more than the minimum required each month, you'll make progress in paying off the debt.

Savings Trick # 2: Deferring Big-Ticket Purchases

A young colleague walked into my office one day and said he had just received a raise of $250 a month. When my eyebrows shot up, he was quick to explain: "I just made my last car payment, so I consider myself as having gotten a $250-a-month raise. It's going straight into my savings." His logic and discipline were impressive.

Cutting your expenses is a great way to boost your savings. Every dollar of expenses that you reduce is actually worth much more to you than an additional dollar of income. That's because of the bite of taxes. Think how much you had to earn for every after-tax dollar you spend. If you are typical, you take home only 63 cents of every dollar you earn, after Social Security (7% of your pay) and federal taxes (27%, if you are in the 27% bracket) and state taxes (3%, on average). Another way of looking at it is that you have to earn $1.60 before taxes for every after-tax dollar that you spend.

If you keep your car for five years after it's paid off and invest the savings, you are making solid progress toward your goals. My friend was looking forward to saving that $3,000 a year in car payments. Even if you acknowledge the additional maintenance and repair expenses that go with owning an older car, you have to admit that my friend would still be better off than if he bought a new car and assumed a new set of payments. It's reasonable to think that he could save $10,000 over the next five years.

Savings Trick #3: Salt Away Those "Extra" Paychecks

If you're like many workers who get biweekly paychecks, you know that there are two months in every year when you get three paychecks instead of two. Some savers have told me they deposit those "bonus" checks into their savings accounts. It's a great idea. If you're accustomed to supporting yourself on two paychecks a month, isn't there a chance you don't need to spend that additional chunk of money?

Savings Trick #4: Add Up the "Slow Leaks"

You'll be surprised at the other potential savings you'll discover if you carefully monitor your spending for a month or so. This exercise doesn't require elaborate spreadsheets; it can be as simple as carrying an index card with you each day and jotting down all of your expenditures. Be sure to keep track of each purchase you make, no matter how small. At the end of the month, look at what you spent your money on and calculate how much each item will be costing you over a year's time. These are like small leaks from your wallet. And as Ben Franklin said, "Beware of small expenses; a small leak will sink a great ship."

As shown in Table 4.2, small savings, invested judiciously, can increase your wealth amazingly. You don't have to live like a miser—just consider the trade-offs you're making every single day. Is a $3.00 cup of coffee each morning more worthwhile than a secure retirement? Remember that it took $4.75 in pre-tax earnings to put that $3.00 in your pocket.

TABLE 4.2   Little Expenses Add Up Over Time

	Annual Cost	Value after 20 Years*
One takeout dinner a week for four	$1,560	$71,389
$5 for lunch each work day (240 days)	$1,200	$54,914
Interest on $5,000 credit card debt (at 18%)	$ 900	$41,186
$3 for a double latte each work day	$ 720	$32,949

*Pre-tax value if the sum is saved and invested each year-end at 8%.

Saving versus Investing

No matter where you put the money, saving is an effective way to accumulate wealth. I'm not the only one who grew up equating saving with bank accounts, rather than investment portfolios. And salting away money in an interest-paying bank account or certificate of deposit is not a bad way to accumulate capital. The advantage of keeping your savings in a bank account or a CD is that your interest rate is assured and the principal is generally guaranteed. Your success in accumulating wealth will depend on how disciplined you are, since it's mostly a matter of how much you put into the account rather than what you earn in interest.

It's okay if you prefer to be a saver, not an investor. Bank savings accounts are sometimes derided as a symptom of financial illiteracy. But some people prefer the security that comes from keeping their savings in a bank account, a certificate of deposit, a Treasury bond, or a money market mutual fund. They simply don't want to accept the risk that's part of investing. They'd rather give up the potential for gains than take a chance on losing any of their principal. If you're a saver at heart, don't let anyone goad you into taking more risk than you want to. As long as you are comfortable with the modest returns you get on savings vehicles, stick with them and skip the rest of this book.

Savings Priorities

Once you've decided to combine a good savings program and an effective retirement investment program, the next question is where to invest that money. Some investors feel overwhelmed because there are so many different tax-advantaged ways to invest long-term savings. There are different kinds of IRAs, as well as 401(k) plans or other employer-sponsored retirement plans, and a range of annuity insurance products.

What's the best investment strategy for your savings program? It depends on the trade-offs you're willing to make. For example, look at the two major kinds of IRAs. Investing in a traditional IRA will get you an instant tax deduction if you meet the eligibility rules, but later in life you'll have to pay income taxes on the proceeds when you begin withdrawing your money. The assumption is that by then you'll be retired and in a lower tax bracket. But perhaps you'd prefer to forgo the upfront tax deduction and invest in a Roth IRA. Then you will owe *no* taxes when you start withdrawing the money (assuming that you follow the rules and don't, for example, draw on the account too soon).

Choosing between a traditional IRA and a Roth IRA means weighing the trade-off between a short-run tax break and tax-free appreciation over the course of a lifetime. For most people, the Roth IRA is a much better choice because there is no tax bite from the payout in retirement. The amount of money retained then far outweighs the taxes paid on the money initially invested. Once you clarify trade-offs, decision-making becomes much easier.

For most people who are investing for retirement, the best priority list is this one:

1. Contribute to your 401(k) plan up to the employer's matching contribution percentage.
2. Contribute to a Roth IRA up to the contribution limit.
3. Contribute to your 401(k) plan up to the contribution limit.
4. Once you've maxed out on the tax-advantaged opportunities, consider putting your additional savings in a combination of tax-efficient mutual funds, including tax-managed and index funds. (We'll discuss tax-efficient investing in greater detail in Chapter 10.)

I've omitted variable annuities from this list, although financial planners and insurance agents often heavily promote them as a good way to save for retirement. Variable annuities aren't for everyone. Essentially, a variable annuity is an insurance contract whose value fluctuates depending on the value of the underlying investments. The benefits of these investments include lifetime income payments, a death benefit, and tax deferral. They can make sense for you under these conditions: *If* you've contributed up to the maximum on your 401(k) and your IRA; *if* you have a very long time horizon; and *if* you will be able to leave that money untouched.

The biggest drawback of variable annuities is that most of them charge such high fees that they don't offer good value. Read the fine print, and before you invest, ask about surrender fees, agent commissions, and other expenses. And never hold a variable annuity within your IRA—you're already getting tax deferral within the IRA, and the variable annuity provides no additional tax advantage.

One More Incentive to Start Saving Early

The key variables in any investment program are how much you invest, how much time the investment has to grow, and how much return your investments earn. You can control how much you invest and how early you start. But you can't do much to influence your return—or can you?

Here's something interesting that most people don't realize. The more time you have in your investment program, the more risk you can afford to accept. The converse is equally true: The less time your investments have to compound, the less risk you can afford to accept. A person who begins saving for retirement at age 50 probably would not want to risk losing any of her principal by investing in aggressive stock funds. She would be likely to choose lower-risk investments (including other kinds of stocks) that provide a lower return. But a teenager who begins investing in an IRA as soon as she is old enough to earn money by mowing lawns or babysitting can afford to invest aggressively. After all, she won't be tapping that money for 45 years or more. Who cares if the account has a bad year and loses 20% of its value? She has decades to let the market and her account recover.

Why is it good to take on more risk? Because that should mean a bigger return. And over a long period, just a percentage point or two in added return makes a difference much larger than you might expect. Example: Suppose you contribute $3,000 a year to an IRA for 25 years, and you earn an average return of 6% a year. In the end, you'd have $174,000 in your account. Not bad? Well, now assume that you invest a bit more aggressively and get an average return of 8% a year. This time you wind up after 25 years with nearly $237,000. And if your investments should bring you an average of 10% a year, you will end up with nearly $325,000.

Longer investment periods magnify the benefits of taking on increased risk. You have enough time to recover from down years, and extra time to allow the outsized returns of good years to compound. As you can see, over long periods the advantages are impressive. In the long run, time dampens the effects of the extra volatility you have to put up with while maximizing the impact of a higher return.

In a Nutshell

You can transform yourself into a disciplined saver by:

- **Signing up for automatic investment programs.** If you funnel money from your paycheck right into your investment accounts, you're paying yourself first.

- **Participating in a 401(k) or other tax-deferred retirement plan at work.** Tax deferral and the convenience of having the money withheld from your paycheck make saving easier.

- **Capturing additional savings opportunities.** Direct "extra" paychecks and windfalls into savings instead of spending them. Identify the little expenses that are undermining your efforts to accumulate wealth.

chapter five

HOPE FOR THE BEST—BUT PREPARE FOR SOMETHING LESS

Now that we've discussed how to save, the next question to raise is: How can you know whether you're saving *enough*?

People tend not to ask themselves that question when making decisions about saving. They decide how much they think they can afford to save and then hope that they'll end up with sufficient money for their goals. But your notion of what you can afford to save could change if you made some quick calculations.

If you're really serious about accomplishing a specific goal, you'll want to first discover how much it's going to cost and then figure out how much to save to get there. To obtain the answer, you have to work backward. You look at (1) the size of your goal, (2) the amount of time you'll have, and (3) the amount of investment return you can reasonably expect to achieve. Then you do a little math. For instance, say you hope to amass $50,000 for your child's college education over the next 18 years, and you think you can earn 8% a year on your investments. A calculator or a spreadsheet will tell you that you'll need to invest $103.46 at the start of every month to accomplish your goal. Those projections, like all the ones we'll use in this book, assume that you reinvest all your earnings and don't make any withdrawals from the account during the period.

Is 8% a fair projection for your investment returns? It depends.

Over the very long term—the 76 years from 1926 through 2001—U.S. stocks have gained an average of 10.7% a year. Bond returns have averaged 5.7% a year. Annual returns on cash investments have averaged 4.0%. You'll hear those numbers again and again as you invest. People will tell you it's reasonable to expect similar returns in your own portfolio over the course of many years.

But you should not think of those figures as guaranteed. The particular 5, 10, or even 15 years when *you* are investing to meet a goal might have a very different pattern from the long-term average. Inflation will be a factor. So will the timing of your contributions. And you can't know in advance what the markets will be like when it's time for you to draw on your investments.

In this chapter, I'll discuss how to go about making the financial assumptions that are the foundation for your investment program. I'll share some stories from my own experience as well as some hypothetical scenarios based on real market events.

When Inflation Rears Its Ugly Head

When they look to the future, many people forget about inflation—but don't let yourself make that mistake. Inflation is the general increase in the prices of goods and services that tends to occur over time. It reduces everyone's purchasing power—meaning, literally, that a dollar this year doesn't buy as much as a dollar did last year. High rates of inflation are an investor's greatest enemy. Bond investors are particularly vulnerable because much of their return consists of interest payments, which are worth a little less each year. That's why most long-term investors need to hold a significant stake in stocks, which not only provide dividends, but have a chance to increase notably in value.

No measure of inflation is a perfect match for your spending habits, but the one that's relied on most for financial planning is the U.S. Consumer Price Index, which tracks the prices of some 80,000 goods and services purchased by consumers. In the 1990s and the first years of the twenty-first century, inflation was very low, and many people seemed to have forgotten that it was a threat. Older investors will remember, though: In the late 1970s, inflation reached double-digit levels. For the 1973–1982 period, the annual inflation rate averaged 8.7%. When inflation is running at 8.7%, the car that previously cost you $15,000 costs $16,305. And of course, it's not just the big-ticket items that are affected by inflation. Virtually everything you buy is costing you more.

The long-run average for U.S. inflation, going all the way back to 1925, is about 3%. That sounds low, but look at the results: At a 3% annual inflation rate, something that costs $10,000 now will cost $24,300 in 30 years. At a 5% inflation rate, that $10,000 item would sell for $43,200 in 30 years. From 1960 through 2001, inflation has been a little higher, averaging 4.4% a year.

It's safe to assume that inflation will be a factor to one degree or another during the years in which you are accumulating assets and also the years when you are spending from them. During your working years, your salary increases are likely to keep up with inflation. But your investment returns might take a hit. For these reasons, it's vital to think about inflation when you calculate how your investments will grow with time.

When you check the historical returns on different kinds of investments, be sure to look at figures that are adjusted for inflation. These are called *real* returns. Figures that haven't been adjusted for inflation are called *nominal* returns. Most of the historical investment returns you'll see are given in nominal terms, so if you are using them for your projections, you will need to adjust for inflation on your own. It's simple to do: You just choose a hypothetical inflation rate and subtract it from the average return figure. You could use a 3% to 4% inflation rate, or if you are very conservative, you could project inflation at a slightly higher level.

As shown in Figures 5.1 and 5.2, the differences between nominal and real returns can be substantial.

Future Investment Returns

We don't have crystal balls, so we can't know with any certainty which numbers will provide the most accurate projections of future investment performance. Recognize that even small differences in the assumptions can have a big effect on your calculations. If your projections are too rosy, you could end up far short of your goal, as the next case study shows.

Back in January 1992, an investor named Andrew decided to open an investment account in a stock mutual fund with the goal of accumulating $50,000 by December 31, 2001. He chose a fund whose return was pegged to the S&P 500

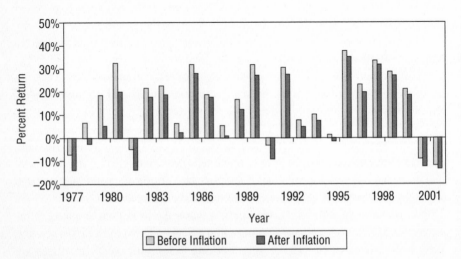

FIGURE 5.1   S&P 500 Index Total Returns: 1977–2001

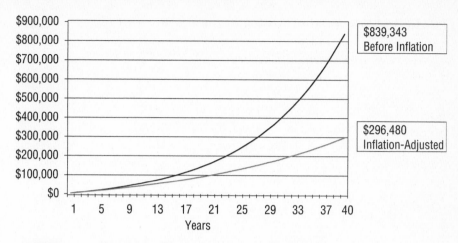

FIGURE 5.2   How Inflation Affects a Long-Term Investment

This chart assumes that a person invested $3,000 in a tax-sheltered account at the start of each year for 40 years. It also assumes that the account earned an annual investment return of 8% after expenses and before adjusting for inflation at 4% a year.

Index. To figure out how much he'd need to invest at the start of each year, Andrew tested a set of different assumptions about market performance, as shown in Table 5.1. He found that, if he assumed that the S&P 500 would continue to perform for the next decade as it had in the last decade—gaining 18% a year, on average, from 1982 to 1991—he would need to invest $1,801 at the start of each year to reach his goal. But if Andrew was a little less optimistic and assumed future average annual returns of 10%—a return closer to the long-term average— he would need to invest an additional $1,051 a year, for a total of $2,852. And if he were more conservative, assuming an 8% annual return, he would need to invest an additional $1,395 a year—a total of $3,196.

Plainly, the effects of different projections are pretty dramatic on a 10-year investment scenario. Imagine how wide the variations would be if extended over 30 years. Though our example is based on investments made in a lump sum at the beginning of the year, the lesson also holds true if you are making monthly or bimonthly contributions, as most investors do.

Only time will tell how accurate your own projections of future returns are. Note that for Andrew the investor, the "realistic" projection would have meant bad news. Actual stock market returns averaged an excellent rate of just under 13% a year during the 1992–2001 period when Andrew was investing, so it turned out that he would have needed to invest $2,410 a year to reach his $50,000 goal. If he had relied on an 18% rate of return, he would have come up short at the end, with an account valued at $37,358.

TABLE 5.1   Annual Investing to Reach a $50,000 Goal: 1992–2001

	Projected Average Annual Total Return	*Annual Investment Needed at Start of Year to Reach $50,000 on December 31, 2001*	*Value of Account at End of Period Based on Actual Return*
"Realistic" Estimate (based on past 10-year return)	18%	$1,801	$37,358
"Conservative" Estimate	10%	$2,852	$59,158
"More Conservative" Estimate	8%	$3,196	$66,294
Actual S&P 500 Index Return	13%	$2,410	$50,000

Don't Count on Present Investment Conditions Continuing

When I entered the investment business in 1982, the conventional wisdom was that stocks could be expected to return 9% or 10% a year over the long run. But stocks then proceeded to compound at an astounding average rate of 15.2% a year for the next 20 years. Looking at that 10% figure, an investor who began 1982 with a $100,000 nest egg could reasonably hope to end up with $673,000 after 20 years. At the actual figure of 15% a year, he or she would have wound up with $1.6 million. What an incredible effect those outsized returns had on investors' expectations!

Amid those booming bull market years, I received a sobering note from an older business acquaintance. On the occasion of my tenth anniversary at Vanguard, in July 1992, he wrote:

> Congratulations on your first 10 years at Vanguard. It won't always be that easy. The stock market's average annual gains were 19% during the past decade. They were 3.5% during my first 10 years in the business.

The note was a striking reminder of how deeply an investor's perspective is colored by personal experience. Because my friend had endured a very different investment climate, he had a far different point of view on the present.

Investment experts often treat historical returns from periods as short as 10 years as a basis for future projections, but returns from a decade can be distorted by prolonged market downturns (as in the 1970s) or upturns like the ones we experienced in the 1980s and 1990s. During the 1982–2000 boom in the stock market, people began to think that a permanent change had occurred in the economy, and that long-term returns going forward would be much better than in the past. Indeed, the standard measurement of long-term investment results—the average yearly return for the past 10 years—was 14% at the end of 1990, much higher than the 8% it had been in 1980.

At Vanguard, we wanted to discourage investors from being unrealistically optimistic, so in our shareholder communications we began discussing long-term investment performance in terms of 15-year stock market returns, which were lower than 10-year returns. Frustrated shareholders would write to us, "Now you are changing the rules of the game, and you're telling me that long-term is 15 years, not 10 years?"

By 1997, even 15-year historical returns averaged 18% annually, so it was yet harder to convince investors that the stock market's prolonged turbocharged performance was a transitory phenomenon. As crazy as it seems now, many investors began to believe that the historical very-long-term averages were no longer relevant and that, in fact, negative years were no longer possible. As of June 30, 2002, the stock market had lost a cumulative 33% since its peak in March 2000—a sobering and painful lesson for those who believed that the markets had evolved to an entirely new state of nature.

The Problem with the Long-Term Averages

When you are making projections about the growth of your investment portfolio, even the long-term historical averages need to be taken with several grains of salt. Long-term averages are a mathematical construct. In real life, people don't earn a constant rate of return year after year. The reality is that very few investments appreciate at a steady rate. If you were to chart the value of your portfolio over decades, you would have a bumpy line, not a smooth line, with your balance taking lots of ups and downs while (we hope!) following a generally upward trend over time.

While stock returns averaged 11% a year from 1926 through 2001, there have been just a handful of years when the actual return came close to matching that figure. Returns have also varied for 5-, 10-, and even 20-year chunks of the entire 75-year period. Table 5.2 shows the ranges of total returns for a variety of rolling time periods, such as the 5-year periods 1926–1930, 1927–1931, and so on, and the 20-year periods 1926–1945, 1927–1946, etc.

TABLE 5.2   S&P 500 Index Annualized Returns for Rolling Periods: 1926–2001

	High	*Low*
1-Year Periods	54.2% (1933)	–43.1% (1931)
5-Year Periods	28.6% (1995–1999)	–12.4% (1928–1932)
10-Year Periods	19.9% (1949–1958)	–0.9% (1929–1938)
20-Year Periods	17.9% (1980–1999)	3.1% (1929–1948)

In your own investment program, you will earn good returns in some years and not-so-good returns in other years. There's no way of knowing when the market will be up and when it will be down, but one thing is true: The *timing* of those ups and downs in your life cycle will be important to your success in reaching your goal. As shown in Figure 5.3, anyone who was investing over the 25-year period from 1977 to 2001 experienced a wide range of annual returns.

Let's assume that you are investing for a period of four decades and your portfolio of stocks and bonds has an average annual total return of 10% over that period. Let's also assume that you are contributing regularly to your savings, so that your portfolio starts out small and nears $1 million over time.

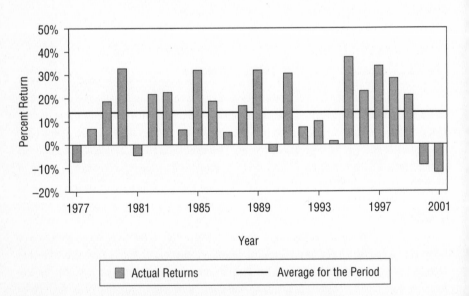

FIGURE 5.3   S&P 500 Index Annual Total Returns: 1977–2001

If your portfolio had an unexpected gain of 40% in the early years, you would probably be very pleased. But wouldn't you be even happier to receive that 40% gain in the fourth decade, when the balance in your account has grown much larger? Forty percent of $800,000 ($320,000) is much more pleasing than 40% of $8,000 ($3,200).

Losses are a different issue. If you had a 40% loss on your $8,000 portfolio early on, your portfolio would still have many years to recover. But suppose that the 40% drop occurred in the fourth decade. A 40% loss on $800,000 is a huge setback, and you'd have little time to recover. (This is why it's generally wise to transition to a more conservative mix of investments as you get older.)

Because you have no way of foreseeing the path that your investments will take, you have a choice to make when developing your financial plan: You can pay a financial planner a fee to perform what's called *time-path dependency testing*. He or she will do all sorts of calculations and then tell you a range of possible outcomes for your portfolio, depending on what financial conditions occur. For example, your planner might tell you that, in 60% of the scenarios she tested, you would have met your financial goals, but in the other 40% you would have come up short. If that doesn't satisfy you, you could ask her to assume you'll invest more and re-run the numbers, continuing this until you arrive at a monthly investment contribution that results in your desired probability of success.

But you don't have to pay someone to do elaborate scenario testing to protect yourself from unfavorable conditions. You can be very successful with a do-it-yourself approach. Just be sure to use very conservative planning assumptions.

Scenario-Planning Tools

Your financial planning can be as unsophisticated as punching in numbers on a handheld calculator and jotting down projections on the back of an envelope. But you can also find plenty of sophisticated tools to help you project how much you need to save at a given rate of return in order to reach the goals that you have set. A number of calculators are available online from mutual fund firms and other financial providers. Or you can use one of the many financial-planning software packages now available.

The benefit of these planning tools is that you can compare different what-ifs: What if inflation is 5% instead of 3%? What if your investments earn 6% a year instead of 9% on average? What if you want to retire at 62 instead of 65? All of those factors will affect the answer to the big question: Will you have enough money for your goals? This scenario planning is particularly useful in figuring out how to deploy your savings for retirement.

Not-So-Great Expectations

Conservative assumptions about future investment performance are inherently safer than "realistic" assumptions based on recent market data. By definition, the lower your assumptions about future investment returns, the more money you will need to supply to your investment program to reach the same end point. If you assume that your experience won't be all roses, you will become a disciplined saver and a conservative investor. If it turns out that your projections were too conservative, the worst thing that happens is that you're pleasantly surprised. You'll have more money in your portfolio than you expected.

You face a very different set of potential consequences if you're overly optimistic in your assumptions—and wrong. If you take the rosy view about future returns, you will conclude that you don't need to supply as much capital to your investment program because the market's bounty will get you where you need to be. If the market isn't as fruitful as you anticipate, or if the timing of the market's ups and downs isn't favorable, you could end up with much less money than you expected.

Just remember that it's always tempting to use the most optimistic assumptions. That's why you shouldn't start your financial planning by first deciding how much to save and only then go on to figure out how much it will earn for you. You can always come up with assumptions to justify an acceptable answer. Want to be able to "find out" that you'll be okay if you save only a little for retirement? Just assume that you'll be earning 20% a year and inflation will be negligible. But will that optimistic scenario occur? I don't think so. In most of the hypothetical scenarios in this book that involve stock investments, I have based my projections on 8% average annual total returns—a slightly more conservative number than historical data suggest.

In my own personal planning, I am even more conservative. To stay on the safe side, I always assume that my pay increases will occur at a slow rate, and I project investment returns that will stay slightly ahead of inflation—real returns of about 3.5%. Back in the 1980s, when I was deciding how much money to save for my children's college educations, very few sophisticated financial-planning tools were available. So I did my number-crunching by hand on a calculator. I always made conservative assumptions, projecting an investment return of 1% to 3% a year after inflation. When the reality proved to be better than that—as is usually the case when assumptions are as conservative as mine—I felt very lucky.

If you take a conservative approach to your financial planning, you'll be the one who wins in the long run. Conservative projections will drive you to save more. You will consume less. As a result, you'll be a more satisfied investor, because the surprises will usually be on the positive side. If you're too conservative and you end up with more money than you expected, well, that's not so painful a prospect, is it?

I always believe in Murphy's Law: "Anything that can go wrong, will." But I believe even more strongly in O'Toole's Corollary: "Murphy was an optimist." Remember O'Toole's Corollary if you want to accumulate wealth.

In a Nutshell

It's wise to be conservative about future investment returns when deciding how much money you need to invest to achieve your goals. Here's why:

- **A dollar won't buy as much in the future.** Inflation will eat away at the purchasing power of your investments, so you're likely to need more money than you think.

- **There is no guarantee that your investments will earn returns that match the historical long-term averages.** If you're overly optimistic about future returns, you could fall short of your objectives.

PART TWO

Construct a
Sensible Portfolio

chapter six
BALANCE AND DIVERSIFICATION HELP YOU SLEEP AT NIGHT

Let's say you've identified your goals and decided to design an investment program to achieve them. Now you're probably ready to hear about how to select investments. I'll tackle that very topic soon, but first we need to address a major strategic issue. To construct a sensible portfolio, you must first decide on the *types* of investments you need. In this chapter, I'll be talking about how to figure that out by using some basic, commonsense principles. Choosing the specific stocks or stock funds, bonds or bond funds, or other vehicles comes later.

In truth, you can do pretty well as an investor by keeping just two fundamental principles in mind: *balance* and *diversification*. Balance means owning different types of investments—assets that typically behave differently enough from each other that they are unlikely to all disappoint you at once. Diversification means spreading your money around enough that no individual holding can hurt you significantly if it takes a dive. Balance and diversification help to manage the risks that are inherent in investing. (Notice that I said *managing* risk—not *minimizing* risk. As I've said before, you have to take on some level of risk to get any meaningful reward in investing. With balance and diversification, we're talking about tools for making sure you don't take on more risk than you intended to.)

If you hold a portfolio that's balanced across the asset classes and diversified within those asset classes, you'll avoid the risk that goes with pinning all your hopes on one company's stocks or bonds. Your balanced, well-diversified portfolio will be less volatile than one that has concentrated holdings. A volatile portfolio is one that zigs and zags between highs and lows like a person who's subject to frequent mood swings. If you have a portfolio that's better equipped to ride out the ups and downs in the markets, you're likely to sleep easier at night. This isn't just academic theory. It's a real-life strategy that works.

The terms *balance* and *diversification* are often tossed around as if they were interchangeable, so let's look at them a bit more closely:

- A **balanced portfolio** is one that's invested across at least two of the three major asset classes—stocks, bonds, and cash investments.

- A **diversified portfolio** is one that's invested in a variety of securities issued by different kinds of companies or other entities. A diversified stock portfolio is not concentrated in any single stock or industry. A diversified bond portfolio is not concentrated in debt from any single type of bond issuer.

Balance and diversification are a powerful combination when they are both employed. They're the team of oxen you want to have pulling your wagon.

Let's apply these principles to an imaginary portfolio that's invested in individual securities. Suppose your investments are split evenly three ways: A third in Company A's stock, a third in Company B's bonds, and the rest in Bank C, where you have an interest-bearing savings account and some short-term certificates of deposit. That's certainly a balanced portfolio, because it is invested in all three of the asset classes. It is not diversified, however. If a major business reversal struck Company A or Company B, you could lose a great deal of money.

Suppose you diversified your portfolio by buying the stocks of 100 companies, not just one, and owned bonds from 100 issuers as well. Then you'd be much less likely to be hurt financially if one of those companies ran into trouble.

Why Balance Really Works

Even if you are new to investing, chances are you already understand the value of balance in other aspects of life. If given the choice, most people would probably rather eat ice cream than broccoli. But we know that wouldn't be very healthful. We know we will have more energy and probably live longer if we consume a prudent variety of nutritious foods every day.

Balance is equally important to your financial health. Whether the portfolio is a multibillion-dollar endowment fund or a modest-sized IRA account, investing across the three major asset classes is a good way to reduce risk. Stocks, bonds, and cash investments typically don't rise or fall at the same time. When one type of asset has a bad year, it's likely that at least one of the others will fare better.

Let's look at some historical performance statistics to understand why you need to invest with balance. While stocks do tend to outperform bonds and cash over the long haul, there have often been extended periods—sometimes lasting years—in which stocks came in last. Table 6.1 shows that stocks did better than bonds and cash during 14 years of the 1977–2001 period. But there were 11 years in which stocks were outperformed by either bonds or cash—or both. In those years, if you had all your money in stocks, you might have felt pretty bad

TABLE 6.1   25 Years of Returns

Year	Stocks Broad Stock Market	Bonds Long-Term Corporate Bonds	Cash 90-Day Treasury Bills
1977	–2.64%	1.98%	5.50%
1978	9.27	0.01	7.39
1979	25.56	–4.21	10.35
1980	33.67	–3.03	11.89
1981	–3.75	–0.70	15.05
1982	18.71	45.45	11.32
1983	23.46	6.57	8.93
1984	3.05	16.84	10.02
1985	32.56	28.24	7.82
1986	16.10	18.95	6.23
1987	2.27	0.69	5.91
1988	17.94	10.05	6.76
1989	29.17	15.59	8.64
1990	–6.18	6.86	7.90
1991	34.21	20.59	5.75
1992	8.97	8.64	3.61
1993	11.28	12.75	3.09
1994	–0.06	–5.78	4.24
1995	36.45	26.55	5.75
1996	21.21	1.54	5.25
1997	31.29	13.53	5.25
1998	23.43	10.22	5.06
1999	23.56	–6.53	4.74
2000	–10.93	12.70	5.96
2001	–10.96	11.79	4.09
Average Annual Return	**13.73**	**9.36**	**7.02**

Returns are for the Wilshire 5000 Index, the Lehman Brothers Long Credit AA Index, and the Salomon Smith Barney 3-Month Treasury Bill Index.

about it, especially if you unexpectedly had to draw on your investments. One of the main reasons for having balance in your portfolio is that it helps you to keep *your* balance when one part of your portfolio is doing poorly. Knowing that stocks have long-term returns of 11% a year isn't much comfort in a period like 2000–2001, when stocks *lost* 11% a year.

The key thing to remember about balance is that at any point in time, it will look like a dumb strategy. For example, let's look at the years 1980, 1981, and 1982, when the top-performing asset varied each year (Table 6.2). Suppose you held a balanced portfolio through that period. At the end of 1980, you might have thought, "I should have had all my money in stocks!" At the end of 1981, it might well have been: "I should have had all my money in money market funds!" And a year later, at the end of 1982, you would have been tempted to say, "Why in the world am I holding anything but bonds?"

Whenever you find yourself questioning the wisdom of balance, remember the difference between tactics and strategy. Tactics focus on short-term benefits; strategy looks to the long term. Tactics may win you a battle, but you need strategy to win the war. With a balanced portfolio, it's true that you'll never be earning as much as you'd get if you managed to put all your money in the asset class that was destined to be the year's top performer. The problem is, there is no way to know in advance which one it's going to be. A balanced strategy keeps you from kidding yourself about your ability to predict the future.

You'll see the upside and downside of balance in Table 6.2. As shown in the table, a balanced portfolio underperformed the all-stock portfolio for the 25-year period from 1977 through 2001. A $10,000 investment would have grown to $249,436 in the all-stock portfolio, but it would have grown to only $171,518 in the balanced portfolio. But during 6 years out of the 25, stocks lost money, and although the balanced portfolio also lost money during those years, it usually lost less. During those tough times, holding a balanced portfolio could have given you the courage to keep on investing.

There will be times when you are sorely tempted to abandon balance. Over the years, many investors have told me stories about giving up on a balanced portfolio when one asset class got so far ahead that they just couldn't stand it anymore. They shifted all of their money into the hot-performing class. Then, invariably, the returns on that type of asset reverted to something much more in line with the long-term averages, and the investors found that their portfolios had shrunk.

In the early 1980s, money market funds—which historically have returned about 4% a year on average—were providing 14% and 15% yields because of that era's high inflation. Money poured in. But those outsize yields lasted only for a period of months. Investors who sank everything into money market funds would have had to move fast in order to benefit fully when stocks rallied suddenly—and continued to outperform throughout most of the 1980s and 1990s.

TABLE 6.2   How Balance Provides a Buffer: Annual Returns of the Three Major Asset Classes versus Those of a Balanced Fund, 1977–2001

Year	Stocks — Broad Stock Market	Bonds — Long-Term Corporate Bonds	Cash — 90-Day Treasury Bills	Balanced Portfolio — 60% Stock/ 30% Bond/ 10% Cash
1977	−2.64%	1.98%	5.50%	−0.44%
1978	9.27	0.01	7.39	6.31
1979	25.56	−4.21	10.35	15.11
1980	33.67	−3.03	11.89	20.48
1981	−3.75	−0.70	15.05	−0.95
1982	18.71	45.45	11.32	25.99
1983	23.46	6.57	8.93	16.94
1984	3.05	16.84	10.02	7.88
1985	32.56	28.24	7.82	28.79
1986	16.10	18.95	6.23	15.97
1987	2.27	0.69	5.91	2.16
1988	17.94	10.05	6.76	14.46
1989	29.17	15.59	8.64	23.05
1990	−6.18	6.86	7.90	−0.86
1991	34.21	20.59	5.75	27.28
1992	8.97	8.64	3.61	8.34
1993	11.28	12.75	3.09	10.90
1994	−0.06	−5.78	4.24	−1.35
1995	36.45	26.55	5.75	30.41
1996	21.21	1.54	5.25	13.71
1997	31.29	13.53	5.25	23.36
1998	23.43	10.22	5.06	17.63
1999	23.56	−6.53	4.74	12.65
2000	−10.93	12.70	5.96	−2.15
2001	−10.96	11.79	4.09	−2.63
Ending Value of a $10,000 Account	$249,436	$93,742	$54,566	$171,518

Returns are for the Wilshire 5000 Index, the Lehman Brothers Long Credit AA Index, and the Salomon Smith Barney 3-Month Treasury Bill Index. Returns for the balanced portfolio are also based on those indexes.

Pitfall: Don't Invest Too Heavily in Your Employer's Stock

If you invest a large part of your assets in your employer's stock, as many 401(k) participants do, you may not be as diversified as you ought to be.

Thanks to Enron Corporation, I don't have to belabor that point very much. As surely everyone knows, in the Enron blowup of 2001, thousands of the company's employees—some of them at or near retirement—saw a lifetime of retirement savings evaporate. Over a period of six weeks, about $1 billion was lost by 401(k) investors as the company's stock price sank from above $30 to pennies a share, according to news accounts. There have been many other instances in recent years when employees put their faith and their retirement savings into their employer's stock and then lived to regret it.

Let me be clear: There are valid reasons for companies to include their own stock in employee retirement plans. Owning company stock allows employees to participate in their company's financial success. From an employer's perspective, encouraging employees to invest in company stock can create a shared commitment and an incentive for greater productivity.

What should you do? If you are investing in your employer's stock, be sure you know how much exposure you have. What percentage of your retirement savings is in company stock? If it's more than 10% to 20%, you should consider bringing it down to within that range if possible. The rules of your retirement plan will govern what you can do. For example, you may be able to redirect future contributions to a diversified mutual fund instead of to the company stock, or you may be able to exchange some of your company-stock shares for shares in a mutual fund. (*Tax note:* Transactions within a company-sponsored retirement plan usually don't trigger any taxes, but if you want to sell or exchange shares outside your retirement plan or IRA, check the tax implications before you act.)

Some employers match their employees' retirement-plan contributions with shares of company stock. Such plans may forbid the employees to sell those shares until they reach a specified age or have owned the shares for a certain length of time. If your plan has restrictions like these, and if the company stock makes up an oversized part of your retirement portfolio, you need to make a firm decision to sell some shares as soon as you are able to do so. Until then, you can take steps to reduce the concentration of company stock in your account by (1) making sure you contribute as much as possible to your retirement plan and (2) directing those contributions to other investments, preferably broadly diversified mutual funds. In other words, diversify the portion of the 401(k) that you contribute yourself.

Employees typically underestimate the risk of owning company stock in their retirement plan. Since they're familiar with their own company, they feel that its stock is safer than shares in other companies or mutual funds. But that's faulty logic. Even if all the confidence in management is justified, the reality is that outside market forces—not just employee confidence—determine the value of company stock. That old notion that you should invest in what you know best can lead you astray with your 401(k).

Many investors assume that they'll be able to recognize the point at which one market cycle ends and another begins, but in my experience, virtually no one can do so. Market shifts tend to happen very suddenly, and when they are occurring, they are nearly imperceptible—to professionals and nonprofessionals alike. The fact that we've seen a major change becomes obvious only *after* the fact.

The first such change I encountered was the beginning of the bull market, which happened just a month after I joined the mutual fund business in the summer of 1982. No one could see that the market was about to enter one of the longest bull runs in its history. In fact, stocks were looking pretty drab. I thought I was making a good career move because of the fine company I was joining, but I'd never have guessed that my firm and many others would soon be growing apace as the markets soared.

It's no wonder that people were pessimistic about stocks in the summer of 1982. Stocks had returned an average of 6.5% a year from 1972 to 1981, a period when the annual inflation rate averaged 8.6%. Subtracting inflation, you were actually losing 2.1% a year by investing in stocks! Why would anyone have wanted to own a risky investment like that when money market funds were yielding 15%? But the bull market took root on August 13, 1982, and for the next 10 years, stocks would gain 17.5% a year and money market funds 7.3% a year, on average.

With the benefit of hindsight, we can see that there have been plenty of other times in recent decades when the performance momentum quietly shifted from one asset class to another:

- **January 11, 1973.** Stocks returned 19% in 1972, but as 1973 began the worst bear market of the post–World War II era was just around the corner. Stock prices peaked on Thursday, January 11. The bear market would last until October 1974. For the next decade, stocks would return 6.7% a year, on average.

- **December 31, 1981.** Investment-grade bonds had returned –1.4% a year, on average, for the five years ended in 1981. But the New Year was bringing good news—they would gain 44% in 1982, and would produce average annual total returns of 16% for the next 10 years.

- **August 25, 1987.** Stocks had been booming when prices peaked on Tuesday, August 25, having returned about 35% for the previous 12 months. But the crash of October 1987 was about to occur. The stock market would lose 22.6% of its value in a single day on October 19, erasing $500 billion in investor wealth. The effects would pull down historical averages for a decade.

- **March 10, 2000.** This date saw the peak of the dot-com bubble as the Nasdaq Composite Index reached an all-time high of 5,048, bringing its 12-month return to a whopping 44%. Over the next five weeks, the Nasdaq plunged –34%.

The lesson from these pivotal moments is that it's very, very difficult to recognize a shift in momentum from one type of asset to another, or from one industry sector to another. If you decide to try to pick the right time to move your portfolio from stocks to bonds or from bonds to stocks, you are unlikely to get it right. And think of the wasted energy. Better to commit to a balanced strategy and save your energy for more rewarding pursuits, such as living your life.

Diversification Is Good for You—But Sometimes It Hurts

Diversification is the other word to remember when constructing your portfolio. If you are invested in a broad variety of stocks, bonds, and money market securities, your portfolio is not only balanced, but diversified. Diversification reduces the risk associated with having far too much of your money invested in a single company's stock or bonds. Finance experts use the term *specific risk* for the danger associated with such an investment. An academic could give you a long, sophisticated presentation on specific risk, but in my view it's as simple as that old warning about not putting all your eggs in one basket.

Let's consider how a diversification strategy might work in a portfolio of individual securities. (I'm going to name some specific companies as examples, but please don't construe this as a recommendation to buy these stocks!) Suppose you spread your dollars among General Electric, IBM, and Johnson & Johnson—three companies that have fared very well competitively over long periods. Through GE you are invested in many industries; through IBM you're in computers and services; and through J&J you're in health care. But you can further reduce the riskiness of your portfolio by including companies such as Procter & Gamble, Wal-Mart, Ford, and Citigroup, which represent, respectively, the consumer products, retailing, automobile, and financial services sectors. Let's not stop there. Now add in Exxon, John Deere, and Heinz, which represent energy, farming equipment, and food. With this 10-stock portfolio, you have broad exposure to high-quality, globally competitive American companies. And you have taken on far less specific risk than you would have by investing in just one or two of them. Keep in mind, however, that your portfolio is still far more concentrated, and therefore far more risky, than a broadly diversified mutual fund, which may hold hundreds of different stocks.

Investors sometimes ask whether certain companies are safer investments than others and can be held in concentrated amounts. If you think about it for a moment, you'll see why the answer is no—unless you have the benefit of hindsight! Though a company may be active in many different industries, the whole enterprise is still in the hands of one leadership team. And all of those leaders are human beings who can make mistakes. People often cite General Electric as an example of a very diversified, extraordinarily well-run company. Although GE has many different lines of business, don't forget that it has just one chairman and one board of directors. It's a fine company, but you would be taking on a great deal of specific risk if you invested a significant portion of your money in its stock.

Over the years, many companies have been hailed as supremely sure things only to hit the skids for one reason or another, such as a drop in profits or exposure to legal liabilities. Large, well-established companies have been known to suffer drastic declines even though business is booming for everyone else. In the years after the oil crises of the 1970s, many companies that were used to operating in a cheap-energy environment struggled to adapt to a new set of circumstances.

Diversification's virtues also apply to bonds. If you own one company's bonds, you are vulnerable to changes in its credit quality due to management mistakes or other factors. That could mean you'd lose money if you had to sell the bonds—or, worse, you could lose all of your investment if the company defaulted on its debt. Surprises do happen! Enron's credit rating was lowered from investment-grade to below-investment-grade on November 28, 2001, and the company filed for bankruptcy four days later. Holding the bonds of a variety of issuers reduces your risk. In a mutual fund that holds bonds from hundreds of issuers, the failure of one issuer to pay interest or principal has only a slight effect on investment performance.

Keep in mind that there will be many times when you regret holding a diversified portfolio, just as you sometimes will regret pursuing a balanced strategy. By definition, diversifying means that you give up some of the gains you could get if you knew which of your holdings were going to do best over the next year or so. In a diversified portfolio, there will always be a few star performers, just as there will be a few laggards. How you handle your emotions in those situations will be critical. You could smack yourself in the head and say, "I wish I'd had the sense to put all my money in Wal-Mart" (or whichever company is the current star). Try this instead: Look at your *worst* performer and be glad you didn't put all your money there.

Of course, diversification also applies to a portfolio made up of mutual funds. Funds concentrating on just part of the market carry significant risk. Some technology-sector funds posted triple-digit gains in 1999, only to decline significantly in 2000 and 2001. But at the height of the bubble, plenty of people—professionals as well as ordinary investors—scoffed at diversification as an outmoded idea. Indeed, an investor who stuck with balance and diversification missed out on the boom in technology stocks. But when the dust had cleared, the balanced investor was better off.

Here's a tragic example of giving up on diversification. In the months after the bursting of the dot-com bubble, I spoke to a rueful investor near retirement who had moved her entire account out of a broadly diversified Vanguard stock fund and into a technology fund at another firm in 1999, at the height of the dot-com frenzy. When the tech sector and growth stocks in general tumbled, she lost 80%

of her money. If she had stayed in the broad stock market fund, the loss would have been only about 15%. She went on to say, "Mr. Brennan, as soon as my technology fund gets back to even, I'll move the money back to Vanguard." Sadly, she may be waiting for that moment for many years. It's dangerous to hope that an inappropriate investment will get back to even, as we'll discuss later.

A Case Study

Let's take a closer look at how diversifying a stock portfolio reduces risk. For this example, we at Vanguard created a series of 12 imaginary stock portfolios and examined how they would have performed during the five-year period ended March 31, 2002. In terms of diversification, they ranged from Portfolio #1, which was invested in just one sector, to Portfolio #12, which had holdings evenly spread across all of the stock market's 12 broad sectors, or industry groups. Portfolio #1 was devoted entirely to the technology sector, the most volatile industry group for the five-year period. Portfolio #2 was evenly split between the technology sector and the energy sector, the second-most-volatile sector in the period. And so on through Portfolio #12, which had exposure to everything.

As shown in Figure 6.1, we significantly reduced the volatility of the portfo-

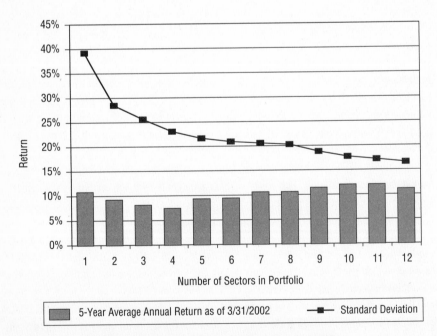

FIGURE 6.1   How Diversifying Your Portfolio Reduces Volatility

Sources: FactSet, S&P 500 Index; sectors are those used by Frank Russell Company.

lio without substantially reducing the return when we diversified it. To compute this type of risk, we used a measure called standard deviation, which is based on the extent of up-and-down swings in returns over a given period. (I'll discuss standard deviation in more detail in Chapter 11.) Portfolio #12 was less than half as risky as Portfolio #1, but its five-year return was very similar—11.8% versus 11.3% for the period ended March 31, 2002.

Wellington Fund—The Enduring Appeal of Balance

Balance in investing is like a navy-blue blazer—you can joke about it being stodgy, but over and over again, it has demonstrated its reliability. Let me tell you the story of Vanguard Wellington Fund. If funds had clothes, Wellington would be attired in a blue blazer and gray flannels.

You could say that the nation's first balanced mutual fund was out of step the day it began operations on July 1, 1929, near the top of the "Roaring Twenties" boom. As a balanced fund, Wellington Fund was dedicated to reducing risk by investing in a sensible mix of stocks and bonds. Its founder, Walter Morgan, was a conservative investor in an era of feverish speculation. Who cared about bonds? Who cared about risk? Speculating in stocks had become the national pastime. But the stock market peaked that summer, and its worst crash in history was just three months away. Thanks to Mr. Morgan's conservatism, the new fund would survive both the crash and the horrific Great Depression that followed.

Wellington Fund, initially named the Industrial and Power Securities Company, went on to weather World War II, the turbulent 1960s, the recession of the 1970s, and much, much more. It has outlasted nearly all of the 677 other funds that were in business in 1929. Most of them were highly aggressive stock funds that invested with borrowed money, and their share prices sank like stones after the crash.

Today, Vanguard Wellington Fund is the nation's oldest balanced mutual fund. It is also one of the largest funds in the world. The fund has gone in and out of favor over the years as the concept of balance has fallen in and out of favor with investors. From 1970 to 1984, more money left the fund than came in each year. But its story proves that a conservative, balanced approach is a strategy for all times.

Over a 30-year period, from 1972 to 2001, Wellington Fund produced an average annual return of 11.4%, compared with 12.2% for stocks as measured by the S&P 500 Index for the period. Not bad for a fund that maintains a 65%/35% ratio of stocks to bonds—meaning that it is only about 65% as volatile as the S&P 500. Someone who put $10,000 into Wellington Fund at the start of that period and left it there untouched for 30 years would have had a balance of $251,958 at the end of 2001, before taxes. My point is not to brag about Wellington Fund specifically, but to demonstrate that balance and diversification are proven strategies that really work.

In a Nutshell

Balance and diversification are investment strategies that will pay off in the long run if you commit to them and stick to them when the going gets rough.

- **Balance smooths your ride.** Holding a balanced portfolio—one that's made up of stocks and bonds, and perhaps cash too—can make it easier to endure the inevitable ups and downs in the stock market.
- **Diversification reduces risk.** Holding a diversified portfolio—one that's invested in the securities of a variety of issuers—protects you from the risk that goes with putting all your eggs in one basket.

chapter seven

YOU NEED A PERSONAL INVESTMENT POLICY WHETHER YOU START WITH ZILLIONS OR ZIP

The very first step in assembling an investment portfolio is to decide how to spread your dollars among stock, bond, and cash investments. This is your *asset allocation plan*, and it is the most critical investment decision you will make. That's right—your asset mix will be a bigger factor in your investment returns than any decisions you will eventually make about the merits of individual mutual funds or securities. This statement may sound odd—after all, lots of people in the financial business want you to believe success depends on shrewd stock picking or having the right mutual funds. But they're wrong.

Think of your asset allocation plan as your personal *investment policy*. Just as multibillion-dollar pension and endowment funds adopt investment policies based on a target asset mix, so should you. The idea is to develop a simple allocation that you can stick with through thick and thin, modifying it only as your situation changes—not in response to the ups and downs of the financial markets. I'd recommend that you put it in writing and file it away with your important financial records to reinforce the commitment you're making to yourself.

Should you invest your entire portfolio in stocks? Or should you divide it among stocks and bonds—or perhaps stocks, bonds, and cash investments? It depends. Your asset mix should suit your financial situation, time horizon, and risk tolerance. In this chapter, we'll again encounter that familiar risk/reward trade-off as we examine how to go about discovering the asset allocation plan that is right for you.

Why You Should Care . . . *a Lot*

There's an important reason for making such a big deal about asset allocation. It really matters! A landmark 1986 study found that decisions about asset mix had a far greater influence on investment results than decisions about specific funds. Because of this study—"Determinants of Portfolio Performance," by Gary P. Brinson, L. Randolph Hood, and Gilbert L. Beebower[1]—it is now widely accepted in the investment business that the first step in constructing an individual portfolio is to make a conscious, deliberate decision about how to apportion your assets among stocks, bonds, and cash investments.

Unfortunately, many investors don't spend much time thinking about their asset mix. They leave it to chance. They may change the mix willy-nilly every time the investment climate shifts, moving their money into stocks when the market is rising and then into bonds when the stock market slumps. Or they may waste energy agonizing over whether to invest in Coca-Cola or PepsiCo, or over which of the hundreds of large-cap growth funds to buy, without giving a thought to their overall investment plan. Either approach is likely to lead to disappointing results. Asset allocation is a strategic decision. If you get the strategy right, the tactical decision about which securities to buy is not so difficult—or crucial, for that matter.

Kicking the Tires on Some Different Portfolio Models

Before you can decide on your asset mix, you need to understand the trade-offs involved. Each possible weighting of stocks, bonds, and cash carries a different level of risk and potential reward. We've already discussed the fact that riskier assets tend to provide higher long-term returns with less stability, while less-risky assets provide more stability and lower long-term returns. Accordingly, it will come as no surprise to you that returns from stock-heavy portfolios have historically been more volatile than those of bond-heavy portfolios, and also have been higher over the long haul. Conversely, portfolios dominated by bonds have provided lower but more stable returns.

Table 7.1 illustrates the trade-off in practical terms. It shows, for example, that a conservative growth portfolio composed of 40% stocks and 60% bonds provided average yearly returns of 8.1% from 1926 to 2001. Along the way, this portfolio posted losses in 16 of the 76 years—roughly one year in every five. In contrast, an aggressive all-stock portfolio returned 10.7% a year, on average, while enduring losses in 22 out of 76 years—a decline roughly every 3½ years. (Both portfolios had their worst year in 1931, when the conservative portfolio lost

---

[1]Brinson, Hood, and Beebower: "Determinants of Portfolio Performance," *Financial Analysts Journal* (1986, 1991).

TABLE 7.1   Asset Mixes and Their Past Performance: 1926–2001

Goal of Mix	Components	Average Annual Return	Worst 1-Year Loss	Number of Years out of 76 with Losses
Stability	10% stocks 80% bonds 10% cash	6.2%	−6.7% (1969)	10
Income	20% stocks 80% bonds	7.0%	−10.1% (1931)	13
Conservative Growth	40% stocks 60% bonds	8.1%	−18.4% (1931)	16
Balanced Growth	50% stocks 50% bonds	8.7%	−22.5% (1931)	17
Moderate Growth	60% stocks 40% bonds	9.1%	−26.6% (1931)	19
Growth	80% stocks 20% bonds	10.0%	−34.9% (1931)	21
Aggressive Growth	100% stocks	10.7%	−43.1% (1931)	22

Stock returns are based on the S&P 500 Index. Bond returns are based on high-quality corporate bond indexes. Cash returns are based on the Salomon Smith Barney 3-Month Treasury Bill Index.

18.4% and the aggressive portfolio lost 43.1%.) Obviously, if you are the owner of the aggressive portfolio, you may need strong nerves to stick with it long enough to earn a higher long-term return.

Your Personal Asset Allocation Plan

You can design your own portfolio to achieve the level of risk/return that suits your needs. To decide just what these needs are, you'll want to consider a few simple factors: your financial situation, your time horizon, and your risk tolerance. Let's look at these key factors in order.

Financial Situation

How secure is your job? How much money have you saved? How much debt do you have, and when is it due? Those are the kinds of questions that will help you to clarify the priorities in your overall investment program. If you are tucking away a significant sum, you won't need to take on as much risk to reach a particular goal as you would otherwise. For instance, if you were investing a lump sum of $100,000 and hoped to reach a $500,000 goal after 20 years, you would need average annual gains of 8% to get there. But if you had only $50,000 to invest, you would need to receive an exceptional 12% average annual return to get to $500,000 in 20 years.

There are additional issues to consider. It would be unwise to focus all your energy on developing a stock portfolio if your job is not very secure and you don't have an emergency fund. Your first step is to get that emergency fund in place by building up short-term bond and cash investments. Those reserves would come in handy if you lost your job. If you put your rainy-day money into stocks, you run the risk of being forced to sell them for cash at an inopportune time, such as in the midst of a market downturn.

Time Horizon

How soon will you need the money you hope to accumulate? Will you have to withdraw it as a lump sum, or can you draw on it gradually over a long period?

Questions like these will further guide you in allocating your dollars. Generally, the longer you have until you'll need to tap your money, the greater your ability to try for a higher return by holding volatile investments like stocks.

Two general rules of thumb apply:

1. If you have an investment horizon of less than five years, you probably should not be investing in stocks. That's because of the volatility risk—the stock market might be heading downward just when you need to sell your holdings. For instance, if you are saving up to make a down payment on a house in three years' time, you should play it safe and invest the money in short-term bonds or a money market fund rather than in stocks.

2. If you have a very long time horizon—20 years or more—then you probably should invest a good portion of your money in stocks, if you can stand the volatility. While money market funds and other very-short-term investments are good for preserving capital, they typically don't grow as much as stocks over long periods, and they may even lose ground to inflation.

If you're somewhere in the middle of these two extremes—say, with a time horizon of 10 to 15 years—a mix of bonds and stocks is probably appropriate. But other factors in your situation will help guide your asset mix for these intermediate-term goals.

One more comment about your time horizon: It might be longer than you think. After all, you're unlikely to be withdrawing every cent of your retirement account or your child's college savings on a certain day. The retirement phase of your life could last 20 years or more, and college payments could take 4 or more years.

Don't Overlook Bonds

Long-term investors are often quick to embrace stocks but less interested in bonds. Some people simply think bonds are boring; others are intimidated by them. The next chapter goes into more detail about bonds. But since I've been discussing the role of bonds in a portfolio, I want to say a few words on their behalf here.

- **Bonds aren't just for retired people.** Many people think of bonds as an investment for retirees or others seeking a regular source of income. It's true that the regular interest payments do make bonds an attractive choice if you are looking for a steady source of cash, as many retirees are.

  But you don't have to be a retiree to benefit from investing in bonds. As I've discussed previously in this book, holding bonds in a portfolio helps to offset the volatility of stocks. When the stock market plunged in 2000, plenty of investors found that their boring old bond funds were very reassuring investments.

- **You don't have to have the "bond gene" to invest in bonds.** A very smart person I know insists that she'll never be able to understand how bonds work because she was born without the bond gene. Granted, bonds can be complex, but you don't have to understand all of their intricacies in order to use them effectively in your portfolio.

- **If you've ever ridden a seesaw, you can understand how bonds behave.** The most important thing to understand about bond investments is that bond prices and interest rates move in opposite directions. When interest rates are rising, bond prices are falling. And when rates are falling, bond prices are rising. This is a confusing concept to new investors, but you'll remember it if you think of bond prices and interest rates as a seesaw.

  Why does it happen? Suppose you invest in a 20-year Treasury bond that pays 5.5% in interest. If prevailing interest rates rise to 6.5%, other investors will be able to buy new bonds that pay better. No one in his right mind would be willing to pay full price for a 5.5% bond, so if you wanted to sell your bond you would have to take less than its face value. But if interest rates fall instead, and new Treasury bonds are offered with a 4.5% rate, you'll probably be able to sell your bond for more than you paid.

- **Long-term investors should ignore the bond seesaw.** If you are investing in bonds as part of a long-term strategy, you shouldn't worry too much about their price declines. In fact, although it may seem counterintuitive, long-term investors in bond funds should celebrate the news that bond prices are falling. Bond prices fall when interest rates are rising, and that means that your fund will be able to invest in new bonds that pay higher interest rates. Over the long term, those reinvested interest payments will be the source of most of the wealth accumulated in your bond fund account. At higher interest rates, you'll accumulate wealth faster. An investment earning 7% a year doubles in 10 years. One earning 6% doubles in 12 years. See "The Rule of 72" on page 167.

Risk Tolerance

Do you find yourself worrying a lot about things you cannot control? Or do you just take events as they come, accepting bad news as inevitable from time to time? Questions like these will help you assess your tolerance for risk. Although your current financial situation and your time horizon are fairly straightforward to assess, your risk tolerance is very subjective. No one else can know how much or how little you'll be distressed if your portfolio suffers a loss. Many people don't even know for themselves until they have experienced it. Try this: Imagine that you get your next account statement, and it shows that a fifth of your savings have vanished. In fact, a lot of people have experienced this very situation in the 2000–2002 period. If your stomach churns at the mere thought of such a loss, you would not be comfortable with a portfolio that's entirely invested in aggressive growth stock funds.

Pitfall: Beware the Allure of Gold, Real Estate, and Other Risky Investments

In this book, I am focusing on stocks, bonds, and cash equivalents—the three major asset classes. From time to time, you'll hear people tout investments in other assets, such as commercial real estate, gold and precious metals, timber, collectibles, and so forth. It's true that these investments provide good returns from time to time. Also, I suppose you could argue that they help with portfolio diversification because they may behave very differently from stocks, bonds, and cash. But they are very risky, and certainly not essential to a solid investment program.

While these assets can add diversification to a large portfolio, they also add complexity, and they may be expensive in terms of management fees or your time. Your best bet is to leave them out entirely. Broad stock and bond funds will give you exposure to those sectors, so you'll benefit from any booms in timber or commercial real estate or gold mining without being overly exposed to the risks. If you feel that you must invest in them, never weight them as heavily as you would stocks, bonds, or cash investments.

You'll see what I mean about the riskiness of gold in Figure 7.1. The average annual total return on the Salomon Smith Barney World Gold Index for the 20-year period from 1982 through 2001 was 2.87%. Subtracting inflation, the real return was actually negative: A $10,000 investment made in 1982 would have been worth just $8,978 at the end of 2001. There will of course be periods when gold provides attractive returns, but generally, the risks outweigh the rewards, in my view.

Although other factors might seem to point you toward an aggressive portfolio, if you are not a risk-tolerant person, that should trump everything else. While you will probably want to hold some stock investments to reach your long-term goals, you should balance them with enough bonds and cash investments to let you sleep soundly at night even when the markets are volatile. Holding bonds can give you the courage to hold stocks. (We'll examine risk tolerance in greater detail in Chapter 11, "Risk: Give It the Gut Test.")

Asset Models for Retirement Investing

Let's consider how asset allocation can affect a retirement portfolio, since that is likely to form the biggest chunk of your investments. Financial planners have come up with various asset allocation models geared to the "typical" investor.

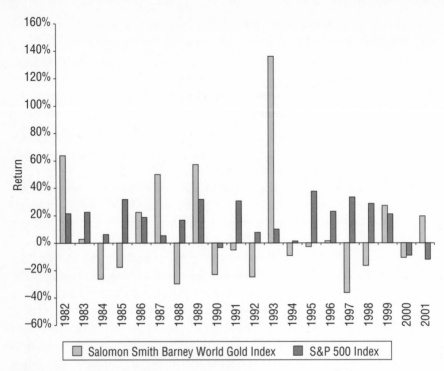

FIGURE 7.1   Gold Index Returns: 1982–2001

These models generally assume that the investor's allocation should change over time, with the level of risk dropping as retirement approaches. Most recommend that you start out in your twenties by investing entirely, or almost entirely, in stocks, and then gradually add bonds to your portfolio over the years. For example, a model might recommend that you start with 100% stocks in your twenties, move to 80% stocks/20% bonds in your thirties, go to 70% stocks/30% bonds in your forties, and so on. As you approach retirement, many asset allocation models would have you owning more bonds than stocks.

Of course, asset allocation models geared to a "typical" investor won't suit every individual. They focus purely on age, whereas you must also consider your investment objective, personal financial situation, and risk tolerance. If you are 55 and investing for retirement, but you plan to work past 65, your age won't tell the full story about your time horizon. You may differ from the average retirement investor in other ways as well. For instance, if you have other means of financial support and won't need your retirement savings to live on, you may want to invest more aggressively in order to build an estate. In that event, you could increase the stock component of your portfolio above what the models suggest. It just depends on what your goals are.

Your risk tolerance is another factor that might set you apart from the "typical" retirement investor. Suppose you are not at all comfortable with risk. Then you would want to choose a more conservative asset mix than the models recommend. For instance, instead of 70% stocks/30% bonds in your 40s, you might prefer a 50%/50% mix or even a 30%/70% mix. It's quite possible that two investors with different risk tolerance levels would choose different asset mixes even though they had identical goals and time horizons. The great thing about living below your means and being a good saver is that you'll have the flexibility to be *either* more conservative *or* more aggressive with your investment portfolio.

One caveat for those who are getting a late start on saving for retirement: Be very, very careful about taking on extra risk in an effort to make up for lost time. Yes, you can sometimes score big by investing aggressively, but you can also lose big. You can't afford to gamble with your retirement savings. Rather than taking on extra risk, you could work longer, save more, or adjust your plans for your retirement lifestyle.

What about International Markets?

There are pros and cons to investing internationally. The bottom line is that if you're an American investor, you should not feel that you *must* invest in the markets of other nations to properly diversify your portfolio. You already have some exposure to those overseas markets if you invest in the stocks and bonds of U.S. companies. America's stock market is the world's largest; our largest companies derive a significant portion of their profits from markets around the world.

However, there are some worthwhile reasons to invest internationally. A major one is the growing opportunity offered by businesses abroad. Many leading companies in important industries are based outside the United States. In addition, there are very attractive opportunities in the unification of Europe's monetary and economic systems, the growth of capitalism in Eastern Europe, the enterprise of the Pacific Rim, and the growth possibilities of emerging-market economies in Asia, Europe, South America, and Africa.

Investing in international stocks can also add a degree of diversification to your long-term portfolio. The returns of foreign stocks can move in different directions from those of U.S. stocks. Thus, holding international stocks can help to offset the ups and downs of U.S. stocks in your portfolio. To capture the benefits of portfolio diversification without taking on too much risk, limit your international stock holdings to no more than 10% to 20% of your overall stock holdings.

A few caveats:

- **International stocks carry added risks.** One risk is that currency movements will have an effect on your investments. A stronger U.S. dollar diminishes the value of foreign assets owned by U.S. investors, while a weaker U.S. dollar will increase their value. A second factor to consider is political risk, the possibility that events in other nations could lead to problems for your investments. Political risk is a special concern in the markets of less-established, developing nations.

- **International funds typically charge much higher fees than other types of stock funds.** Research may be more expensive, and transaction costs are higher in smaller markets. The average expense ratio for international stock funds in 2001 was 1.69%, but there are low-cost funds charging far less.

- **International stocks can be more volatile than U.S. stocks.** History shows that international stocks have the potential for more serious short-term declines than U.S. stocks.

Because of these factors, a few rules of thumb make sense: If you want to obtain exposure to foreign markets, the best way is through very broadly diversified low-cost mutual funds. Index funds are a wise choice here, just as they are domestically. Some international funds focus on stocks from many countries, while others focus on a particular region or country or a category of countries with similar economic conditions. I suggest that you avoid single-country international funds because they are very risky. You can find index funds that track the major foreign markets in Europe, the Pacific region, and developing nations.

Resist the temptation to buy or sell international funds based on your views or the views of experts about where the dollar is headed. That's another form of market-timing.

In a Nutshell

You're establishing a personal investment policy when you decide how to spread your dollars among stock, bond, and cash investments. This is a critical first step in constructing an investment portfolio. Should your stock/bond mix be 80%/20%, 60%/40%, or some other blend? Take the "OTROC" approach by addressing these issues:

- **O**bjectives. What is your purpose in investing?
- **T**ime horizon. How soon will you need to use the money? Some investments are better suited to short-term, mid-term, or long-term purposes.
- **R**isk tolerance. How much stomach do you have for the risks of volatile markets?
- **O**ther investments. What holdings do you already have, and what do they offer in terms of balance and diversification?
- **C**hoose. Decide your portfolio's asset mix accordingly.

chapter eight
MUTUAL FUNDS: THE EASY WAY TO DIVERSIFY

There is an old saying that the three most important words in real estate are location, location, location. If there are three most important words in investing, they are diversification, diversification, diversification. Diversification will help you manage the risk that's an inevitable part of investing in stocks and bonds.

You can choose to diversify for yourself by choosing a variety of individual securities, or you can diversify by investing in packaged investment products like mutual funds, where professionals have done the work for you. I'm a firm believer in mutual funds—not because funds are what I do for a living, but because of what they can do for me while I earn my living.

Which approach is the right one for you? I'm going to be blunt. Despite all that you read in the papers, most people should not attempt to invest in individual securities with their "serious" money. Why? It's too risky. Recent studies indicate that to adequately diversify a stock portfolio may require up to 100 stocks, carefully chosen to include all major industries and both large and small companies.

When professional financial analysts pick securities, they weigh a variety of financial ratios and other indicators as well as competitor data and industry trends. Even so, successful results are far from guaranteed. The pros who spend their entire careers—40 to 60 hours a week—studying these things don't bat a thousand. In fact, most stock pickers fail to beat the performance of the broad market, and for two reasons: (1) It's *really* difficult to pick winners. (2) Transaction costs cut into investment returns. Chances are, your own batting average won't be any better. Nonprofessionals face all the same challenges that the pros do, and they cannot match the time, resources, and experience of a professional investment manager.

It's extremely difficult to make the right decisions and avoid the wrong decisions when you are managing a portfolio of many different securities. Suppose you are evaluating a company with a new chairman that has just spun off a division at a time when the industry is going through major upheaval. You need to decide whether those developments bode well for the company. Better hurry, because it's just one of 100 companies you are investing in, and the investment climate is constantly changing for all of them.

If that's not enough to juggle, remember that you've got to be managing your emotions, too. Investors tend to make emotional decisions; even the experts do, sometimes. It's tough to resist the temptation to be a momentum investor, betting that the markets will continue to move in a certain direction. When markets are climbing, the temptation is to buy in. When markets are falling, the temptation is to bail out.

For all of these reasons, most individuals will find that easily the best way to achieve diversification is by investing in mutual funds. Many funds hold securities from hundreds or even thousands of issuers. In fact, it is possible to obtain exposure to the entire universe of U.S. stocks and bonds very efficiently with just two mutual funds—a total-market stock index fund and a total-market bond index fund.

The virtues of diversified mutual funds are regularly demonstrated by events. In the late summer of 1998, when the stock market took a dive after the collapse of a big-name (but poorly run!) hedge fund, mutual fund investors fared better than investors in hundreds of individual stocks. By year-end, 1,282 stocks out of the total of 7,168 listed for public trading had lost 50% or more of their value. In sharp contrast, just two (yes, two!) mutual funds had losses of 50% or more—two out of 3,404 U.S. stock funds in existence for the period.

How Mutual Funds Work

In my view, mutual funds are the greatest invention ever in financial services because they provide ordinary people with easy access to diversified investment pools at a relatively low cost. Today, millions of investors from virtually every walk of life entrust their savings to mutual funds to reach their financial goals. The existence of these investments has been a key reason for America's evolution from a nation of savers to a nation of investors. The fund industry started with the introduction of a single mutual fund in 1924, and today manages almost $7 trillion in assets. Nearly half of all U.S. households invest in mutual funds.

The idea behind the mutual fund is simple: Many people pool their money and pay a professional to invest it for them in a particular market or market segment. Each investor shares proportionately in the investment returns. Every fund has a professional manager who invests the fund's assets in accordance with the objectives stated in the fund's prospectus. The objective could be, for example, long-term growth, high current income, or reasonable income along with stability of principal. Depending on its objective, a fund may invest in common stocks, bonds, cash instruments, or a combination of all three.

Basic Information: How You Make Money As a Mutual Fund Investor

You invest in a mutual fund to make money. So before you put up any cash, you should understand exactly how a fund proposes to make money for you. The way a fund produces earnings can make a big difference to you in several respects.

The first thing you need to understand is that there are three potential ways to make money by investing in stocks, bonds, and other securities.

- **Interest.** You earn interest on bonds, money market instruments, and other debt securities.

- **Dividends.** You earn dividends on stocks when a company distributes some of the profits it makes to its shareholders. Not all companies pay dividends; some have no profits to pay out to shareholders, while others retain all of their earnings to reinvest and keep the business growing.

- **Capital appreciation.** You can benefit when the price of an investment that you hold goes up.

Mutual funds earn money in the same ways: They get income—dividends or interest—from stocks or bonds they own. And they have capital appreciation when their holdings go up in price. When a fund sells appreciated securities for a profit, then it has a realized capital gain. The fund is obligated to pass its income and capital gains along to you, the owner. It does so by making *distributions*, usually expressed in terms of a dollar amount per share.

But that's not the whole story about how you can make money from a fund. You also can sell your fund shares or exchange them for shares in another fund—which is, in effect, a sale. If your fund shares are worth more when you sell them than what you've invested in them, you have a profit. Selling those shares locks in your profit and gives you a realized capital gain.

Unless you hold the fund in a tax-deferred retirement account, you'll owe taxes on income or capital gains distributions that you receive. However, you don't owe taxes on capital appreciation in your fund shares until you sell the shares. The IRS taxes income and capital gains differently, and the amount of taxes you'll owe also depends on your tax bracket. (Income from tax-exempt bond or money market funds usually is free from federal income tax. But capital gains distributions are taxed, even if they are from a tax-exempt fund.)

We'll discuss tax issues in Chapter 10, but for now, just remember that you generally won't keep all the money you make on your mutual funds in taxable accounts. Even if you reinvest your earnings in the funds instead of taking them in cash, you'll owe taxes.

I'll discuss the basics of mutual funds in the sidebars to this chapter. But if you haven't invested in a mutual fund before, you should know some of the key points that make them different from other types of investments.

- Mutual funds pass along all their earnings—after expenses—to their shareholders.

- Each mutual fund is a company in itself, owned by its shareholders. However, funds are usually sponsored by a different company, typically the one that provides management services to the fund (and is paid by the fund to do so).

- Share prices of mutual funds are established just once a day, after the markets close. A fund's share price is called its *Net Asset Value*, or *NAV*. To calculate the NAV, the fund adds up the market value of its assets, subtracts its liabilities, and divides the result by the number of fund shares outstanding. Hence the "net" in "net asset value."

- A mutual fund investor can redeem, or sell, shares in the fund at any time.

- A fund's performance is expressed as *total return*. Total return has two components: (1) any change in the share price, and (2) any dividends or capital gains that the fund passed along to shareholders.

When mutual funds report their performance, they are required to state it in terms of 1-year, 5-year, and 10-year periods (or "since inception" if the fund hasn't been around that long). For each multiyear period, the fund must calculate a yearly average, which is generally labeled the *average annual total return*.

The Advantages of Mutual Funds

The mutual fund industry has enjoyed a level of public trust that is unknown in most other parts of the financial industry. That's partly because mutual funds are the most strictly regulated segment of the U.S. securities industry. Every fund is required to provide full disclosure of its policies, objectives, and risks, as well as its operating costs and any fees or commissions, on a regular basis. To date, the fund industry's reputation has not been marred by major fraud-related scandals such as those that have afflicted other financial businesses.

A key reason for this tradition of integrity is the regulatory framework. The two primary watchdogs are the U.S. Securities and Exchange Commission and the National Association of Securities Dealers. The primary law regulating mutual funds is the Investment Company Act of 1940—a pretty miraculous piece of consumer-protection legislation whose effectiveness has stood the test of time. The law contains numerous provisions designed to ensure that mutual funds are operated in the interests of the shareholders rather than the interest of the fund sponsor. I won't list them all, but one example is that mutual fund boards must include a majority of independent directors whose duty is to serve the interests of investors.

For investors, the attractions of mutual funds can be summed up succinctly:

- **Diversification.** Combining your money with that of thousands of other shareholders makes it possible to invest in far more securities than you could buy as an individual. That reduces your risk of loss from problems affecting the securities of any single company or institution.

- **Professional management.** You don't have to make decisions about which securities to buy and sell. An experienced investment manager who has access to extensive market information and works with skilled securities traders makes those decisions for you.

- **Liquidity.** You can sell your shares back to the fund on any business day, so you have easy access to your money. That is not always the case with individual securities.

- **Convenience.** You can monitor the price of your fund shares daily in newspapers and other sources. You can also take advantage of a variety of services that make it easy to monitor your accounts not just by mail, but by telephone or the Internet. Most major fund companies offer extensive recordkeeping services to help you track your transactions and obtain tax information.

- **Low cost** (*in some, but not all cases*). Compared with other means of investing, many mutual funds are quite cheap. Economies of scale enable them to hold down overhead and transaction costs far beyond what you could achieve on your own.

Caveats to Consider

Mutual funds aren't perfect. Like any other investment, they have some shortcomings. These are the major ones:

- **You can lose money in a mutual fund.** Unlike bank accounts, mutual fund accounts are not insured or guaranteed by the Federal Deposit Insurance Corporation or any other government agency. Your share price can go down, and so can your income from dividends or capital gains payments. Of course, you could run those risks with individual securities as well.

- **Diversification has a penalty.** Just as diversification keeps you from being seriously hurt by the problems of a single security, it keeps you from making the "big score" that you might get by piling everything into a single stock or bond whose value then shoots up.

- **Costs can vary.** As I just noted, you can invest more cost-effectively with mutual funds than by buying individual securities through a broker. However, you must be *very* careful about where you buy your funds and what you are paying in expenses. Mutual funds are an unusual product in that two nearly identical offerings can have widely different costs—there are high-cost funds that charge operating expenses 5 to 10 times higher than those of low-cost funds. Paying sales commissions on top of high expense ratios will reduce your investment returns even further.

- **You get the share price at day's end.** Mutual funds trade at the price established at the market close. That means your trade won't reflect whatever the market is doing at a given moment. But that's only a problem if you're a market-timer—in which case, you should have quit reading by now.

In truth, today there are mutual fund products you *can* trade at changing current prices. They are called *exchange-traded funds*, and they do have some benefits when used wisely. But they also have some drawbacks, and overall they're a topic for more specialized needs than this book is addressing.

Pitfall: Some Mutual Funds Are Less Diversified Than Others

Just because you're investing in a mutual fund doesn't mean you're diversified. Some mutual funds are very concentrated.

Generally speaking, the least diversified stock funds are those that invest in industry sectors such as health care, technology, energy, real estate, or precious metals. A sector fund might be fine for a small portion of your assets, but it's too risky a choice as a core holding for your portfolio.

For an illustration of the risk, we need look no further than the technology funds that sprouted like weeds during the late 1990s. Many of these funds boasted double-digit returns in those days. Where are they now? When the technology craze ended, many of them changed their names and their investment focus, or they were merged into other funds. Shame on the fund industry for bringing out so many of those funds at the top of the market for tech stocks. Egged on by the news media and by fund industry ads, thousands of investors put their hard-earned savings into the tech funds just as the joyride was ending. They bought high and ended up selling low.

There are also varying degrees of diversification among bond funds. You can invest in a fund that gives you exposure to the entire bond market or to a significant part of the market (such as short-term Treasury bonds or intermediate-term corporate bonds). Or you can invest in something with a much narrower focus, such as a fund specializing in high-yield bonds—the bonds of riskier companies, which are commonly called *junk bonds*. Say the fund owned 150 different issues; that would make you a diversified investor within the "junk" market, but it's still a tiny part of the overall bond market and quite a risky one to boot. Issuers of junk bonds are vulnerable not only to problems within their own companies but to adverse developments in the economy or in the markets. It would be unwise to make a junk bond fund the core of your portfolio.

In a Nutshell

It's extremely difficult for an individual investor to construct and manage an adequately diversified portfolio made up of individual securities. Mutual funds offer multiple advantages as the building blocks of your portfolio:

- **Diversification.** You can invest in hundreds or even thousands of individual securities through a single mutual fund.
- **Professional management.** Funds are run by professionals, so you don't have to make the decisions about which securities to buy and sell.
- **Cost efficiency.** You can invest more cost-effectively through mutual funds than with individual securities. (Just be sure to avoid high-cost funds.)
- **Liquidity.** You can sell your shares back to the fund on any business day, so you have easy access to your money.

chapter nine

HOW TO PICK A MUTUAL FUND (AND HOW NOT TO)

Once you have decided how to allocate your assets among stocks, bonds, and cash securities, you'll be ready to think about selecting specific investments. In this chapter, I want to show you a straightforward way to go about selecting mutual funds. I won't recommend specific funds. (Although I would love to!) Rather, my objective is to give you an understanding of the trade-offs that are involved in choosing one fund over another.

The goal is to "buy right and sit tight"—that is, pick funds that will suit your needs and serve as durable components of your portfolio for a long time. It's counterproductive to change your investments as often as you change the oil in your car. By choosing funds judiciously, you can construct a portfolio that will serve your needs for years—perhaps decades—and require relatively few adjustments. That's the route to investment success.

First, just to be clear, here's how *not* to select funds:

- Don't buy whatever is recommended in the latest financial magazines.
- Don't buy a fund purely because it led the performance charts over the past 12 months.
- Don't buy a fund just because it is currently top-ranked by fund-rating organizations.
- Don't buy a fund because you've seen the manager interviewed on TV and he or she sounded very smart.

Plenty of investors rely on fund rankings and magazine "top ten" lists, but they are often disappointed by the results. The trouble with rankings and hot-performer lists is that most of them are based heavily on past investment performance, ignoring cost and risk. And past performance proves absolutely nothing about the future. There's a boilerplate phrase that's a legal requirement in mutual fund prospectuses: "Past results are no guarantee of future performance." This boilerplate also happens to be one of the eternal truths of investing.

Of all the ratings and rankings, Morningstar's star-based system—just overhauled in 2002—is perhaps the best known. Morningstar provides excellent data on funds, and it uses an objective set of criteria for awarding stars. The company is careful to point out risks and to warn consumers that its ratings don't foretell the future. Yet people treat the star system as a shopping tool, just as they might rely on the appliance ratings in *Consumer Reports* to select a new washing machine.

"Well, why not?" you may ask. Why *shouldn't* a fund's past performance give a clue to what investors can expect? There are a variety of reasons: Markets change. Managers change. Bad news happens. Investment strategies or sector allocations that succeed in one period may do poorly in the next. It's also possible that the top funds in any given period may have taken on extra risk to produce stellar returns. And these factors aren't just theoretical; the real force behind the warning comes from long, hard *experience*. Anyone who has spent significant time in the investment industry has seen, over and over again, how quickly and completely the tide can turn, sometimes for reasons that no one fully understands. Here again, the late 1990s offer a telling example: If you were making an investment in December 1999, and you decided to choose between a growth stock mutual fund and a value stock fund on the basis of their 10-year performance records, you'd probably have sunk all your bucks into growth. Growth funds were *way* ahead at that point. But starting in March 2000, the wind changed and value-oriented stocks took the lead. There's just no telling when any of these changes might occur.

If you need more proof that past performance can be a poor predictor of future returns, look at Table 9.1. We examined how 1990's 10 top-performing domestic stock funds fared in subsequent years. If you bought them because of their performance, you would have been disappointed in the results.

A Process for Constructing a Portfolio

Constructing a portfolio is a four-step process:

1. Decide how to allocate your money among stocks, bonds, and cash investments.
2. Choose where to invest within each asset class.
3. Decide whether you want actively managed funds, index funds, or both.
4. Evaluate specific funds.

The rest of this chapter looks at each of these steps in detail.

TABLE 9.1   Hot Funds That Turn Cold

The top 10 general U.S. stock funds in 1990 did not always do so well in later years. Their rankings in subsequent years are shown below.

	1990	*1991*	*1994*	*1999*
Number of funds evaluated	*567*	*623*	*1,182*	*3,695*
Fund A	1	127	880	518
Fund B	2	52	1,089	186
Fund C	3	80	1,029	562
Fund D	4	617	1,109	3,132
Fund E	5	200	198	2,025
Fund F	6	594	78	2,569
Fund G	7	69	37	19
Fund H	8	8	856	816
Fund I	9	602	670	1,647
Fund J	10	241	919	1,097

Step #1: Stocks, Bonds, Cash? It's Time to Decide

By now you know the importance of making a conscious, deliberate decision about how to allocate your dollars among stocks, bonds, and cash investments. To get your portfolio started, you need to settle on an asset allocation—be it 100% stocks; 80% stocks/20% bonds; 60% stocks/30% bonds/10% cash; or any other combination that fits your tolerance for risk and your goals.

Once you know your target asset mix, you can put together a portfolio without much more effort if you want to keep things simple. The easiest way to set up a balanced, broadly diversified portfolio is to buy two or three mutual funds that offer broad exposure to the markets. A broad stock market index fund, a broad bond market index fund, and a money market fund will give you everything you need. If you are seeking a 60/30/10 asset mix, you would set up your savings program to funnel 60% of your money to the stock fund, 30% to the bond fund, and 10% to the money market fund.

You can even base your portfolio on a single balanced fund, assuming there is one that matches your target allocation. A balanced fund is one that invests in both stocks and bonds; some employ cash investments as well. You can choose a balanced fund that holds more stocks than bonds, or the reverse; or you can find one that is divided 50%/50%. Some balanced funds enforce their allocations fairly strictly, while others may change the proportions to take advantage of market trends (an approach that's a bit riskier but has the potential for greater reward). Balanced funds let you gain exposure to both asset classes with a single investment.

Of course, you don't have to take the simple approach. You could decide to build a portfolio with several funds selected to create a more tailored strategy. I'll give you some guidelines for choosing them, with just this word of warning first: No one should need more than 10 mutual funds, and fewer than that is better.

Step #2: Where to Invest within an Asset Class?

If you want to go beyond a broad-market fund to represent stocks or bonds, you need to look at subcategories of these markets. There are different types of money market funds as well. Here I'll describe very generally how to consider specific sectors within the major asset classes. In choosing among funds representing these sectors, you will be establishing your *sub-asset allocation*. (There is a more detailed discussion of these options in Appendix A to this book; see "A Guide to Stock and Bond Funds.")

Money Market Funds

Money market mutual funds are among the safest places to put your savings. I must emphasize that they are not insured by the Federal Deposit Insurance Corporation or any other government agency, so they can't boast the same protection that bank accounts have. But money market funds are strictly regulated to enforce the characteristics that make them safe. They typically invest in very-short-term debt securities from very-high-quality issuers, such as major corporations, banks, or the federal government. Because these securities mature so rapidly, there is little chance that an issuer will default (companies' credit problems usually take awhile to develop, so money market managers have time to hear the warnings and avoid the securities).

Of course, being so safe means that money market funds normally don't earn very high yields compared with other fixed income investments. That's why, as I noted earlier, a money market fund shouldn't be the core of your long-term portfolio. Your money won't grow enough in such a fund to keep you comfortably ahead of inflation.

Money market funds generally fall into three groups:

1. **U.S. Treasury funds.** These are the most conservative, since they invest principally in direct U.S. Treasury obligations—possibly the safest investments in the world.

2. **U.S. government funds.** Also called *federal* funds, these invest in securities from government agencies other than (or in addition to) the Treasury. They may also buy issues from nongovernment agencies that are backed by the U.S. government.

3. **General funds.** These are often called *prime* funds. They invest principally in issues from large, high-quality corporations and banks.

What trade-offs do you make in choosing among these three groups? It's mainly a matter of risk versus yield. Treasury funds, being the safest, usually pay the least in income. Government funds pay a bit more. General funds, which are considered the riskiest since they invest in corporate securities, typically provide the highest yields among money market funds. For most investors, the higher yield is well worth the slight extra risk.

For example, at the end of June 2002 (a period of very low interest rates), three Vanguard money market funds were providing these yields: 1.66% for the general money market fund; 1.64% for the federal money market fund; and 1.57% for the Treasury money market fund. An investor who opted for the Treasury fund was giving up 0.09 percentage points of yield (5% of his income) in order to feel ultra-safe. The yield differences between these funds are sometimes wider.

If you are in a high tax bracket, you might want to look at a fourth type of money market fund—the municipal money market fund, also called a tax-exempt money market fund. The income on these funds is exempt from federal income taxes and sometimes from state and local income taxes as well. But there is a trade-off: The pre-tax yields are typically lower than those provided by taxable money funds, so some analysis is required to determine if they make sense, given your tax bracket. For example, Vanguard's tax-exempt money market fund was yielding 1.39% at the end of June 2002, compared with the 1.57% yield of a taxable Treasury money market fund. (Chapter 10 includes more discussion about tax-exempt funds, including an explanation of how to compare yields of taxable and tax-exempt bond funds.)

Bond Funds

Before deciding among bond funds, you need to be clear about exactly what role you want bonds to play in your portfolio. That's because with bonds, the risk/reward trade-offs can lead to very different results. If you're looking for the highest current income available from bonds, you will have to expect some notable ups and downs in your account value. If you'd rather have more price stability, then lower your expectations for income from bonds.

With that in mind, let's look at the major types of bond funds. If you're new to these funds, the first thing you need to know about one of them is where it falls within each of these categories:

- **Tax status.** Taxable or tax-exempt?
- **Credit quality.** High, medium, or low?
- **Maturity.** Short, medium, or long?

The first of these I'm going to dispense with quickly. Never pick tax-exempt funds for an IRA or a 401(k) or any other account that already is sheltered from taxes. And you shouldn't consider a tax-exempt bond fund for your taxable accounts unless you are in a relatively high tax bracket and have done the calculations to make sure the fund is a wise choice. That's because tax-exempt funds typically have lower yields than similar taxable funds. (See Chapter 10.)

The other two bullet items are directly related to the question of risk versus reward. You should not buy any bond fund—taxable or tax-exempt—until you understand how it fits within these categories.

The style box shown in Figure 9.1 provides an easy way to visualize bond fund classifications. For example, a fund that invests primarily in long-term Treasury bonds, considered to have unimpeachable credit quality, would occupy the top right-hand box in Figure 9.1. A fund that invests primarily in short-term "junk" bonds, which are considered low in credit quality, would occupy the lower

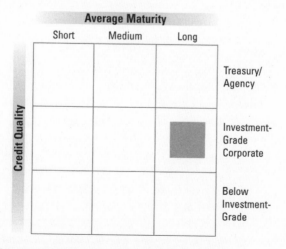

FIGURE 9.1   Sample Style Box for a Taxable Bond Fund

This example shows a long-term investment-grade corporate fund.

left box. Just keep in mind that style boxes illustrate the *primary* investment emphasis of a fund. They're not perfect tools, because some funds straddle the categories.

Credit quality. The credit quality of a bond relates to the issuer's ability to pay interest on the bond and, ultimately, to repay the principal upon maturity. A bond with a lower credit rating typically will pay you higher interest to compensate for the greater risk that principal and interest won't be repaid on time. Conversely, a bond with a higher credit rating can be expected to pay lower interest.

Major sources of credit ratings include Moody's Investors Service and Standard & Poor's Corporation. They conduct analysis to determine the business strength of companies that want to issue bonds. You don't need to know the intricacies of bond credit ratings, but it is helpful to have a general awareness of the levels. U.S. Treasury bonds have the highest quality because they are backed by the "full faith and credit" of the United States. At the bottom of the credit list are high-yield or junk bonds, issued by companies viewed as having the potential to default.

Average maturity. This is the average time until all of a fund's bond holdings reach maturity. For a short-term fund, average maturity should be less than 5 years; for an intermediate-term fund, 5 to 10 years; and for a long-term fund, more than 10 years. As you might imagine, bond funds with longer average maturities are more sensitive to changes in prevailing market interest rates. A statistic called *duration* (see Chapter 11) is a handy way to judge this interest rate sensitivity. The longer the average maturity, the steeper a fund's share-price swings tend to be when rates change. But longer-term bonds typically pay higher interest rates than shorter-term bonds to compensate investors for the risk that future events (rising interest rates or inflation, for example) will erode the value of the bond investment.

Selecting bond funds. Let's deal with the credit-quality trade-off first. If you are risk-averse, my advice is to stick with higher-quality bonds for the vast majority of your long-term bond allocation. That means investing in funds that hold U.S. Treasury bonds, high-quality corporate bonds, or insured mortgage-backed bonds. If you're in a higher tax bracket, and tax-exempt bonds make sense for you, stick to high-quality bonds issued by financially strong states and municipalities. I suggest higher-quality bonds as your main focus because the whole idea of owning bonds is to get regular income and to balance out the risks of owning stocks.

But for investors who understand the associated risks, high-yield bonds can be an attractive part of your fixed income portfolio because of the higher yields they provide. Just be sure that the high-yield bond fund you pick is very diversified.

As to average maturity, again there's a trade-off: If your investment time horizon is long-term—more than a decade—then base your bond allocation on an intermediate- or long-term fund. In doing so, keep your eyes open to the fact that the fund's share price will be more volatile than would be the case with a shorter-term bond fund. You'll be putting up with that volatility for the sake of the added income you'll get from the mid-term or long-term fund.

If your time horizon is only a few years, *don't* use a long-term bond fund. You won't be paid enough to offset the risk that the share price will fall just at the time you need the money. Instead, find a short-term fund for your bond allocation.

Stock Funds

To be a thoughtful stock investor, you need to know something about the way stocks are classified. Frankly, some of the terms you'll hear are jargon. Words like *growth* and *value* have acquired a financial meaning that isn't always in sync with what most people assume or the way fund managers think about stocks. But such words are so commonly used that you simply must be familiar with them if you're going to understand what you read and hear about stock mutual funds.

Stock funds are typically classified according to two criteria: market capitalization and investment style.

Market capitalization. This category tells you about the size of the companies a fund invests in. For an individual stock, market capitalization is equal to the number of shares outstanding multiplied by the current share price. For example, a company with 2 million shares trading at a current price of $10 a share has a market capitalization of $20 million. For a fund, the term refers to the median market cap of all the stocks it owns. Stock funds are typically grouped as *large-cap*, *mid-cap*, or *small-cap*. While there is no industry standard for the dollar amounts associated with those terms, fortunately they are fairly intuitive. For example, you can assume that most of the holdings of a large-cap fund will be familiar big-company names. But the fund might also own mid- and small-cap companies. Why should you care about market capitalization? One reason is that it's a risk factor. *As a group*, small companies are considerably riskier than big ones, and mid-size companies fall in between. So you wouldn't want your core stock allocation to consist only of small-cap funds. The other reason to care about market caps is diversification—you want to have some exposure to small-caps and mid-caps because there are times that these smaller stocks do way better than large-cap stocks.

Investment style. Stock funds are also classified in terms of whether they invest primarily in *growth* or *value* stocks. (If they invest in both, they are called *blend* funds.) I'll discuss growth and value investing in more detail in Appendix A, but

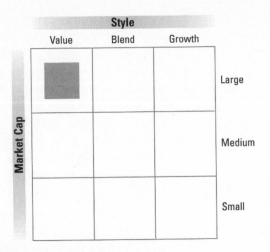

FIGURE 9.2   Sample Style Box for a Stock Fund
This example shows a large-capitalization value fund.

for now I'm going to oversimplify: Growth stocks are pricey by most traditional measures, and they pay little or nothing in dividends. People who buy them are betting that the company is going to grow fast enough to warrant an even higher price in the future. In the 1990s, growth stocks justified that belief for a long time. Value stocks, in contrast, represent companies that the market as a whole does- n't expect to grow very fast. These stocks generally have low prices according to traditional measures of what a company is worth. The idea in value investing is to sniff out companies that are underappreciated or temporarily out of favor with the market and then get a nice price jump when your insights turn out to be correct.

There are a variety of style box models for stock funds, but the one you'll en- counter most often is the Morningstar style box, as shown in Figure 9.2. I think of the style box categories as a set of fish ponds. If you are investing in stocks for the long term, you'll want to fish in all the ponds. The reason for this is that there will be times when the fish are biting in one pond but not in others; times when large-cap stocks outperform small-cap stocks (or vice versa), and when value stocks outperform growth stocks (and vice versa). The idea is to maintain some exposure to all of those sectors at all times instead of thinking you can succeed with a market-timing strategy of moving from one to another. To keep a hook in every pond, pick a single stock fund that invests broadly across all sectors of the stock market or a number of funds that invest in different sectors.

Some investors like to think of themselves as intensely value-oriented or growth-oriented and will passionately argue the long-term merits of their strat-

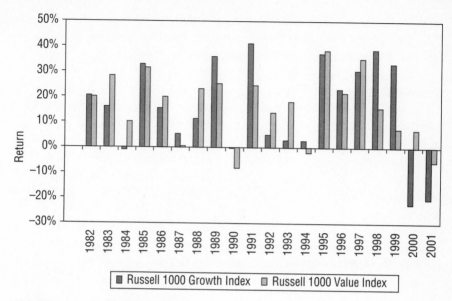

FIGURE 9.3   Growth versus Value

egy. But over the long run, the returns of growth and value stocks have been pretty similar, as shown in Figure 9.3. I wouldn't recommend a big bias in either direction. Stay broadly diversified.

Step #3: Actively Managed Funds, Index Funds, or Some of Each?

You can build a mutual fund portfolio using either actively managed funds or index funds—or a mix of both. There are some interesting differences between the two strategies, and their relative merits have provoked a great debate ever since index funds surfaced in the 1970s. Here's my position: Index funds have advantages so powerful that you should use them for the core of your portfolio. Indeed, an *all*-indexed portfolio can work very well. If you want to invest in actively managed funds, let them play a supporting role. Let's look at the differences between the two approaches.

The manager of an "active" fund tries to beat the market by shrewdly selecting which stocks or bonds to buy. The manager bases decisions not only on experience and market savvy but also on sophisticated security analysis and research into economic, demographic, or other trends.

In contrast, an index fund tries to match—not beat—the market. To do so, the fund buys and holds all (or a large representative sample) of the securities in an established market benchmark. That might be the S&P 500 Index or the Wilshire 5000 Index for stocks, the Lehman Aggregate Bond Index, or any of dozens of other well-known indexes tracking markets or market segments.

What's so good about index funds? Why do I recommend that you do without the shrewd selection, market savvy, research, and all that? It's because history has shown that, despite those factors, active managers don't beat the indexes even half the time. One of the biggest reasons that they don't is costs—the money that active funds have to spend on research and analysis and trading fees. Index funds have no research expenses and do relatively little trading, so they have a big cost advantage over actively managed funds. That cost advantage translates into a big head start for the investors. A fund that takes less of a cut from its gross returns to cover its expenses is passing along a bigger chunk of return to you.

We investors as a group make up "the market," so as a group we earn whatever return it provides—after expenses are subtracted. Index funds work because (1) very few active managers can consistently beat the markets, but index funds *can* consistently match the markets, or at least come close, and (2) index funds minimize the drag of costs.

It's pretty hard to argue against the logic of index investing, but some diehard proponents of active investing still do. You may hear them say that index investors are settling for average or mediocre returns. They'll ask you: Why not reach for something better by investing in an actively managed fund that tries to beat the indexes? In fact, very few actively managed funds manage to beat their benchmark indexes, as shown in Figure 9.4. The facts suggest that there's a great deal of wisdom in aspiring to be average. *And* frugal.

Market indexes outpaced most active fund managers over the 15-year period ended in 2001. The data in this table actually understate the advantages of indexing because of *survivorship bias*—it doesn't include data from funds that went out

	Value	Blend	Growth
Large*	80%	74%	66%
Medium*	56%	67%	62%
Small*	79%	56%	29%

FIGURE 9.4   Percentage of Actively Managed Funds Outperformed by Their Index Benchmarks: 1986–2001

*The table is based on data from Morningstar and the following Russell indexes: Russell 1000 Index (and its value and growth subsets); Russell Midcap Index (and its value and growth subsets); and Russell 2000 Index (and its value and growth subsets).

of business during the 15 years. Funds that close usually do so because of poor performance. In the small-cap growth category, many funds gained an edge over the index in this period by stretching their mandate to include larger stocks.

Step #4: Evaluating a Fund

Let's assume you've determined that you want to invest in a particular fund category. Perhaps it's an intermediate-term Treasury bond fund or a large-cap value stock fund. Now you need to know how to identify and evaluate some funds that could fill the bill.

Think Like an Owner: Eight Important Reasons to Read the Prospectus

When you buy shares in a mutual fund or shares of stock in a corporation, you're not buying mere pieces of paper. You are becoming part-owner of a company (remember, a mutual fund is a company, too). So in evaluating a possible investment, it's best to think like an owner.

As a potential owner, start by reading a fund's prospectus. I know, *prospectus* sounds like a Latin word meaning dull and boring. But mutual fund prospectuses are easier to read these days, thanks to "plain English" rules the SEC enacted a few years ago. Becoming familiar with the prospectus is part of your homework as an investor.

In case you don't have the time to read the prospectus from front to back, take 10 or 15 minutes to skim through it, highlighter in hand, and mark the answers to the following questions. (You'll locate many of them in the summary near the front of the booklet.) I guarantee you'll be a more informed investor as a result.

1. **What is the fund's investment objective?** Make sure you understand what the fund is trying to accomplish. A money market fund's objective is to provide current income while keeping the share price constant, which keeps your investment from shrinking. An aggressive growth fund's objective is capital appreciation—it is trying to buy stocks that will rise in value over time. A balanced fund or an equity income fund may be trying to produce both current income and long-term capital appreciation.

2. **How will the fund go about making money for you?** Look for the section on investment strategy to learn how the fund manager will try to reach the stated objective. This should tell you the types of securities the fund typically holds, and provide some basic information about the methods the manager uses to select the securities. If you find the strategy hard to fathom, don't invest until you have asked more questions and gained at least a general understanding of how the fund works.

3. **What risks will you encounter?** Read the section about primary risks and then look for everything else the prospectus has to say about risks. These risks are *real*; I assure you, the fund company doesn't list them there on a whim! But remember, your goal isn't to avoid all risks—every fund has some type of risk—but instead to understand the specific risks you'll face.

4. **Who's running the fund?** The prospectus will include a section about the fund's "investment adviser," the manager (or team of managers) in charge of the fund. You want to know how long the manager has been running the fund; its past results may be less meaningful if the manager has changed recently. How many years has the manager been in the investment business, and what are his or her credentials?

5. **What are you paying?** In the summary at the beginning of a fund prospectus, you'll find a full list of the fees and expenses charged by the fund, including its expense ratio and any sales commissions, purchase or redemption fees, low-balance fees, and the like. To help you see the impact, there will be a table illustrating how much these fees would cost you on a $10,000 investment in the fund.

6. **How long has the fund been around?** There are plenty of sound, established funds with long track records. A newer fund may be a fine investment, but you should be aware that its track record might not be very meaningful and that its results when new and small might be hard to sustain as it gets older and larger.

7. **What services does it offer?** Make sure that the fund or its sponsoring company provides the services you want and that you know what they'll cost you. Do you want to write checks against your fund account? Do you want to conduct transactions online? Is there a limit on the number of checks or transactions in a given time period? The prospectus should answer these questions and most others you might have.

8. **How has the fund performed?** I listed this item last because past performance really is not a good indicator of how a fund will perform for you. The prospectus will tell you a fund's average annual returns for the past 1-, 5-, and 10-year periods (or since the fund began), and it provides a helpful comparison of those results against a market index as a benchmark. Look at the "financial highlights" portion of the prospectus to see the fund's past distributions of capital gains and income dividends—this will give you a sense of how the fund may affect your tax bill.

One sensible approach is to choose a few sound fund families and then compare similar funds offered by those firms. Here are some things to keep in mind when you compare.

- **Make sure you understand what you are buying.** Doublecheck that the fund or funds you are considering are "fishing in the right pond" for your investment objective. There are truth-in-labeling rules for mutual funds, but opinions can differ about what a term like *growth* or *value* or *high level of income* means. A fund's prospectus discloses its investment strategies. Make sure that you understand where it invests—for example, does it also hold foreign securities? And check to see that you understand its level of risk.

You can find other essential information about a fund's strategies and risks in its prospectus. Today's prospectuses are a lot easier to deal with than they used to be, but I'm well aware that they're still not exactly a breezy read. That's why I've included the sidebar titled "Think Like an Owner: Eight Important Reasons to Read the Prospectus," on page 97.

- **Choose low-cost funds.** Costs are a drag on your investment returns—the more you're paying, the more of a drag they are. We'll talk more about costs in a future chapter; the key point here is that you should always examine a fund's costs before investing in it. You don't have to buy the lowest-cost fund that's out there, but you should be very selective in evaluating expense ratios and fees.

  I honestly can't think of *any* reason to invest in *any* type of fund with above-average costs. But cost is especially important when you're choosing bond and money market funds. Indeed, with money market funds, it's by far the dominant factor in achieving competitive returns. Since all such funds have to invest in pretty much the same groups of securities, it's hard for any one of them to pull far ahead of the pack in terms of returns. If you are choosing between two very similar funds, look at their costs.

- **Gauge the quality of management.** Check to see who manages the fund and how long they've been at it. Experience matters. Throughout the modern era of professional money management, there have always been flashes in the pan who fare incredibly well in a bull market or make a single prescient call about a bear market or guess right on a hot market sector. It is pretty easy to be right once, but it's much harder to be right consistently over time. To make sure you are entrusting your hard-earned money to investment advisers who have proven themselves over time, look up the tenure of the portfolio managers in the fund prospectus or in sources like Morningstar (available in libraries and online at www.morningstar.com).

- **Verify that the fund has pursued its strategy consistently over time.** Has the fund recently changed advisers or basic investment policies? If it has, be sure to find out why. A fund can make money by following any of a number of investment strategies, but it has to follow that strategy consistently and over a long time to succeed. In the process, the fund will have to weather periods in which its investment approach produces good results and periods when its results are subpar. Sometimes a rocky spell will provoke a fund company to change its strategy, but such shifts often prove to be ill-timed. One way to check is to consult Morningstar, whose fund snapshots include the investment style history. (Sometimes funds are reclassified by Morningstar or other rating services even though nothing has changed but the categories, so you do need to inquire further.) If you see that a fund's practices appear to have changed, feel free to call or write the fund company and ask why.

- **Is the fund sponsored by a broad and deep and credible organization?** As a prospective investor, you are, in effect, considering entering into a partnership with a fund provider. Because you hope to achieve a satisfying, long-lasting partnership, before you go further you should decide whether you are comfortable with how the company does business. There are many fine companies that provide mutual funds, but they're certainly not "all about the same." It can be needlessly risky to buy an off-brand mutual fund when you can obtain the same product from established, high-quality fund sponsors. Might there be an occasion when you would do business with a small or new fund provider because of the specialty products it offers? Sure. But to buy a core bond fund, money market fund, index fund, or balanced fund from a non-mainstream provider makes no sense whatsoever, in my view. You will most likely pay higher costs, you will receive limited services, and you won't be absolutely sure that the fund provider has the kind of stability a long-term investor needs.

- **Look at past performance.** I began this chapter by saying that past investment performance shouldn't be your first criterion for choosing a fund. But at some point, you'll definitely want to evaluate the history of a fund that you're considering. While past returns are no guarantee of future performance, they *do* provide an indication of how consistent a fund has been and how well it has performed relative to its benchmark and its peers.

  The SEC requires all fund marketing literature and ads discussing performance to report 1-, 5-, and 10-year total returns as of the most recent calendar quarter. One-year returns aren't very meaningful for determining the relative merits of two funds. Instead, look at their returns over a decade. In addition to the 10-year average annual total return, also examine year-by-year returns, if you can, to gain an understanding of how the funds' performance varied over time. Keep in mind that the underlying financial and economic environment always has an effect on returns. For example, most stock funds benefited from exceptional gains in the 1990s, but most of them suffered in 2000 and 2001.

You will also want to know how a fund compared with its benchmark index and other similar funds. If it is an actively managed fund, the index comparison will tell you whether the fund manager added value over what you could have earned by investing in an index fund. Two caveats: Be sure to compare a fund to the index that is most relevant. (See the sidebar on "The Major Market Indexes.") And remember that an index fund's return will not match the return of its target index exactly, because the fund incurs expenses while the unmanaged index does not.

To sum up, here's what you ultimately want in a fund:

- **Low costs.** You can't predict that a high-performing fund will continue to perform well, but you can predict that a high-cost fund will continue to have a drag on its performance.

- **Solid performance.** While it is misguided to think that you have to have the top-ranked fund in its category, it does make sense to limit your selections to funds that have ranked in at least the upper half of their peers over time. Avoid the true stinkers. Bottom-quartile performers tend to stay at the bottom of the long-term performance rankings. The reason is that those funds tend to have the highest operating costs.

- **Consistency.** You want a fund that has had relatively predictable returns in the past. If a fund's returns seem erratic compared with those of peers having similar investment objectives, it could signal a lack of discipline.

The Major Market Indexes

Stocks

Dow Jones Industrial Average. Oldest and best-known barometer for the stock market, although it tracks just 30 major company stocks.

Standard & Poor's 500 Index. Tracks 500 large-capitalization stocks representing more than 75% of the value of all U.S. stocks.

Nasdaq Composite Index. Tracks more than 5,000 stocks traded on the Nasdaq Stock Exchange; during the 1990s, it became a widely watched barometer for technology stocks.

Wilshire 4500 Completion Index. Tracks the portion of the U.S. stock market not included in the S&P 500.

Wilshire 5000 Total Market Index. Tracks the entire U.S. stock market—now more than 5,800 stocks.

Russell 1000 Index. Tracks the 1,000 largest U.S. stocks.

Russell 2000 Index. Tracks 2,000 small-capitalization stocks.

Morgan Stanley Capital International Europe, Australasia, Far East (MSCI EAFE) Index. Tracks the world's major non-U.S. stock markets.

MSCI Europe Index. EAFE subindex that tracks European stocks.

MSCI Pacific Index. EAFE subindex that tracks Pacific Rim stocks.

Bonds

Lehman Brothers Government Bond Index. Tracks U.S. government agency and Treasury bonds.

Lehman Corporate Bond Index. Tracks fixed-rate, nonconvertible, investment-grade corporate bonds.

Lehman Mortgage-Backed Securities Index. Tracks fixed-rate securities of the Government National Mortgage Association (GNMA), Federal National Mortgage Association (FNMA), and Federal National Loan Mortgage Corporation (FNLMC).

Lehman Aggregate Bond Index. The broadest measure of the taxable U.S. bond market, tracking most Treasury, agency, corporate, mortgage-backed, asset-backed, and international dollar-denominated issues.

Lehman High Yield Index. Tracks corporate bonds with credit ratings that are below investment-grade.

Lehman Municipal Bond Index. Tracks investment-grade tax-exempt bonds that are issued by state and local governments.

In a Nutshell

To construct a portfolio methodically, follow this four-step process:

- **Determine your asset mix.** How will you allocate your dollars among stocks, bonds, and cash investments?
- **Allocate your dollars *within* those asset categories.** What kinds of stock funds, bond funds, and money market funds will you pick?
- **Weigh indexing versus active management.** Will you invest in index funds, actively managed funds, or some of both?
- **Compare and evaluate specific funds.** Of the funds that are in the categories you're seeking, which offer low cost, solid returns, and consistency in performance?

chapter ten
IT'S WHAT YOU KEEP THAT COUNTS

Investing is an inherently risky activity, full of uncertainty. In truth, we individual investors have no control over the market forces and economic cycles that affect the performance of our investments. But we do have control over a few important things, and those will be the focus of this chapter and the next.

In investing, it is what you keep that counts. And what you keep has everything to do with two simple things: (1) The costs you pay your investment provider; and (2) the taxes that you pay on your earnings. Table 10.1 shows just how hard costs and taxes can hit a hypothetical mutual fund account. It demonstrates that for you as an investor, the bottom line is your profit *after* costs and *after* taxes.

TABLE 10.1 Profit Statement for a $10,000 Fund Account Earning 10%

	Return
Gross investment gain (10% before expenses)	$1,000.00
– Fund expenses (1.34% of average account balance of $10,500)*	– 140.70
Net investment gain	$ 859.30
– Income taxes (30%)	– 257.79
After-tax profit	$601.51

*1.34% was the average expense ratio for all mutual funds in 2001, according to Lipper Inc.

All investments have costs. Most gains get taxed sooner or later. Although you can't avoid costs and taxes altogether, there are some steps you can take to minimize the bite, and you don't need an accounting or law degree to do this. If you keep a few simple things in mind when you structure your investment program, you'll be able to keep more of your returns. In this chapter, I'll explain:

- How to choose low-cost, tax-efficient mutual funds.
- How you can avoid behavior that hurts you on taxes and costs.
- Why it pays to be judicious about which kinds of mutual funds you hold in your tax-deferred accounts and which ones you hold in taxable accounts.

Costs: Are You Leaving Too Much on the Table?

As a financial entrepreneur, you need to become vigilant about costs. Many investment firms want you to ignore what they charge you. Their advertising campaigns dwell on investment performance or wise advice, as if these have value beyond price. Meanwhile, some investors lose track of the total amount they're paying as the same firms layer on fees and charges. Individual investors don't give nearly as much attention to costs as they ought to. It's sad to see people work so hard to get the money to invest and then be so careless about costs. They might as well be walking around with big holes in their buckets.

If someone tells you that costs don't matter, ask him or her why institutional investors—pension funds, endowments and the like—negotiate so hard with investment companies to keep advisory costs low. Institutional investors have long understood that costs eat into investment returns and that the effects are magnified over time by compounding.

There's plenty of other proof that costs matter. According to a 2002 study by the Financial Research Corporation, a fund industry consulting firm, expense ratios are the *only* factor that can be reliably linked to the future performance of mutual funds. Researchers examined 10 characteristics of mutual funds to see whether they could have been used to predict how the funds actually performed over a given period. The characteristics included Morningstar ratings, expenses, turnover, manager tenure, net sales, asset size, and four mathematical measures of risk or volatility. What the researchers found, after examining five broad fund categories, was this: Funds with lower expenses delivered "above-average future performance across nearly all time periods." The study called lower expense ratios an "exceptional predictor" for bond funds and a "good predictor" for stock funds.

All mutual funds have costs, but some funds cost much more to own than others. The average mutual fund expense ratio was 1.34% in 2001, but there were funds out on the market charging as much as 6% and more. Some funds also levy sales charges or other fees on top of their expense ratios.

All the fees and expenses you pay reduce your investment returns *directly*, because they are deducted before you receive your return. It pays to shop around and to remember three easy tips.

Three Simple Tips for Reducing Your Investment Costs

Cost Reduction Tip #1: Avoid Sales Charges or "Loads"

If you buy a fund through a broker, financial adviser, or other intermediary, you will usually pay a sales charge. This is often called a *load*, with several cheery variations: a *front-end load* is a fee taken from your initial investment, whereas a *back-end load* typically comes out of your earnings when you sell your shares. (Front-end loads typically range from 3% to 6%. Sometimes you have to pay them even when you reinvest dividends in additional shares. You may be able to avoid paying a back-end load by holding the investment for a certain period of time.)

Investing $20,000 in a fund that charges a 5% front-end load means, in effect, that you are starting out with a $1,000 loss. Only $19,000 of your $20,000 is invested for you, and you'll need to earn 5.3% on that $19,000 in the first year just to get back to what you started with. By the same token, back-end loads, including deferred sales charges, hit you when you redeem your shares, taking a bite out of any gain (or worsening any loss!) you have realized.

The most cost-effective funds are no-load funds—the ones that don't have sales charges. It's simple to buy them: You call the firm's toll-free number to request a prospectus and then send back the completed account application with your check. These days, you may be able to do it all online.

Cost Reduction Tip #2: Choose Low-Cost Funds

Every mutual fund has an expense ratio, which it has to report publicly. The ratio represents the percentage of the fund's assets that were used to pay operating expenses in a given period. The expenses covered include legal and accounting services, telephone service, postage, printing, and other administrative costs, as well as fees paid to the fund's investment adviser—which can be a big item. All of these expenses are subtracted from the fund's gross investment return before you, the shareholder, see any of it.

Most funds have expense ratios between 0.2% and 2.5%, which translates into $20 to $250 a year on an investment of $10,000. You should expect to pay slightly above-average expenses for actively managed funds that require significant investment research; for example, aggressive small-company funds and international funds. But be skeptical about any fund whose expense ratio is higher than the industry average, which was 1.34% in 2001. And be especially skeptical about any fund that charges 12b-1 fees. These fees cover distribution-related expenses, including advertising and broker fees—so you are in effect paying for the fund to market itself to other investors.

The 12b-1 fees are assessed as a percentage of your average net assets and must be included in the fund's stated expense ratio. (Note that sales charges, or loads, are *not* reflected in the expense ratio.) I'll talk about 12b-1 fees again in a sidebar later in this chapter.

Cost Reduction Tip #3: Be Aware of Transaction Costs Paid by the Fund

Mutual funds incur transaction costs when they buy and sell securities. Brokerage commissions are one type of transaction cost. Another cost occurs as a result of the spread between buy and sell prices. These are hidden costs, but they create a drag on investment returns. Money that the fund pays to brokers is money unavailable to pay to you.

The more frequently a fund buys and sells securities, the higher its transaction costs are likely to be. (Keeping these costs down is one of the advantages of index funds, which do relatively little trading.) To find out how frequently a fund buys and sells, look up its *turnover rate*, a statistic that's listed in prospectuses, fund

---

Fees and Expenses

The following table describes the fees and expenses you may pay if you buy and hold Investor Shares of the Fund. The expenses shown under *Annual Fund Operating Expenses* are based on those incurred in the fiscal year ended December 31, 2001.

	Investor Shares

SHAREHOLDER FEES *(fees paid directly from your investment)*

Sales Charge (Load) Imposed on Purchases:	None
Purchase Fee:	None*
Sales Charge (Load) Imposed on Reinvested Dividends:	None
Redemption Fee:	None
Exchange Fee:	None
Account Maintenance Fee (for accounts under $10,000):	$2.50/quarter**

ANNUAL FUND OPERATING EXPENSES *(expenses deducted from the Fund's assets)*

Management Expenses:	0.18%
12b-1 Distribution Fee:	None
Other Expenses:	0.02%
Total Annual Fund Operating Expenses:	**0.20%**

*The Fund reserves the right to deduct a purchase fee from future purchases of shares.

**If applicable, the account maintenance fee will be deducted from your quarterly distribution of the Fund's dividends. If your distribution is less than the fee, fractional shares may be automatically redeemed to make up the difference.

FIGURE 10.1   Vanguard Total Stock Market Fund Fee Table (Investor Shares)

reports, and many other sources. Average turnover rates for stock mutual funds have trended higher over the years and lately have approached 100%—meaning that funds on average hold their stocks for one year. Some funds have turnover rates as high as 300% to 400%. At the other extreme, some funds have turnover rates as low as 5%, meaning that on average they hold stocks for 20 years. Keep in mind that a high turnover rate doesn't necessarily mean you should skip the fund. But it certainly is a warning sign.

You Can Look It Up

Remember that you can find out about fees, expense ratios, and turnover in the fund's prospectus, in its annual and semiannual reports to shareholders, or in information provided by companies such as Morningstar or Lipper. You also can simply call up the fund company and ask; most have toll-free numbers. In addition, the major fund companies and many smaller ones provide all this information on their websites.

Prospectuses are a particularly good source, because the SEC requires mutual funds to disclose all fees and expenses in a consolidated table placed near the front of the booklet. The fee table shows all expenses that an investor would pay on a hypothetical $10,000 investment at the end of 1, 3, 5, and 10 years, assuming a 5% annual return. Figure 10.1 gives an example.

'But It's Just a Few Percentage Points . . .'

Perhaps you're tempted to think that a difference of a percentage point or two is hardly worth worrying about. Many people felt that way during the late 1990s when stocks had annual gains in the teens or higher. When you're seeing double-digit returns, an expense ratio of 2% or 3% may well seem trifling. Costs become more punitive as returns become more average. On a gross gain of 8%, a 2% expense ratio is eating up a 25% of your return.

Over the long run, even small costs have a big impact. Remember compounding? It magnifies not only returns, but the damage of costs, too. Table 10.2 shows the impact of costs over time on three imaginary funds, each earning gross returns of 8% annually.

- Fund A is a no-load fund with an expense ratio of 0.28%.
- Fund B is a no-load fund with an expense ratio of 1.25%.
- Fund C has an expense ratio of 1.41%. In order to have a villain, we'll also make it a load fund that charges 3% on purchases. (Plenty of funds charge more—up to 8.5%)

TABLE 10.2   How Costs Affect Returns Over Time

	Fund A	*Fund B*	*Fund C*
Initial Investment	$10,000	$10,000	$10,000
Value on Day 1	$10,000	$10,000	$ 9,700
Value after . . .			
5 years	$14,489	$13,798	$13,276
10 years	$20,992	$19,037	$18,169
15 years	$30,415	$26,267	$24,867
20 years	$44,068	$36,242	$34,033

This example assumes an 8% annual return, reinvestment of dividends, and annual compounding net of expenses. *Source:* SEC Cost Calculator.

Pitfall: If You Must Buy from a Broker, Be Wary of 12b-1 Fees

While no-load funds are always the most cost-effective, many people prefer to invest in funds through intermediaries such as brokers, financial planners, insurance agents, and banks. All these middlemen have to be paid, of course, and sometimes they get their money indirectly. If you buy your funds through an intermediary, be aware that you have a choice in how that person or company is compensated. But it's up to you to ask the right questions.

Some funds sold through agents charge front-end or back-end loads (as explained in this chapter) and share the money with the intermediary. At least those loads just hit you once. The type of charge to be most wary of is the 12b-1 fee, which amounts to paying a commission year after year.

A 12b-1 fee is a method of charging marketing and distribution-related expenses directly against fund assets. (The term refers to the SEC rule that permits the practice.) Nearly half of all mutual funds charge 12b-1 fees. You'll see a fund's 12b-1 fee listed as part of its expense ratio. These fees normally run between 0.15% and 1% of the fund's net assets. If you are charged a 12b-1 fee of 1%, you are paying $10 a year for every $1,000 in your account.

If you expect to remain invested in a particular fund for a long time, you need to recognize that, over extended periods, a 12b-1 fee takes a bigger bite out of your wealth than an upfront load. Here's an illustration: Suppose you put $10,000 in a tax-free account and leave it there for 20 years, reinvesting all your dividends. Let's assume that the fund earns an average annual return of 8%. Table 10.3 lists the ending account values in some hypothetical funds with varying sales charges. All of the funds have the same expense ratio before the 12b-1 fee is added.

The lesson should be plain: Always ask about the fees before you buy.

If you're unsure about the impact of a mutual fund's fee structure, check out the SEC's Mutual Funds Cost Calculator at http://www.sec.gov/investor/tools/mfcc/mfcc-int.htm. This is a great tool for comparing the impact of expense ratios and loads.

TABLE 10.3   How Costs Affect the Growth of Your Portfolio

	Initial Investment	Average Annual Total Return	Value after 20 Years
Fund A (no-load)	$10,000	8%	$46,610
Fund B (5% load)	$ 9,500	8%	$44,279
Fund C (no-load; 1% 12b-1 fee)	$10,000	7%	$38,697
Fund D (no-load; 0.50% 12b-1 fee)	$10,000	7.5%	$42,479

After 20 years, Fund A would grow to $44,068. An investment in Fund B would come to $7,826 less because of its higher expenses. And the investment in Fund C, impeded by the 3% sales load, would be worth $34,033 in the end—$10,035 less than was earned in Fund A. If that is your retirement money, which of the three would you rather have?

As an investor, *you* put up the capital and *you* take the risk. It makes sense to minimize costs so that you—not the investment provider—will earn the bulk of the returns.

Pitfall: Beware of Fee Waivers

Beware of funds that have temporarily waived management fees as a marketing ploy. A temporary fee waiver can boost a fund's yield and total return. That's great—while it lasts. Usually it doesn't last very long. Fund sponsors can restore full fees without notice or raise them gradually, leaving unsuspecting shareholders in a higher-cost fund that is now yielding much less.

You usually see fee waivers offered for money market funds because fees have such a dramatic effect on their yields. Waivers are less common with stock and bond funds, but they do occur.

Funds must disclose these waivers in their prospectuses. Turn to the fee table; there the fund is required to show its full charges and list any waivers in an accompanying footnote. With this information you can assess whether the fund truly offers good value or will merely seem to do so for a while.

Should you ever take advantage of a fee waiver? There's nothing wrong with doing so in the case of a money market fund—if you have the time and energy to monitor the expenses and move your money to a lower-cost fund when the fee waiver expires. But be careful about pursuing fee waivers in stock or bond funds; when the waiver ends and you want to move your money out, you could find yourself confronting capital gains taxes that would wipe out what you saved in expenses.

Taxes Are Costs, Too

Most mutual fund managers focus on maximizing the pre-tax returns they provide to their investors, so it's up to you to pay attention to your after-tax returns. As a mutual fund investor, you can minimize your tax bill in three ways:

1. Resist the temptation to trade a lot.
2. Choose tax-efficient funds.
3. Use tax-deferred and taxable accounts wisely.

Tax Tip #1: Resist the Temptation to Trade a Lot

One of the old jokes in the business is that the quickest way to make a small fortune is to start with a large fortune and trade it a lot. It's all too true, and taxes are one of the reasons. If you trade your fund shares frequently, you may be incurring big tax liabilities. A quick refresher: When you sell some or all of your shares at a profit, or you exchange shares of one fund for shares of another, you can reap a capital gain on which you'll have to pay taxes. Just how much you owe will be determined by your tax bracket and the length of time that you held the shares.

For example, if you buy 100 shares of mutual fund X for $20 a share and sell them all six months later for $22 a share, you will owe short-term capital gains taxes on your $200 profit. If you are in the 31% marginal tax bracket, that's $62 you must pay to the government. However, if you hold on to the shares for more than 12 months before selling them, your profit is considered a long-term capital gain. Then it will be taxed at a maximum rate of 20%, so you will owe no more than $40. The tax code rewards patience.

Basic Information: Taxes and Mutual Funds

As a mutual fund investor, you can incur taxes in three ways:

1. When the fund distributes income dividends. These distributions reflect all interest and dividend income earned by the fund's holdings—whether cash investments, bonds, or stocks—after the fund's operating expenses are subtracted.

2. When the fund distributes capital gains from the sale of securities. These reflect the profit the fund makes when it sells securities. A fund is said to "realize" a capital gain when it makes such a profit. It realizes a capital loss when it sells securities at a price lower than it paid. If a fund's total capital gains are greater than its total capital losses, it has *net realized capital gains*, which are distributed to fund shareholders.

3. When you sell or exchange fund shares at a profit.

   You must pay taxes on distributions regardless of whether you receive them in cash or reinvest them in additional fund shares. There are a couple of exceptions:

- **U.S. Treasury securities**, whose interest income is exempt from state income taxes.

- **Municipal bond funds**, whose interest income is exempt from federal income tax and may also be exempt from state taxes.

   When your fund distributes capital gains, an important factor in how much tax you owe on them is the holding period—that is, how long the fund held the securities before they were sold. Profits on securities held for one year or less before being sold are called *short-term capital gains*.

Your mutual fund will provide you with the information you need to declare these distributions properly at tax time. Distributions of income and short-term capital gains are taxed as ordinary income at your marginal tax rate (anywhere from 15% to 38.6% in 2002, depending on your overall income and your marital filing status). Distributions of capital gains on securities held longer than one year are taxed at a maximum rate of 20% (a maximum rate of 10% for taxpayers in the lowest tax bracket).

Tax Tip #2: Choose Tax-Efficient Funds

Most people don't realize it, but a significant portion of their pre-tax returns on U.S. stock funds ultimately goes into federal income-tax coffers, not into their pockets, unless those returns are sheltered from taxes in a retirement account. This is a particularly important issue for people in high tax brackets. According to some research we have done at Vanguard, taxes reduced the return of the average domestic stock fund by an average of 2.5 percentage points a year during the 1990s. Bond and money market funds (except for tax-exempt funds, of course) typically surrender an even larger percentage of their returns to taxes.

How can this be? It's because mutual funds have to distribute to you any income or capital gains they receive from the securities they own—which then become *your* income or capital gains. You don't feel the tax pinch until you file your annual return; that's why many people never make the connection.

Tax-efficient funds caught on in the 1990s, when economic researchers first realized that the way a mutual fund was managed could have a big impact on shareholders' taxes. Since 2001, mutual funds have been required to disclose how income taxes can affect their returns. To report these *after-tax returns*, a fund applies current tax rates to the income and capital gains it distributed during a given period, and also to the gain (or loss) that an investor would have realized by selling shares. You can find this information in a fund's prospectus, among other sources. The tax burden may not matter much to you when fund returns are generally high, but in slumping markets you may find it galling to owe capital gains taxes on distributions from a fund that is *losing money*.

Though most funds are not managed with the goal of keeping taxes low, some are more tax-efficient, either inherently or by design. There are three types of funds to consider if you are looking for something that's tax-friendly:

1. **Stock index funds**—especially those tied to broad market indexes—are generally tax-efficient because of their buy-and-hold practices. Their turnover is typically very low, on the order of 10% to 20%. They do dis-

tribute capital gains on occasion—for example, when a stock is removed from the target index and thus must be sold by the fund.

2. **Tax-managed funds** are operated in a manner designed to keep taxable gains and income low. These funds may employ an indexing approach to hold down turnover, and they use trading strategies carefully designed to offset capital gains with losses whenever possible. Tax-managed funds may also impose redemption fees to encourage long-term investing.

3. **Tax-exempt funds**, also known as municipal or "muni" bond funds, generate income that is exempt from federal income tax, and in some cases from state and local income taxes as well. However, I want to emphasize that muni bond funds are not for everyone. Muni bonds typically have lower yields than taxable bonds. Generally you won't benefit from holding munis unless you are in the 30% tax bracket or higher—that is, with taxable income of more than $67,700 for single filers or $112,850 or more for joint filers, based on 2002 tax schedules.

To figure out whether to invest in a muni bond fund or a comparable corporate bond fund, you have to do a few simple calculations. Over the years, I've seen a number of investors choose muni funds without bothering to do the numbers, and most of them are hurting themselves by doing so. One of my colleagues pointed out an interesting IRS statistic to me: In 1999 (the latest year for which IRS statistics are available), more than $497 million in tax-exempt interest income was declared on returns by taxpayers who had *no adjusted gross income* to declare. Those taxpayers were so determined to avoid taxes that they were investing in lower-yielding muni bonds even though they didn't benefit from the tax exemption. They could have earned higher returns for themselves by investing at least some of that money in taxable bonds.

So do the numbers before you invest in a muni fund. You need to look at something called the *taxable-equivalent* yield. You get that by doing a bit of math that is more complicated to describe than it is to perform. First, convert your combined state and federal tax rate to a decimal form (a 30% tax rate becomes 0.30, for example). Then, subtract the decimal figure from 1.00 (in our example, $1.00 - 0.30 = 0.70$). Next, divide your result into the muni fund's yield. In our example, if the muni yield was 4.50%, you would divide that by 0.70: $4.5\% \div 0.70 = 6.4\%$. This tells us that the muni bond fund has a taxable equivalent yield of 6.4%. You will now have an apples-to-apples comparison when comparing the muni fund's yield with yields of alternative taxable bond funds.

Tax Tip #3: Use Tax-Deferred and Taxable Accounts Wisely

Preferred domain is a fancy-sounding term that has become an increasingly important investment issue in recent years. The idea is that you need to think about the tax sensitivity of your overall portfolio and choose the right *domain*—tax-deferred or taxable account—to hold assets.

The tax laws make it advantageous to hold certain kinds of investments in taxable accounts and others in tax-sheltered accounts, such as 401(k)s and IRAs. This issue didn't exist 30 years ago, because tax-advantaged accounts hadn't become broadly available. But nowadays more people are recognizing that decisions about where to hold certain investments can make a significant difference at tax time. You're likely to hear more about this issue in the future.

The first point to make about retirement accounts is that, since taxes are deferred, your money can grow more for you there. (Indeed, with a Roth IRA you won't pay *any* taxes in the future, assuming you follow the rules.) That's one reason you should contribute the maximum you can to such accounts.

But there is an additional wrinkle to consider if you're interested in minimizing your current taxes. If your overall investment plan includes some funds more liable to incur taxes than others, see if you can put those less-tax-efficient funds in your retirement accounts. Which funds tend to be less tax-efficient? Remember that income distributions and short-term capital gains are taxed at a higher rate than long-term capital gains. Consequently, bond funds, income-oriented stock funds that pay high dividends, and very aggressive stock funds with high turnover rates all can heighten your tax bill. If possible, hold these kinds of funds in your retirement plan or your IRA.

In a Nutshell

There's little you can do to influence the future performance of your investments, but you *can* exercise control over what you're giving up in costs and taxes. Follow these tips to improve your bottom line as an investor:

- **Avoid sales charges, also known as fund loads.** You're starting out at a loss if you pay an upfront sales charge on your investment.

- **Choose funds with low expense ratios.** The average mutual fund expense ratio was 1.34% in 2001, but there are funds that charge much more. Avoid them.

- **Resist the temptation to trade often in your own account.** In a taxable account, frequent trading can carry tax consequences.

- **Choose tax-efficient funds for your taxable accounts.** Some funds are more tax-friendly than others, either inherently or by design.

- **Use tax-sheltered accounts wisely.** Be strategic in deciding which kinds of funds to hold in tax-deferred accounts, such as 401(k)s and IRAs, and which to hold in taxable accounts.

chapter eleven

RISK: GIVE IT THE GUT TEST

I've been talking a lot so far about the long-term rewards that you can gain as an investor if you are willing to accept a prudent level of risk. Investing in money market funds instead of keeping your money in the bank is one example of taking a prudent risk that carries worthwhile rewards—the rewards being relatively higher yields. In this case, the risk is minimal. But another example of prudence is choosing to invest some of your long-term retirement assets in a well-diversified stock fund instead of keeping them all in a money fund. Although the stock market is definitely risky, most retirement investors find that the potential rewards are well worth the risk, as long as they take care to diversify. In both of these investment scenarios, risk is an ally in your effort to increase your wealth.

Indeed, risk can be both friend and foe, so prudent investors pay careful attention to it when they construct a portfolio. In this chapter, I'll focus on two aspects of risk management:

1. **How to understand the level of risk in your overall portfolio—and to avoid worrying over the risks of specific holdings.** The reason for taking a global view is that the risk factors of some holdings can be mitigated by those of other holdings. For example, the income and price stability of money market funds serve to offset some of the volatility in stock prices.

2. **How to assess whether the level of risk is one that you can tolerate.** There are a variety of statistical tools you can use, but ultimately, your gut is the simplest, best test of your risk tolerance.

Your Investment Risk

In its broadest sense, your investment risk is the chance that you ultimately won't have enough money to meet your long-term goal of a comfortable retirement, a

college education for your kids, or whatever else you want to have. But another way to think of risk is in terms of how you tolerate the price declines that you'll experience from time to time as you pursue your goal. If you can't bear the inevitable bumps in the road, you won't stick with your investment program long enough to meet your goals. So you have to weigh the risk of falling short of your goals against the risk of declines along the way.

Risk is not always apparent, but experts in finance have tried hard to define and quantify it. They have come up with all kinds of names for specific aspects of risk; see "The Many-Headed Risk Monster" on page 123 for a long list of those terms.

Researchers also have come up with mathematical measurements for certain kinds of financial risk. These measures have daunting names, but they're not really all that complicated to use. They focus on how volatile a stock or a fund was over a past period of time or how closely its returns matched those of the overall market. While these numbers can be useful when you are comparing funds, they have some flaws, as I'll explain in a moment. So feel free to skip to the next section of the chapter if you're simply not interested in knowing about them.

- **Standard deviation** measures how much a fund's returns have bounced around its average return over the past three years. Suppose, for example, that Fund A posts annual returns of –5%, +10%, and +25%. Over the three years, that means an average annual return of almost +10%, with a standard deviation of 15. Fund B returns +5%, +10%, and +15%. It too earns an average return of about +10%, but its standard deviation is just 5. Based on standard deviation, Fund A has been three times as volatile as Fund B.

- **Beta** measures how sensitive a fund has been to what the rest of the market is doing. For stock funds, beta is generally measured relative to the S&P 500 Index or the Wilshire 5000 Index; for most bond funds, the mark is the Lehman Aggregate Bond Index. A beta of 1.0 means that the fund has moved in lockstep with the market. A beta of 1.5 means that the fund has been much more volatile than the market—it has tended to gain 1.5% for every 1% rise in the market and fall 1.5% for every 1% decline in the market. On the other hand, a fund with a beta of 0.5 is notably less volatile than the benchmark. Unfortunately, a fund's beta isn't helpful if the fund has little in common with the benchmark it is being measured against. That's where R-squared comes in.

- **R-squared** measures the degree to which a fund's returns go up and down at the same time as the market. (Again, "the market" is defined in terms of an appropriate index.) R-squared can range from 0 to 1.00: 0 for a fund that doesn't match the market movements at all and 1.00 for a fund that is always up when the market is up and down when the market is down. An R-squared of less than 0.70 suggests a low correlation between a fund and the market it is being compared with.

None of these measures should be your primary gauge for investment risk. One weakness they share is that they are based on what happened in the past, and the conditions that existed yesterday may not apply tomorrow. Another weakness is that they cannot be easily used for assessing the overall risk level of a portfolio, especially one that includes a mix of stock, bond, and money market investments.

Duration: A Risk Measure for Bonds

In Chapter 9, I discussed the *average maturity* of bond funds. That's a good thing to know, but a statistic called *duration* is an even better one. Knowing a bond fund's average duration will let you gauge its interest rate risk—how much the share price will change when market interest rates fluctuate.

Average duration is expressed in years, but it is not really a measure of time. Instead, it tells you how much a bond fund's share price will rise or fall for each percentage point change in market interest rates. For example, if interest rates rise by 1 percentage point, a fund with an average duration of five years will see its share price fall by about 5%. And if interest rates fall 1 percentage point, the fund's share price will rise by about 5%.

Calculating a bond fund's average duration involves computing the cash flows from interest payments on the fund's holdings—in short, it's complex. Fortunately, you don't have to calculate duration—you can get the information from the mutual fund company. Once you have the statistic, you can easily use it to compare different bond funds. And it's smart to compare—even two funds with similar average maturities can have significantly different average durations.

Below is an illustration of the trade-off, based on the actual yields of three low-cost U.S. Treasury bond funds in June 2002. In reading Table 11.1, remember that average duration lets you estimate how much a fund's price will move up or down for a given increase or decrease in interest rates. So, if market interest rates were to rise 1 percentage point, the price decline would be about 9.8% for the long-term Treasury fund, 5.3% for the intermediate-term fund, and 2.1% for the short-term fund.

The intermediate-term Treasury bond fund offered 1.39 percentage points more in yield than the short-term Treasury fund, or approximately 40% more income from each dollar invested. But to get that increase in yield, an investor had to take on more than twice as much interest rate risk—a duration of 5.3 years versus 2.1 years. The long-term Treasury fund's 5.35% yield would result in about 14% more income, but the duration figure shows that it has nearly double the interest rate risk of the intermediate fund.

Higher interest rate risk may not be a big concern for long-term investors, who can overlook short-term price declines for the sake of earning higher yields from intermediate- and long-term bonds. If interest rates were to rise, and the share price of the bond fund fell, the investor would have the consolation of having reinvested income put to work at higher yields. A $1,000 investment held for 10 years, with income reinvested, grows to $1,393 at a 3.37% annual yield, to $1,581 at a 4.69% yield, and to $1,684 at a 5.35% yield.

But this example clearly shows that most of the opportunity for gaining additional yield came from going from short- to intermediate-term bonds, rather than

TABLE 11.1   Bond Funds and Duration

Treasury Funds	*Yield**	*Average Duration*
Short-term	3.37%	2.1 years
Intermediate-term	4.69%	5.3 years
Long-term	5.35%	9 years

*As of June 30, 2002.

from moving from intermediate- to long-term bonds. In any case, the idea is to examine trade-offs so you can make an informed judgment about the balance between risk and reward. Investors who reach for higher yields need to be sure they're comfortable with the additional risk involved.

A Simpler Way to Check a Fund's Past Volatility

For a simple gauge of a fund's volatility, just look at its past returns, preferably over a long period. Keep in mind that a fund that is volatile when it's gaining is likely to be volatile when it's losing, too. I can illustrate this point with one of my own company's mutual funds, Vanguard Growth Index Fund. As Table 11.2 shows, if you were thinking about investing in this fund back in 1999, you might have found its historical returns very alluring. In its brief history since inception in November 1992, it had never lost money. But the sharp gains the fund had seen in the 1995–1999 period should have been a signal that sharp declines were also possible. The fund returned –22.2% in 2000 and –12.9% in 2001.

The Gut Test

Once you've assessed the volatility of the individual mutual funds you're thinking of buying, you still need to give your whole portfolio what I call the gut test. The investments you're assembling may look great on paper, but you are the only one able to say whether you can live with the risk they present as a group. To do this, you need a little self-knowledge about your ability to endure volatile periods and short-term losses.

TABLE 11.2   Vanguard Growth Index Fund: Yearly Returns, 1993–2001

Year	Return
1993	1.5%
1994	2.9%
1995	38.1%
1996	23.7%
1997	36.3%
1998	42.2%
1999	28.8%
2000	–22.2%
2001	–12.9%

Historical returns can give you a general idea of what to expect based on your broad asset mix. Let's revisit a table that you first saw in Chapter 7. Table 11.3 shows how various model portfolios have performed in the past. Suppose you are weighing the risk of a conservative growth portfolio with 40% of its assets in stocks and 60% in bonds. As the data show, you could take some comfort in knowing that a hypothetical portfolio with that makeup had losses in only 16 out of the last 76 years. But you also ought to ask yourself how well you would have endured the year 1931, when such a portfolio would have lost –18.4% of its value.

If you suspect you'll lose sleep worrying about the value of your investments in tough times, you'd be wise to opt for a more conservative mix of assets that will maintain some stability in good times and bad. True, a more conservative

TABLE 11.3   Asset Mixes and Their Past Performance: 1926–2001

Goal of Mix	*Components*	*Average Annual Return*	*Worst 1-Year Loss*	*Number of Years out of 76 with Losses*
Stability	10% stocks 80% bonds 10% cash	6.2%	–6.7% (1969)	10
Income	20% stocks 80% bonds	7.0%	–10.1% (1931)	13
Conservative Growth	40% stocks 60% bonds	8.1%	–18.4% (1931)	16
Balanced Growth	50% stocks 50% bonds	8.7%	–22.5% (1931)	17
Moderate Growth	60% stocks 40% bonds	9.1%	–26.6% (1931)	19
Growth	80% stocks 20% bonds	10.0%	–34.9% (1931)	21
Aggressive Growth	100% stocks	10.7%	–43.1% (1931)	22

Stock returns are based on the S&P 500 Index. Bond returns are based on the high-quality corporate bond indexes. Cash returns are based on the Salomon Smith Barney 3-Month Treasury Bill Index.

asset mix might mean you'll have to save more to achieve your goals, but you'll also be likelier to stick with your program through thick and thin if it is not scaring you to pieces at intervals.

How much risk is too much? It depends on your own constitution. Some people can shrug off big market swings. Others cannot; when markets turn down, they worry themselves sick about the possibility of losing money, and they may make emotion-based decisions that they later regret.

Good markets can lull you into thinking you're tougher and more comfortable with risk than you are. When the markets are rising, people tend to think of themselves as very risk-tolerant. All they see is the reward side of the risk/reward trade-off. That's just what happened in the late 1990s, when stocks had been rising so long that many investors decided that the climb would never stop—or at least, that downturns would be brief. They saw no reason to fear investment risk. In the months after the spring of 2000, when the market changed course, those investors discovered that they weren't nearly as risk-tolerant as they had thought. Downward volatility feels very different from upward volatility.

It's a common investing mistake to think you can take a chameleon approach to risk, and change your investment policy whenever the market environment shifts. But as we'll discuss in Chapter 13, most people who try to time the market fail to make the right moves at the right times. If you've suddenly discovered that your portfolio is riskier than you thought, you're likely to be so frightened that you overreact.

Measuring Your Risk Tolerance

The investment industry has developed a variety of diagnostics—quizzes and the like—to help you measure your tolerance for risk, but it has always seemed to me that there are inherent limitations in trying to use objective measures for something so subjective. Risk tolerance can't be measured as easily as your blood pressure or your cholesterol level. Ultimately, you have to trust your gut. I have often taken fancy computerized risk quizzes and ended up with scores that label me as a highly risk-tolerant investor. I know myself well enough not to believe that. I'm in a high-risk job and I am financially very risk-averse.

To gauge your own risk tolerance, ask yourself these questions:

- How would you feel if your portfolio lost 20% of its value in one day? The Dow Jones Industrial Average lost –22.6% on October 19, 1987—its greatest one-day percentage loss ever.

- How would you feel if your portfolio steadily shrank in an extended market downturn? Such things happen periodically. Bonds were stuck in a slump from March 1971 to September 1975—a period of 54 months!

As I've noted before, it can be difficult to assess your tolerance for risk unless you've actually experienced difficult markets. I thought of this recently when I heard a news report about researchers who were trying to measure the effects of combat stress on soldiers. It turns out that, for many years, the researchers had been attempting to discover how soldiers respond physically and mentally to combat by such tests as immersing their arms in cold water or telling them they had to give a speech. Obviously, neither of those even remotely approaches the physical and psychological stress of combat.

A prolonged and painful bear market is also difficult to simulate. You can take all the tests you want, but if all you know about tough markets is what you've read in books, you don't really know how you will respond.

Pitfall: Don't Let Fear of Loss Keep You Out of the Market

Occasionally I talk to someone who is so risk-averse that he's afraid to invest at all. Even during the record-shattering bull market of the 1980s and 1990s, there were investors who knew that they should invest in stocks to reach their long-term goals but were paralyzed by the fear that a downturn could wipe them out.

Over the long term, avoiding risk to this degree is itself an extremely dangerous thing to do. If you don't put at least some of your money into stocks or bonds, you won't be able to stay ahead of inflation. You'll wind up with an account balance that looks bigger than it used to be, but buys less.

Many risk-averse investors find a measure of comfort in a balanced fund of stocks and bonds. A balanced fund is a middle-of-the-road investment that seeks to provide a combination of growth, income, and conservation of capital.

Another useful tactic is to start out slowly—take risk a sip at a time, so to speak. If you have been keeping all of your savings in money market funds, move just a bit of the money into a balanced fund or a short-term bond fund, leave it there a while, and see how you feel. Once you're comfortable, gradually direct additional money into the new investment. Another possibility is to direct only your interest earnings on the money market fund into the new fund. That way, your money market balance remains stable while you gradually build a position in the new fund.

Managing Investment Risk

Just a few final thoughts on risk:

- If you've decided you're truly a risk-tolerant investor, and you intend to invest accordingly, remember the factors that will help you to stay the course when the markets test your mettle: Hold a balanced, well-diversified portfolio. Control your costs. Keep on saving and investing. Time will be your ally, as I'll explain in Chapter 15.

- If you've decided you're truly risk-averse, recognize that being a conservative investor is nothing to be ashamed of. A friend of mine who was an investment professional was a very conservative investor in his private life. Like me, he recognized that he was in a high-risk profession that was vulnerable to market cycles, and to him that meant he ought to minimize the financial risk in his personal life. He was an even more conservative investor than I am. Although he was a highly paid senior partner in an investment-management firm, he kept his long-term savings in a money market fund instead of investing them in the stock market. His colleagues teased him about adhering to his no-stocks strategy even amid the bull market of the 1980s and 1990s, but they had less to say when the bull market was followed by a prolonged bear market.

Basic Information: The Many-Headed Risk Monster

Every investment carries some degree of risk. But there are many types of risk, and they vary with the nature of the investment vehicle. These are some of the major ones you'll see mentioned in mutual fund prospectuses.

- **Market risk.** The chance that the overall securities market will slump, carrying your investment along with it. When you invest in stocks, this is one of the most significant risks you face. It is primarily a shorter-term threat, however. History has shown that, while stock prices have skyrocketed—or plummeted—during relatively short periods, over decades they have trended steadily upward. That's because corporate profits and the U.S. economy have grown over time. You can reduce market risk by holding stock investments for a long time—at least 10 years.

- **Specific risk.** The eggs-in-one-basket risk. Concentrating your portfolio in too few stocks, or in just one or two market sectors, increases the chance that you'll lose money because of troubles at one company or in a single industry group. Stock market leadership can switch suddenly among sectors—say, from technology to energy to retailing companies. And even fine companies with superb track records can stumble or be affected by an unpredictable development. One way to reduce specific risk is to invest in a mutual fund that holds stocks or bonds from many companies (at least 100) across a range of industries.

- **Interest rate risk.** The chance that the value of your bond investment will fall if interest rates rise. The longer a bond's maturity, the greater the interest rate risk. You can reduce—but not eliminate—interest rate risk by investing in shorter-term bond funds. Note that interest rate risk and income risk are opposites and, in a sense, offset each other. If your bond fund's price falls because interest rates go up, the income it earns will rise over time, reflecting the higher rates.

- **Credit risk.** The possibility that you will lose money when a bond issuer defaults. Also, the possibility that your investment will lose value if an issuer's credit rating is lowered, which sometimes occurs in tandem with a merger, buyout, or takeover. (The reason such events can trigger credit downgrades is that a company may choose to finance the restructuring by issuing a large amount of new bonds, debt that could threaten its ability to pay off existing bonds.) For a mutual fund that invests in many bonds, the credit risk from a single default or rating change is reduced.

- **Manager risk.** The chance that the people running your mutual fund will make poor choices that lead to losses or subpar returns. This risk is a factor in all actively managed funds. You can virtually eliminate it by investing in index funds.

- **Income risk.** The possibility that your income from a bond or money market fund will fall if interest rates decline. Income risk is higher for money market funds than for bond funds, and higher for short-term bond funds than for long-term funds. This is because shorter-term investments mature more rapidly, forcing the fund to reinvest the money at whatever interest rates are prevailing.

- **Investment style risk.** The possibility that a strategy based on particular types of securities will fail or go out of favor. Market segments (small-company stocks, for example) and industries (technology, consumer products, etc.) can experience cycles in which they do either better or worse than the overall stock market. In the past, those periods have lasted for as long as several years. This is the risk that you take if you put all your money in growth funds or value funds. You can reduce this risk by making sure your investments cover small, medium-size, and large companies in a wide variety of industries.

- **Inflation risk.** The chance that the purchasing power of your investment will drop. This risk, based on the rising prices of goods and services, is more serious than many people realize. For example, if inflation runs at 3% for five years, the value of a regular $100 interest payment will fall to $86 in terms of actual purchasing power. Inflation risk is a major consideration with money market and bond funds, but you can reduce it by holding some stocks in your portfolio. Why do stocks mitigate inflation risk? Because they have the potential to gain in value at a rate greater than inflation. And in fact, as I have noted elsewhere, historical returns show that, over the very long term, returns on stocks have beaten inflation by a wider margin than those of either bonds or cash investments.

International investments carry some additional risks:

- **Currency risk.** The chance that currency movements will hurt your returns from a mutual fund that invests abroad. Investments that are denominated in foreign currencies decline in value for U.S. investors when the U.S. dollar rises in value against those currencies. Conversely, the investments rise in value when the dollar weakens. There have been prolonged periods when the dollar trended one way or the other.

- **Country risk.** The possibility that events in a specific country—such as political upheaval, financial troubles, or a natural disaster—will drive down the security prices of companies there. You can reduce (but not eliminate) this risk by choosing an international fund that invests in many countries and that focuses on developed nations rather than emerging-markets countries.

- **Liquidity risk.** The chance that your returns will suffer because a fund manager encounters trading difficulties in a foreign market. Sometimes foreign stocks can be tricky to buy or sell, in part because trading volume on foreign exchanges tends to be much lighter than on U.S. exchanges. Liquidity risk means the fund manager might have trouble buying or selling stocks without causing their prices to fall or rise substantially. You can reduce this risk by focusing on funds that invest in countries with well-established financial markets.

In a Nutshell

There are a variety of objective tools you can use to assess the risk in your portfolio, but ultimately, the best gauge is a very subjective one: Can you stomach the range of ups and downs that are likely to occur as you journey toward your goal? When you are constructing a portfolio, consider these factors.

- **How much appetite for risk do you have in general?** You know yourself better than anyone else does. Choose investments accordingly.

- **How would you have handled past volatile markets?** Look at the past performance data for particular funds or particular types of portfolios and ask yourself how you would react to such scenarios.

chapter twelve
KEEP THINGS SIMPLE

Investors often ask me how many funds is the "right" number to own. There is no set answer to the question. As I've noted already, you can build a sound portfolio with several funds, but it is also possible to create a very well-diversified portfolio with as few as one or two funds.

The old notion that if *X* is good, more of *X* is better does not apply to your mutual fund portfolio. If you have more than 10 funds, it's probably too many.

Investing in a large number of funds can actually hurt your returns. That's because a big collection of funds can be difficult to track, making it more complicated to monitor and rebalance your portfolio. It can also provide a false sense of security about how diversified your holdings truly are. At best, a large collection of funds may mimic the performance of a particular market index, but with higher costs and lower tax efficiency than an index mutual fund doing the same thing.

And yet lots of investors make this mistake. In a recent check of our computer records, we learned that more than 8,000 Vanguard shareholders were invested in 20 funds or more. Although that's a relatively small group of people within our shareholder base of many millions, it concerned me. Even more mind-boggling were the 36 investors who held more than 100 funds each. One investor was listed as holding 167 funds, either alone or jointly with other people. I can't imagine how he keeps track of it all.

Investors who accumulate lots of funds may be collecting investments like butterflies, according to Morningstar research director John Rekenthaler: "Something pretty and bright flaps its wings and catches their eye—an article in a magazine or an advertisement with a great total return number—and they get excited and buy some of that fund. That's not an investment strategy; that's investment opportunism."[1]

---

[1] "An Interview with Morningstar Research Director John Rekenthaler," *In The Vanguard* shareholder newsletter, Autumn 2000, page 1.

How Complications Can Set In

When investors end up with a jumble of similar funds, it's usually a result of chasing performance. It's easy to understand how this happens. Funds that performed well during a given period are apt to have followed similar investment styles and objectives. They're the funds near the top of the rankings in newspapers and magazines, and they're the funds whose managers are being profiled or interviewed. Those funds might as well be festooned with neon lights that flash "Buy me. Buy me *now*."

Suppose you loaded up on top-ranked mutual funds in 1998, when large-capitalization growth stocks outperformed large-cap value stocks by 27 percentage points (as measured by the S&P/Barra indexes). Since large-cap growth funds were leading all others, you wound up with several of them. When the market's direction changed in 2000, value stocks outperformed growth stocks by 28 percentage points. If you were still hanging on to your portfolio full of growth funds, you were hit hard. But if you had been diversified, you wouldn't have been hurt as badly.

You'll avoid the risk of accumulating a hodgepodge portfolio if you resist the temptation to chase performance. I repeat this point from Chapter 6 because it is so important: Balance and diversification will do good things for you, but only if you are willing to buy and hold investments in periods when they seem unattractive because of recent "subpar" results.

A Case Study

Imagine starting an investment program in 1999. You scan the mutual fund performance tables. Near the top is Potomac: OTC Plus, up 104.2% in 1998. That figure gets your attention, and the fund gets $10,000 of your money. You're fuzzy on the investment basics, but you know enough not to put all your eggs in one basket. You invest $10,000 in each of four other top-rated funds: Janus Twenty, PBHG: Large Cap 20, Excelsior Large Cap Growth, and Alger Capital Appreciation.

Your colleague, the woman who chats with you about markets at the water cooler, invests $50,000 in just one fund, a broad stock market index fund. You warn her that she might not be very diversified if she holds just one fund.

During 1999, your five-fund portfolio returns 83.7%—three and a half times the 23.8% return earned by your colleague. Your $50,000 has grown to $91,850, while hers is only up to $61,905. Then the tables turn. During 2000, your portfolio loses one-third of its value. In 2001, it shrinks by another third. Your initial investment of $50,000 has shriveled to $43,313. Your colleague's portfolio isn't immune to the tough stock market; she loses almost 11% for two years in a row. But she finishes 2001 with an account value of $49,289.

You're furious. How could you do so badly when you were so diversified?

But you weren't diversified. You made the common mistake of assuming that a large number of funds translates into diversification. You'll understand if you look at the style box in Figure 12.1, which represents the U.S. stock market as a nine-sector grid. On the vertical axis, stocks move from small to large; on the horizontal, from value to growth. (As a reminder, value stocks are those with low prices relative to corporate fundamentals. Growth stocks typically represent fast-growing companies and command relatively high prices.)

Because you were in essence chasing performance, each of your five funds occupies the same corner of the style box. You have no exposure to value stocks or smaller stocks. In essence, you have five funds doing the work of one—a complicated, inefficient, poorly diversified, and needlessly expensive investment plan. Why so expensive? Your growth funds have an average expense ratio of 1.19%, whereas if you consolidated your assets in the cheapest of the five, you could cut your expenses to 0.84%. Indeed, if you invested in a truly low-cost growth fund, you could knock that expense ratio down to 0.30% or so.

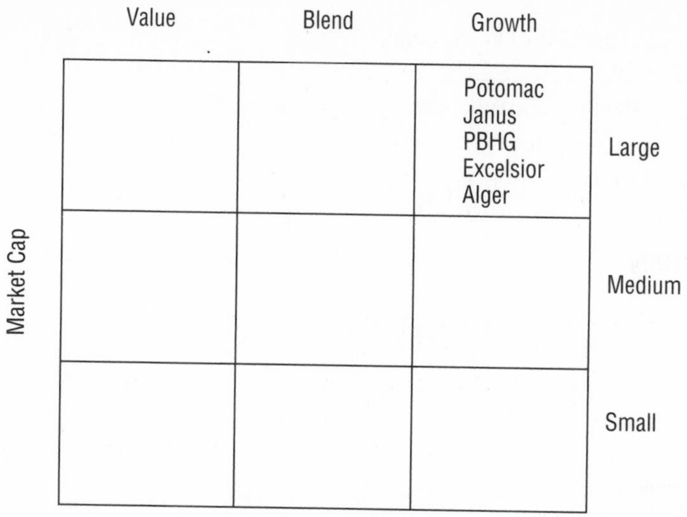

	Value	Blend	Growth	
Market Cap			Potomac Janus PBHG Excelsior Alger	Large
				Medium
				Small

FIGURE 12.1   Stock Fund Style Box Analysis

The five large-capitalization stock funds in the style box are Potomac: OTC Plus; Janus Twenty; PBHG: Large Cap 20; Excelsior Large Cap Growth; and Alger Capital Appreciation.

A better idea would be to select one low-cost large-cap growth fund, keep some of your assets there, and exchange the rest into funds with exposure to other parts of the stock market. Add a large-cap value fund, for example, and balance your large-cap stocks with smaller stocks. The result will be a steadier ride toward your financial goals, as strength in one part of your portfolio offsets weakness in another.

What about your colleague, the daredevil who put everything in one fund? She's much better diversified, as shown in Figure 12.2. The broad stock market fund includes stocks from every sector of the U.S. market—small stocks, large stocks, and growth and value stocks. This approach is a model of simplicity, efficiency, and frugality—exposure to the entire U.S. market through an index fund charging, say, 0.20% of assets.

Whether or not you choose to index your money, the makeup of the broad market is a good template for spreading your assets around. It's good to have exposure to each sector of the market. One index fund is the simplest solution, but you can also put together a portfolio of low-cost actively managed funds, or a mix of indexed and managed funds, to achieve exposure to the broad stock market along with the potential (but not the guarantee) of outperforming the index. Or maybe you want to tilt your investments toward value stocks, or growth stocks, while holding some assets in the other sectors.

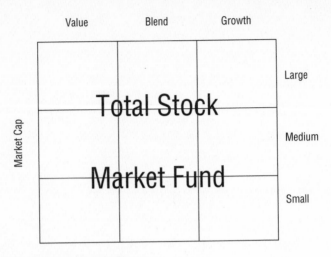

FIGURE 12.2   A Broad Stock Fund

How to Clean Up a Messy Portfolio

If you're wondering whether your own portfolio needs some pruning, here are some questions to ask yourself:

- Do you know why you own each of your funds? Each one should play a definite role in your portfolio.
- Do two or more of your funds share the same investment objective or investment style? If so, you might want to consider consolidating in one fund.
- If you were starting fresh today, would you invest in the funds you now own? In a sense, each day that you continue to hold a fund is like buying it all over again.

If your answers to those questions persuaded you to shear away a fund or two, fine—but don't act right away. There are some potential tax issues to consider first. It's pretty simple to clean up a messy portfolio if your assets are held in a tax-deferred account, such as an IRA or a 401(k). In that case you can move money from one fund to another without incurring capital gains taxes. But in taxable accounts, selling shares could result in a tax bill. If the potential tax cost is high, you may prefer to keep your fund collection, and diversify by making future investments elsewhere or by directing that the distributions you receive from one fund be invested in another.

Just recognize that there's another trade-off confronting you in this situation: If you adhere to a concentrated portfolio out of reluctance to incur a tax bill, or out of general inertia, you may pay a higher price in the long term because you weren't diversified. In general, the risk of not being diversified is too great to justify using tax considerations as a reason for not holding a balanced, diversified mix of assets.

(If the fund you want to ditch has risen in value, one alternative to selling your shares is to use them for a charitable gift. That way you can avoid incurring capital gains taxes and do some good in the world at the same time.)

Of course, the best reason to clean up a messy portfolio is to keep things simple. Trying to keep up with the transactional mechanics of 10 stock funds and 4 or 5 bond funds can be a recordkeeping chore. Multiple quarterly statements aren't the only headache—you also have the tax-season burden of reporting distributions from all of those funds. You probably have better things to do with your time than be a slave to your portfolio. Investing with simplicity is liberating because it lets you live your life.

When I was named president of Vanguard in 1989, I received a congratulatory phone call out of the blue from an older man whose daughters had been elementary school friends of mine. The man, whom I'll call Bob, said some nice things about Vanguard and mentioned that he had financed the college educations of his daughters (I'll call them Kara and Sally) with long-term investments in a single balanced fund, Vanguard Wellington Fund. Bob didn't have to invest so simply—he was a stockbroker with many investment options. But he was wise enough to understand the elegance and effectiveness of simplicity. I'll always remember his words: "Kara and Sally went to college on Wellington Fund." What a valuable and pointed reminder about the power of simplicity.

In a Nutshell

Strive for simplicity in your investment program. A portfolio that is a jumble of funds is not just an administrative headache; it's also likely to be costlier, less tax-efficient, and riskier than it needs to be. To keep things simple:

- **Make sure each fund serves a distinct purpose in your portfolio.** To achieve diversification, you should have exposure to every sector of the broad market, whether it's through a variety of funds or one or two broadly diversified funds.

- **Resist the temptation to chase performance.** People with portfolios full of similar funds often got there by loading up on "hot" performers.

- **Think about doing some pruning if you have more than 10 funds in your portfolio.** You can assess whether you are overexposed to some sectors of the markets and underexposed to others by using a style box to plot the investment focus of your funds.

PART THREE

Manage Your Investments with Focus and Discipline

chapter thirteen
BUY AND HOLD REALLY WORKS

I was attending a Vanguard client conference in Pittsburgh one night in 1997 when a man introduced himself and shared a terrific story. Back in 1958, when he was in his teens, he had earned $1,200 and had asked his father what he should do with the money. Father and son consulted a financial adviser, who recommended that they invest in a new mutual fund called the Wellington Equity Fund. There the money sat untouched for the next 39 years, accumulating reinvested distributions at an average rate of 13% a year. By 1997, this man's account in Vanguard Windsor Fund (as it is known today) had grown to $145,000—more than 100 times his original investment. He just wanted to say thanks!

If you're determined to succeed at investing, make it your first priority to become a buy-and-hold investor. As the story of the investor from Pittsburgh shows, picking sound investments and keeping them for the long term really works. Not only will this simple strategy enable you to accumulate wealth, it will allow you to live your life without devoting a lot of time and energy to managing your investments.

In this chapter, we'll discuss why a buy-and-hold strategy succeeds and how to implement it with your own portfolio. After that I'm going to be very blunt about two short-term strategies that *don't* work: frequent trading and market-timing.

Developing the Buy-and-Hold Habit

You can establish the buy-and-hold habit through a strategy known as dollar-cost averaging—putting a fixed dollar amount into a designated investment on a set schedule. Dollar-cost averaging creates a discipline of investing, and that systematic approach will help you avoid the temptations of market-timing and frequent trading.

And there's something even better about dollar-cost averaging: Over a given period, it can buy you more shares than you would have gotten by investing at the average share price during the period. That seems counterintuitive, so let me explain. The key is that, whether the markets are up or down, you're investing the same amount of money in the same fund or funds at regular intervals. That fixed sum buys more shares when the price is lower and fewer when the price is high. For example, say you invest $250 every month in a mutual fund. If your fund is selling at $10 a share in the first month, your $250 investment buys 25 shares. If the price declines to $8.50 per share in the second month, the same $250 investment buys 29.4 shares.

As a result, the average cost of your shares is lower than the average market price per share during the time you were investing. In our two-month example, the share price averaged $9.25 on the market, but the price you paid for your 54.4 shares averaged $9.19 apiece. Tables 13.1 and 13.2 show two different dollar-cost-averaging scenarios.

Dollar-cost averaging needn't mean you have to remember to write a check every month. In fact, you might already be using the strategy without having planned it—for example, if you are participating in an employer-sponsored retirement plan with a regular payroll deduction. You can also set up dollar-cost averaging in your other accounts by arranging for regular electronic transfers from

TABLE 13.1 How Dollar-Cost Averaging Works in a Rising Market

Month	*Investment*	*Share Price*	*Shares Acquired*
1	$400	$ 5	80
2	$400	$ 8	50
3	$400	$10	40
4	$400	$10	40
5	$400	$16	25
Total shares purchased			235
Total investment			$2,000
Average price per share*			$9.80
Average cost per share**			$8.51

*Average share price = $9.80 ($5 + $8 + $10 + $10 + $16 = $49; $49 ÷ 5 months = $9.80)

**Average share cost = $8.51 ($2,000 ÷ 235)

TABLE 13.2   How Dollar-Cost Averaging Works in a Falling Market

Month	Investment	Share Price	Shares Acquired
1	$400	$16	25
2	$400	$10	40
3	$400	$8	50
4	$400	$8	50
5	$400	$5	80

Total shares purchased	245
Total investment	$2,000
Average price per share*	$9.40
Average cost per share**	$8.16

*Average share price = $9.40 ($16 + $10 + $8 + $8 + $5 = $47; $47 ÷ 5 months = $9.40)
**Average share cost = $8.16 ($2,000 ÷ 245)

your bank into your mutual funds. This way you'll make investing almost automatic.

There are two things you need to remember to make dollar-cost averaging effective.

1. **You must continue to make regular purchases through thick and thin—** even through periods of market decline. Psychologically, this can be very difficult, so it's vital to remind yourself why you began dollar-cost averaging: to take a disciplined investment approach.

2. **You must stick to the same investment allocation.** Putting a fixed sum into the same investment month after month is dollar-cost averaging; putting a fixed sum into bonds one month and into stocks the next isn't dollar-cost averaging.

Of course, dollar-cost averaging cannot eliminate the risks of investing in financial markets. It doesn't guarantee you a profit, nor does it ensure that you'll be protected from loss in falling markets. But it sure has worked for a lot of people over the years.

You *Will* Be Tempted to Abandon Your Buy-and-Hold Strategy

There will be times when you become dissatisfied with one or more of the funds in your portfolio. It's a reality that sometimes an investment will quit working for you and you'll need to move out of it. But it's also true that every good mutual fund hits a bad patch now and then. When that occurs, you may question your judgment in picking the fund. If you are like many other investors who have written me letters over the years, you will also question the competence of the portfolio manager!

As a buy-and-hold investor, you should be reluctant to abandon an investment unless you have very good reason to assume it is no longer sound. That's because that jumping out can cost you—a lot.

At Vanguard, we recently examined how an investor would have fared if he or she stuck with—or abandoned—a couple of our funds that suffered extended periods of weak performance. Before I show you the results, I want to stress that you should not read *too much* into them. Investment returns are very dependent on the period you're studying, so our results might have been different in another span of years. Nonetheless, while the following case studies don't prove that you can always expect to be rewarded quickly for "staying the course," they do show the potential penalties in abandoning a buy-and-hold strategy.

Case #1: Windsor II

Vanguard Windsor II Fund, a value fund with a distinguished track record, was a laggard in the late 1990s when growth stocks were beating the stuffing out of value stocks. By early 2000, Windsor II's three-year performance numbers looked pretty bad next to the gains of the S&P 500 Index and even those of the average value fund. Some shareholders wrote us letters demanding that the fund managers be fired; others were so frustrated that they sold out and left. Redemptions from the fund reached their highest level in the first quarter of 2000.

Like Windsor II's investors, we were concerned about the fund's performance. But we monitor funds closely, and we had faith in the managers because their strategy, their teams, and their processes hadn't changed. We were confident that the fund's style of investing would eventually come back into fashion, but, of course, we had no way of knowing that the change would arrive so soon. Just as departures from the fund reached their peak, the bull market in growth stocks came to an abrupt end. For the year 2000, Windsor II gained 16.9%, while the S&P 500 Index saw its first decline in a decade, losing 9.1%.

With the benefit of hindsight, we recently looked at how things might have worked out for an investor who abandoned Windsor II in March 2000. The short answer: It didn't pay to make a switch.

Table 13.3 is based on the hypothetical case of an investor who put $10,000 in Windsor II on March 31, 1997, in a tax-free account, and three years later had to decide whether to stay put or switch. We've assumed that an unhappy Windsor II shareholder may have considered moving his money to another actively managed value fund (which is represented in the table by the average peer fund) or to

TABLE 13.3   Vanguard Windsor II Fund: Staying the Course versus Switching

Investment	*Value of Account*		
	3/31/1997	*3/31/2000*	*3/31/2002*
Windsor II Fund	$10,000	$14,275	$16,770
S&P 500 Index	$10,000	$20,677	
Russell 1000 Value Index	$10,000	$16,438	
Russell 1000 Growth Index	$10,000	$25,680	
Average Large-Cap Value Fund	$10,000	$16,840	
After Switching from Windsor II to S&P 500 Index on 3/31/2000	—	—	$11,208
After Switching from Windsor II to Russell 1000 Growth Index on 3/31/2000	—	—	$ 8,013
After Switching from Windsor II to Russell 1000 Value Index on 3/31/2000	—	—	$14,941
After Switching from Windsor II to Average Large-Cap Value Fund on 3/31/2000	—	—	$13,909

one of several index funds: a broad market index fund, a value index fund, or a growth index fund (represented in the table by various indexes). Remember, at the time our hypothetical investor couldn't know which way the market was headed. He would know only that Windsor II was trailing other investments, as you can see in the second column.

As the table shows, the investor would have done best to fight off his doubts and stay with Windsor II. If on March 31, 2000, he had removed his $14,275 from the fund and put it into one of the other investments, he would have ended up two years later with as little as $8,013 and at best only $14,941. If he left the money in Windsor II, it would have grown to $16,770.

Case #2: PRIMECAP Fund

Vanguard PRIMECAP Fund, a growth fund that also has produced an impressive performance record over the years, has also hit the occasional rough spot. At the start of the 1990s, PRIMECAP Fund was lagging both the broad stock market and the growth sector. By the spring of 1992, PRIMECAP investors were writing anguished letters. But as shown in Table 13.4, investors who gave up on PRIMECAP Fund in April 1992—at the peak of redemption activity—did not fare better with other obvious options they might have adopted. Three years later,

TABLE 13.4   Vanguard PRIMECAP Fund: Staying the Course versus Switching

	Value of Account		
Investment	*4/30/1989*	*4/30/1992*	*4/30/1995*
PRIMECAP Fund	$10,000	$13,655	$23,385
S&P 500 Index	$10,000	$14,827	
Russell 1000 Value Index	$10,000	$13,517	
Russell 1000 Growth Index	$10,000	$16,160	
Average Large-Cap Growth Fund	$10,000	$15,482	
After Switching from PRIMECAP to S&P 500 Index on 4/30/1992	—	—	$18,453
After Switching from PRIMECAP to Russell 1000 Value Index on 4/30/1992	—	—	$19,270
After Switching from PRIMECAP to Russell 1000 Growth Index on 4/30/1992	—	—	$17,704
After Switching from PRIMECAP to Average Large-Cap Growth Fund on 4/30/1992	—	—	$17,720

a stay-the-course investor would have had $23,385—ahead of the switchers by $4,115 to $5,681.

An important note: In both of these case analyses, we used the actual index performance figures. In real life, of course, an investor could not invest directly in an index; he would have to use an indexed mutual fund. That would mean slightly lower returns, since a fund, unlike an index, has costs.

The lesson from these examples is that a buy-and-hold strategy takes discipline, but it can serve you well in the end. You don't have to remember Windsor II and PRIMECAP Funds. Just remember the story of my friend in Pittsburgh. Patience really pays off.

Why Frequent Trading *Doesn't* Work

According to the tired old adage, the way to make money in the markets is to "buy low, sell high." Obviously, that's a great idea. You just figure out what's going to go up and then buy it, and you sell it when it reaches its peak. Simply repeat that process again and again as you trade your way to immense wealth. And the faster the better, right?

Unfortunately, it's *so* much easier said than done. But the theory is so simple, and the prospective rewards so great, that it's not surprising that plenty of people say to themselves, "*I'm* an intelligent person; I can see when stocks are going up and when they're going down. This isn't rocket science!" And pretty soon they're using their online brokerage accounts to buy and sell stocks every day. Or maybe they're not quite that aggressive, but they feel very cool about jumping in and out of mutual funds several times a month based on what they hear in TV gabfests or Internet chatrooms.

Don't try it! The odds are stacked against you. In stock trading, even the professionals have a hard time coming out ahead, and they have all kinds of specialized knowledge and research to help them. Without those resources, you would almost have to be psychic to win at trading, especially given that you have to pay to play. Need proof? A few years ago, two professors from the University of California at Davis, Brad Barber and Terrance Odean, studied the impact of frequent trading on the investment returns of 60,000 households that were clients of a discount broker from 1991 through 1996. Their finding[1]: The most frequent traders earned average annual net returns of 11.4%, while the market returned 16.4%. And that was during a bull market, remember; these days, the figures would be much lower, or even negative.

Frequent fund traders have little chance of success as well. To analyze why, we examined how stock mutual funds fared in comparison to the broad stock market over the 20 years from 1982 through 2001. During that time, the market returned 14.3% a year, on average, as measured by the Wilshire 5000 Index. Of the 233 "general equity" funds—that is, funds investing in companies of varied sizes and types—in existence for the entire period, 72 did better than the index and 161 did worse. So the chances were more than 2 to 1 against picking a "winning" fund. Not good odds. (And actually, the odds were much worse than I stated, because our analysis didn't include the performance of 100-plus funds that went out of business or were merged into other funds between 1982 and 2001.) Now take a close look at the *margins* of outperformance and underperformance in Figure 13.1, and you'll see why the odds of picking a fund with a *big* win are extremely long.

Only three of the funds that beat the index over the 20-year period were ahead by an annual average of three percentage points or more. Most of the relatively few funds that beat the index did so by less than one percentage point a year on average. But the margins of defeat were much wider among the 161 funds that underperformed the index. While more than two-thirds of them fell within three

[1]Brad Barber and Terrance Odean: "Trading is Hazardous to Your Wealth: The Common Stock Investment Performance of Individual Investors," *The Journal of Finance* (April 2000).

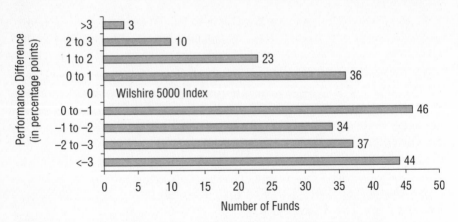

FIGURE 13.1   General Equity Funds versus Wilshire 5000 (1982–2001)

During the 1982–2001 period, the broad stock market returned 14.3% a year on average, as measured by the Wilshire 5000 Index. Very few of the general equity funds that existed throughout the period managed to do significantly better than the market, as the chart shows. While three funds beat the index by 3 percentage points or more, most of the outperformers were within 0 to 2 percentage points of the Wilshire return. In contrast, the funds that lagged the Wilshire generally did so by much wider margins. The data suggest that investors had little chance of picking an actively managed stock fund that would beat the market both consistently and by a notable margin.

percentage points of the index's performance, the remainder trailed by more. The lesson in this example is that when you try to pick a winning stock fund, you have a slight chance of beating the market by a little bit, and a very large chance of trailing it by a lot.

There are two reasons that most frequent traders don't succeed: One is the unpredictability of the markets; the other is the issue of costs and taxes.

The Unpredictability of the Financial Markets

Although some people claim to have a system for picking hot-performing securities or sectors, the fact is that no one has yet proven to have clairvoyance concerning the markets or individual stocks. Even legendary investors make mistakes. Just look at all the professionals who got burned when the technology stock craze ended. And who could possibly have predicted the accounting scandals that are upending several major corporations as I write? Not I; probably not you.

The Cost Penalty

Whether you are trading mutual funds or individual securities, the cost issues can be significant. If you trade mutual funds frequently, you may incur transaction fees from the funds, and if you're dealing through an intermediary you might have fees there too. If you trade individual securities frequently, you will incur brokerage commissions, and you'll also absorb the *bid–asked spread*—the difference between "bid" prices offered by potential buyers of a security and the higher "asked" prices at which potential sellers are willing to part with it. These costs seem negligible, perhaps, but I assure you that they add up rapidly, and their impact is magnified over time because the money lost to costs is not there to grow via compounding.

An even bigger hit is likely to come from capital gains taxes. You will owe a capital gains tax if you make a profit by selling shares in a taxable account (but not if you trade in a tax-deferred account, such as an IRA or a 401(k) plan). The active traders who make profits tend to realize short-term gains, which are taxed at rates approaching 40%. By contrast, long-term gains on securities held for more than a year have a tax ceiling of 20%. On a short-term gain of $5,000, an investor in the top bracket would owe $1,930 in taxes—almost twice the tax bill on a long-term gain.

Why Market-Timing Doesn't Work Either

Market-timers try to guess when to jump into the market and when to be out of it entirely. They wait to invest until the stock market or bond market seems attractive, and they switch out of the market when they foresee rough seas ahead.

Now, the "system" that a market-timer uses to trigger such moves may be a sophisticated computer program that crunches all sorts of financial ratios or that looks for signals based on past patterns. Or a timer might simply jump in or out of the market based on comments from some Wall Street "expert" or a newsletter.

However beautiful the theory, however logical the premise, the fact is that market-timing systems don't seem to consistently enrich anyone, with the possible exception of the brokers handling the market-timers' transactions. If market-timing did work for long periods, the timers themselves would top the lists of the world's richest individuals. You'd certainly never see a buy-and-hold investor like Warren Buffett leading the pack.

The world is simply too unpredictable a place to depend on patterns, or momentum, or logical assumptions that have worked in the past to prevail in the future. Some very smart and very well-heeled people running sophisticated hedge funds have gone belly-up simply because the markets behaved in unexpected—perhaps irrational—ways that were not anticipated by the sophisticates' computer models.

Besides, in spite of the analytical approach that many market-timers employ, most of them are subject to emotional decisions like everybody else. All too often, they either panic and sell at a loss when prices fall, as happened in both the bond and stock markets in 1987, or they jump on the proverbial bandwagon too late.

Myths about Market-Timing

I've already explained why market-timing doesn't work; now I'll share a few silly sayings about timing that are potentially misleading. Let's debunk these myths before we move ahead.

- **Myth #1: The January effect.** Historical data show that small-capitalization stocks have tended to outperform other market segments in the month of January. This has led to a widespread belief that smart investors should buy into small-cap stocks at year-end and sell them in January after their prices go up. People who study the markets have attributed the so-called January effect to a number of factors. One popular theory is that it's all due to tax-loss selling, a result of the volatile nature of small-company stocks. The idea is that every year a large number of investors who have losses on small stocks decide to sell them before December 31 to get a tax deduction; this depresses prices, which then bounce back in January. The problem with trying to profit from the January effect is that it has become so well-known. These days, so many investors have begun buying small-cap stocks at year-end in order to capitalize on the January effect that they've started to drive up the stocks' prices sooner. So now you have investors trying to capitalize on a "November effect," and at this rate, who knows, maybe there will soon be an August effect. You should ignore the whole scene.

- **Myth #2: Sell in May and go away.** This old saying was based on the idea that you should sell your holdings in the spring because the summer tended to be a slow time for trading and prices would fall. Nowadays some people claim that the opposite is true—that some sectors go up in the summer, so you should "*buy* in May and go away." Both versions make the same amount of sense: none. Such market patterns may occur from time to time, but there's no underlying basis for assuming they will continue or for acting on them.

- **Myth #3: Fear all fund distributions.** The conventional wisdom is that you shouldn't buy mutual fund shares in November or December for a taxable account because you will be saddled with a tax liability when the fund makes its year-end capital gains distributions. And this is based on some truth—many funds do make year-end distributions, and you might incur some tax liability by "buying the distribution." But that fact *on its own* should not dictate the timing of your investment decisions. A misguided attempt to save a few dollars in taxes could cause you to miss out on a few percentage points of return. We've seen that the stock market's gains in any given year tend to occur in short bursts instead of being spread out evenly over 52 weeks. If you are sure you want to invest in a certain fund, think hard before you decide to wait a few weeks to avoid a distribution. You can hurt yourself badly by being out of the market at the wrong time.

TABLE 13.5 Growth of $100 Invested in the S&P 500 Index: 1992–2001

	Ending Value	10-Year Compound Annualized Return
Total Period	$337.54	12.94%
Minus the Index's Best-Performing Month	315.13	12.16
Minus Its Two Best Months	293.16	11.36
Minus Its Three Best Months	272.06	10.53
Minus Its Four Best Months	249.99	9.55
Minus Its Five Best Months	231.79	8.77
Minus Its Six Best Months	215.60	7.99

Source: Crandall, Pierce & Company.

Another problem for timers is that market rallies often occur suddenly and over very short periods. If you happen to be out of the market during those times, you could miss most or all of the gains for that year. Tables 13.5 and 13.6 show how risky it is to be absent from the markets at the wrong time. As shown in Table 13.5, missing the six best months of the S&P 500 Index's performance over the 1992–2001 period would have reduced your average annual investment gain by nearly 40%—to 7.99% instead of 12.94%. And being out of the bond markets is equally risky. As shown in Table 13.6, missing the six best months of long-term Treasury bond performance during that 10-year period would have reduced your average annual return from 8.45% to 5.43%.

TABLE 13.6 Growth of $100 Invested in Long-Term Treasury Bonds: 1992–2001

	Ending Value	10-Year Compound Annualized Return
Total Period	$225.13	8.45%
Minus the Bonds' Best-Performing Month	216.58	8.03
Minus the Two Best Months	208.48	7.62
Minus the Three Best Months	194.62	6.89
Minus the Four Best Months	184.77	6.33
Minus the Five Best Months	177.57	5.91
Minus the Six Best Months	169.62	5.43

Source: Crandall, Pierce & Company.

Both frequent traders and market-timers are more like speculators than investors. You might think the chances are good that you'll be one of the few who succeed. But ask yourself whether you really want to play the odds with the money you are earmarking for retirement or your other important financial objectives. My advice is to forget timing and let time, and compounding, do their magic.

In a Nutshell

Once you've constructed a sensible, long-term portfolio, let a buy-and-hold strategy dictate how you manage your investment program. Holding on to what you've bought may not always be an easy strategy to stick with, but it is a proven way to build wealth.

- **Buy regularly.** Use dollar-cost averaging to make regular purchases of fund shares in fixed dollar amounts on a set schedule. Do this in up markets and down markets. Resist the temptation to think you can pick and choose when to invest and when to sit on the sidelines. The odds are against you.

- **Hold for the long term.** Hold your investments for years or even decades—don't try to be a frequent trader. Frequent trading is speculating, not investing, and it's a game that's easier to lose than win.

chapter fourteen

MAKING MONEY IS WHAT MATTERS

Your mutual fund returned 7% last year. Are you pleased or displeased?

It depends, doesn't it? It depends on what kind of fund you have and how it performed compared with the markets. Without a comparative dimension, absolute performance tells you only part of the story. Given that we're always comparing performance in other aspects of life—the gas mileage of our cars, the batting averages of baseball players, the developmental milestones of our offspring, and so on—it should come as no surprise that in investing, there's a thing called *relative fund performance*. Relative performance tells you how a mutual fund stacked up against similar funds or a market benchmark over given periods.

Absolute performance and relative performance are the focus of this chapter because they're at the heart of the question in every investor's mind: "How am I doing?" You'll want to use both of those measures to assess your interim progress toward your goals and determine whether you need to make course corrections.

But paying too much attention to relative performance can actually hamper you in your investment program. So let's frame the discussion by getting one thing straight up front: Despite all the news you hear about performance ratings and rankings, making money is ultimately what counts—not how you did last year relative to the Dow.

Getting to Boca

Some investors become so obsessed about beating the market (or other investors) that they lose sight of the reason they're investing at all. They measure their funds

against the S&P 500 Index or the Nasdaq or the Dow from quarter to quarter as if everything depended on staying ahead all the time. But it's misleading to obsess over whether your fund is two-tenths of a point ahead of this index or half a point behind that one. In fact, the only meaningful measure of your success is whether you eventually reach your investment objective, whether that's a down payment on a home or a retirement nest egg.

One of my all-time favorite commentaries on the beat-the-market obsession was a January 2000 column by Jason Zweig in *Money* magazine. Among other things, he pointed out that it's hard to beat indexes because they don't have any expenses, and that many investors who think they are ahead of the markets really aren't. Zweig ended the column with a great anecdote:

> I once interviewed dozens of residents in Boca Raton, one of Florida's richest retirement communities. Amid the elegant stucco homes, the manicured lawns, the swaying palm trees, the sun and the sea breezes, I asked these folks—mostly in their seventies—if they'd beaten the market over the course of their investing lifetimes. Some said yes, some said no. Then one man said, "Who cares? All I know is, my investments earned enough for me to end up in Boca."[1]

---

[1]Jason Zweig, "Did You Beat the Market?" *Money*, Volume 29, Number 1, January 2000, page 57.

We all would do well to think like that investor. Whether your "Boca" is a comfortable retirement, or a college education for your kids, or an estate to bequeath to your heirs or to charity, the idea is to focus on getting there and worry as little as possible about how your portfolio is performing relative to something else.

You Can't Eat Relative Performance

I'll admit to feeling a little conflicted on the subject of relative performance. As the head of a mutual fund firm, I am very interested in how our funds perform against the competition or the relevant indexes. Those results are critical to the success of our business. I'm also chairman of Vanguard's board of directors, and as such I have a fiduciary obligation to our shareholders to see that our investment products serve them well. We aren't serving shareholders well if our funds don't provide good long-term performance relative to their benchmarks and to their peers.

But as an individual investor, I take a different point of view because, like any other investor, I like to make money. If I invest in a fund and it performs well, I tend to feel good about the gain and not to care much if the fund lagged its benchmark by, say, 2 percentage points over a 12-month period. By the same token, I am not happy about a fund that beats its peers but still loses money. Though the professional investor in me may see things differently, it's small consolation to me as an individual that I would have lost even more if I had invested my money elsewhere.

I'm gratified when I receive letters from investors who seem to understand that making money is what counts. Actually, though, most people tend to reveal this knowledge indirectly. For example, I rarely get letters of complaint if one of our funds gains 24% during a year in which its benchmark gains 27%. However, I do often receive letters and e-mails if a fund posts a loss, even if the benchmark had a worse one. Sensible investors don't put too much store in a fund's relative performance. As the saying goes, "You can't eat relative performance."

How to Make Sense of Relative Performance Information

Of course, comparisons can be useful, as long as you employ the information judiciously and appropriately. You'll find relative performance data in a fund's prospectus and its annual and semiannual reports, as well as in numerous other investing resources online and in print. The Securities and Exchange Commission requires that all fund materials that discuss performance report 1-, 5-, and 10-year total returns.

In shareholder reports, mutual funds are required to provide comparative performance data for one broad market index. Many firms also voluntarily list the average return for a peer group of mutual funds. You can use these measures to get a little perspective on your fund's performance: If it's way ahead of the index, is that because the fund manager is brilliant, or is the peer group also ahead? If similar funds are having a great year as well, that's a clue that what's involved is not the manager's brilliance but a market trend. Even better is when the fund firm gives you two indexes to look at: one that measures the broad market and another that measures the specific segment of the market your fund invests in.

Do pay attention to which indexes are being cited. Some of the most widely known benchmarks may have very little relevance to your own fund. For example, the Dow Jones Industrial Average is probably the most-often-quoted benchmark for the stock market, but it is rarely (if ever) a meaningful benchmark for a stock mutual fund. The Dow consists of only 30 of the largest U.S. companies. Much better—but certainly not perfect—market barometers are the S&P 500 Index, which tracks 500 of the largest U.S. companies, and the Wilshire 5000 Index, which is actually based on more than 5,800 stocks.

Other important caveats:

- **Look at short-term *and* long-term performance.** Extended performance is always more meaningful than quarterly or even annual performance. A fund that trounces its peers or the index during a short period may simply have been lucky enough to benefit from a surge in one stock or one sector. It's the 5-year and 10-year numbers that will tell you the trend. Don't be tempted to shift money around because of a single year's results—or, worse, a single quarter's results.

- **Don't count on a hot track record continuing.** There is an overwhelming tendency for the performance of mutual funds to *revert to the mean*, which means that they tend to move closer to the average with time. The farther a fund diverges from the performance of similar funds in a given period, the more likely it is to fall back toward the average—which means that a turbocharged fund is particularly likely to hit a rough patch at some point. I'm always amused when I see fund managers lionized (or vilified) in the press for a year's performance. One of our fund managers was philosophical when he went from hero to zero and back again to hero over the course of a few bumpy years in the stock market. Looking back on a year when he was most out of favor in the eyes of the media, he mused: "I didn't get dumber last year than I was the year before, and I didn't get smarter this year than I was last year."

- **Always compare apples to apples.** A comparison is not fair unless the risk and return characteristics of the underlying investments are alike. Keep this "apples-to-apples" issue in mind when you make casual performance comparisons. Suppose you're investing in a bond fund to reduce the risk in your portfolio. It would be silly to compare that fund's performance with results for the S&P 500 Index. That's an apples-to-oranges comparison. On the other hand, if your fund is a large-cap blend stock fund, it would make perfect sense to measure its performance against the S&P 500.

- **Remember that indexes start with an advantage.** When you compare your fund's performance to what an index did, keep in mind that the index has no expenses to pay; it exists only on paper, so to speak. Funds do have operating expenses, plus the costs of buying and selling securities, and that money has to come out of their earnings. So your fund would actually have to perform better than the index in order to come out even with it after costs. (This is why even index funds typically trail their benchmarks by a little.)

Your Fund's Performance Isn't the Same As Your Investment Performance

In discussing performance comparisons, I've left the most important caveat for last: the uniqueness of your investment program. What's a benchmark for your fund is not a benchmark for *you*.

Obviously, if you own several funds, your overall investment performance is based on a combination of the behavior of each holding and its weighting within your portfolio. If you have a balanced investment plan, as I have so heartily recommended, then you'll expect to see some of your holdings doing better than others.

In addition, your buying and selling activity will make a difference in your actual performance. For example, if you are employing a dollar-cost averaging strategy and contributing to a fund gradually over the course of a year, you won't receive the reported 12-month return on every dollar of your investment. The same will be true if you sell some shares during the year. A number of fund companies are beginning to provide personal performance information based on your actual activity, and that's the best way to answer the question, "How am I doing?"

My Dad's in Boca

My father needed some investment advice from me when he retired 12 years ago and received pension assets in a lump sum. I set him up with a balanced, well-diversified portfolio based on an appropriate asset mix for his situation, and from that day forward he got on with his life and paid very little attention to investment performance. My father's investment program has succeeded; he has been able to live the way he wants to, and he has also been able to give generously to family members and charities without spending much energy on monitoring his portfolio. In fact, I can assure you that this very satisfied, balanced, and diversified investor—who since his retirement has experienced both a long bull market and some dramatic bear incursions—wouldn't be able to tell you how he's doing compared with the Dow or the S&P 500. Figuratively speaking, he's in Boca. What a great place to be at 85 years old.

In a Nutshell

Your best measure of success as an investor is whether you reach your eventual financial goals, not whether your portfolio beat the Dow or the S&P 500 in any given year. To stay focused, remember these things about investment performance data:

- **Short-term performance doesn't matter.** Quarterly (and even annual!) returns are largely meaningless if you are a long-term investor.

- **Hot performance will abate.** Today's top-ranked fund may seem alluring, but it is likely to lose steam with time.

- **A fund's reported return is not necessarily what you earned.** The return *you* earn on an investment will be affected by your buying and selling patterns, so it probably will be something different than the fund's reported return for a given period.

- **Be careful about the comparisons you draw.** Make sure you're comparing apples to apples when you look at performance data on two or more investments.

chapter fifteen

TIME IS EVERYTHING

After 20 years as an investment professional, I continue to be amazed by the miracle of compounding. My first lesson in compounding came when my banker father helped me to open a savings account. Years later, I encountered it again as an economics student in college when I read Paul Samuelson's classic textbook, *Economics*. I rediscovered the wonders of compounding when I joined Vanguard in 1982.

Test your own knowledge of compounding with this exercise: *If an 18-year-old made a single IRA investment of $3,000 and allowed that money to sit untouched, compounding at 10% a year, how much money would she have after 50 years?* Make a guess and then turn to the end of this chapter to see the answer. I think you will be astonished. I still am.

Most people—including investment professionals—underestimate the value of time in an investment program. Compounding is like a snowball rolling down a hill, picking up its greatest momentum toward the end. At the halfway point in the example above—after 25 years in the growth of our $3,000 investment—the value is only $32,504. The account gains half of its ending value in the last eight years.

In this chapter, I'll discuss how you can make time work for you. And if you're one of the many people who haven't gotten as early a start on investing as they wish they had, I'll offer some tips on how to make the most of the time that's available to you.

Make Time Your Ally

If you start saving when you are young, time will be your greatest ally. Year after year, your investments will earn interest and dividends, and those earnings, in turn, will generate additional earnings. If you wait until later in life to begin saving, time will be your greatest enemy. You won't be able to accomplish nearly as much in your investment program.

Suppose it's your goal to accumulate $100,000 by age 65. As shown in Figure 15.1, if you wait until age 60 to start saving and figure on an 8% annual return, you will need to save $1,361 a month to reach your goal. Conversely, if you start saving much earlier, at age 35, you need to save only $67 a month at the same rate of return. When you start your investing earlier, more of your wealth comes from compounding and less from your out-of-pocket contributions.

An early start is a huge advantage. Here's another hypothetical case study as shown in Table 15.1:

- Will starts saving for retirement at age 30. He invests $1,000 a year for 10 years, earning an 8% annual return, and then stops making contributions.

- Conor, who is Will's age, waits until age 40 to begin saving for retirement. He then contributes $1,000 a year for 25 years, also earning 8% annually.

Who has more money at age 65 when they are ready to retire? Believe it or not, the answer is Will. As shown in Table 15.1, his $10,000 in contributions, with many more years to compound, grew to $107,100. Conor's $25,000 only had time to reach $79,000.

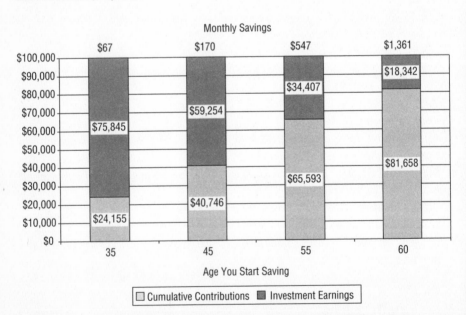

FIGURE 15.1   Monthly Savings Needed to Accumulate $100,000 by Age 65

This chart shows how much you would need to save in a tax-sheltered account each month, depending on your starting age, to reach a $100,000 goal at 65, assuming that you earned an 8% annual return.

TABLE 15.1   Who Has More at 65?

Growth of a Retirement Account at 8% Annual Returns

Age	Will Contribution	Will Value at Year-End	Conor Contribution	Conor Value at Year-End
30	$1,000	$1,080		
31	$1,000	$2,246		
32	$1,000	$3,506		
33	$1,000	$4,867		
34	$1,000	$6,336		
35	$1,000	$7,923		
36	$1,000	$9,637		
37	$1,000	$11,488		
38	$1,000	$13,487		
39	$1,000	$15,645		
40	0	$16,897	$1,000	$1,080
41	0	$18,249	$1,000	$2,246
42	0	$19,709	$1,000	$3,506
43	0	$21,286	$1,000	$4,867
44	0	$22,988	$1,000	$6,336
45	0	$24,827	$1,000	$7,923
46	0	$26,814	$1,000	$9,637
47	0	$28,959	$1,000	$11,488
48	0	$31,275	$1,000	$13,487
49	0	$33,777	$1,000	$15,645
50	0	$36,480	$1,000	$17,977
51	0	$39,398	$1,000	$20,495
52	0	$42,550	$1,000	$23,215
53	0	$45,954	$1,000	$26,152
54	0	$49,630	$1,000	$29,324
55	0	$53,601	$1,000	$32,750
56	0	$57,889	$1,000	$36,450
57	0	$62,520	$1,000	$40,446
58	0	$67,521	$1,000	$44,762
59	0	$72,923	$1,000	$49,423
60	0	$78,757	$1,000	$54,457
61	0	$85,057	$1,000	$59,893
62	0	$91,862	$1,000	$65,765
63	0	$99,211	$1,000	$72,106
64	0	$107,148	$1,000	$78,954
65	Retirement		Retirement	
TOTAL	**$10,000**	**$107,148**	**$25,000**	**$78,954**

Time Reduces Your Risk

If you're a stock investor, having time on your side also provides an interesting fringe benefit in risk reduction. That's because, while stocks are a very risky investment in any single year, the relative risk is diluted over long periods (assuming that your stock investments are diversified). By choosing sound investment vehicles and staying with them for the long haul, you're almost certain to make money, thanks to the accumulation of reinvested earnings along with whatever stock appreciation occurs.

Suppose you'd held an all-stock portfolio invested in the S&P 500 Index for the years 1972 through 2001 (see Figure 15.2). Your yearly returns would have ranged from a gain of nearly 38% in 1995 to a loss of more than –26% in 1974. That's a huge spread! But if you instead look at the returns over rolling 5-year, 10-year, and 20-year periods, the gaps between highs and lows are much narrower. The lesson is that letting the markets and time work for you is a terrific way to minimize the risk in your portfolio.

Table 15.2 shows how differences in return and time period affect the growth of an investment. If you're making annual investments of $1,000 and you have 25 years to invest, you need to earn just 5% a year to accomplish a $50,000 goal. If your time horizon is only a little shorter—20 years—you need annual returns of better than 8% to get to roughly the same goal.

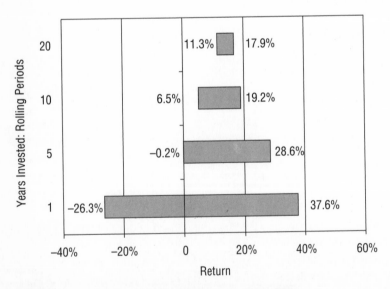

FIGURE 15.2   Range of S&P 500 Returns: 1972–2001

One-year returns fluctuate much more widely than returns over longer rolling periods.

TABLE 15.2   See How It Compounds: Growth of $1,000 in Annual Investments at Different Rates and Different Time Periods

Years	Annual Growth Rate				
	5%	6%	7%	8%	9%
1	$ 1,050	$ 1,060	$ 1,070	$ 1,080	$ 1,090
5	$ 5,802	$ 5,975	$ 6,153	$ 6,336	$ 6,523
10	$13,207	$13,972	$14,784	$15,645	$16,560
15	$22,657	$24,673	$26,888	$29,324	$32,003
20	$34,719	$38,993	$43,865	$49,423	$55,765
25	$50,113	$58,146	$67,676	$78,954	$92,324

How to Make Up for Lost Time

What if you didn't start investing until relatively late in your working career? Is it too late to accumulate a retirement nest egg? The answer is no—absolutely not. It is never too late.

If you are 52, reading this book and regretting the fact that you haven't begun to save for retirement, know that you're not alone. In a survey of financial planners some years back, 29% of the respondents said their clients didn't start preparing for retirement until they were in their 50s. But I encourage you to start *now*.

Actually, you really have no choice. A hundred years ago, the biggest financial risk that ordinary people faced was that they might die too soon to provide for their families. The life insurance industry sprang up to meet that need. These days, longer life spans mean that, for most of us, the biggest financial risk is that we'll outlive our savings. It sounds hard-boiled, but starting an investment program late in life comes down to this choice: Save more now or die early.

You are likely to be living in retirement for 20 or 30 years, so it's not just a matter of accumulating as much as you can by age 65. As I write, a 65-year-old woman is expected, on average, to live to age 85, while a 65-year-old man is expected to live to age 81. And many people live to be much older. To make your savings last for such a long period, you need to be very thoughtful in how you allocate your investments and plan your retirement spending.

A 24-year-old and a 52-year-old who are just starting out as investors need to pursue somewhat different strategies. Their different time horizons will dictate different asset mixes. The 24-year-old probably will want to invest entirely in stocks. The 52-year-old should consider a balanced portfolio made up of funds with relatively conservative risk/return profiles. There are some things they should do alike, however: For instance, each should invest in a Roth IRA because of its very attractive provisions. Withdrawals from a Roth IRA are tax-free after you reach age 59½, provided you've had the account for at least five years and meet other basic conditions.

Working in the 52-year-old's favor are some recently enacted provisions in federal law that are aimed at helping older people "catch up" on saving for retirement. If you are 50 or older and you meet the income limits, you can contribute up to $3,500 a year to your IRA in the years 2002 to 2004—$500 more each year than younger people can invest. The contribution limit for people over 50 rises to $4,500 in 2005 and $5,000 in the years 2006 to 2008. Assuming you are eligible, you could contribute as much as $31,000 to an IRA over the 2002–2008 period.

There are also catch-up provisions for contributions to employer retirement plans. If you are over 50, check with your employer to learn how much of your salary you can put into a 401(k) or 403(b) plan. Plan rules vary, but if you can take advantage of the catch-up provisions, you might be able to sock away as much as an extra $25,000 in your company retirement plan between 2002 and 2008.

If you're starting late, you won't have the advantages that decades of compounding provide, but don't let yourself think that smaller returns and slower accumulation aren't worth pursuing. I've spent a lot of time coaching kids' lacrosse games, and I always emphasize to my players that it's just as important to be able to scoop up loose ground balls as it is to make flashy passes. In lacrosse, the team

TABLE 15.3   Investment Goal: $1 Million at Age 65

Age at Which Investing Begins	Monthly Savings at 8% Annual Returns
Birth	$38
5	$56
10	$84
15	$126
20	$190
25	$286
30	$436
35	$671
40	$1,051
45	$1,698
50	$2,890
55	$5,466
60	$13,610

that's best at the apparently unglamorous work of getting ground balls *always* wins the game. In investing, even unglamorous returns will make a difference over time. If you earn 6% a year, you will still double your money in roughly 12 years.

Whatever your situation, don't overlook the chance to get your children, or the children of your friends and relatives, started early on their investment programs. Dazzle them with this simple but powerful data. Table 15.3 shows the monthly savings required to reach the lofty goal of having $1 million at age 65. I've assumed the money is invested at an annual gain of 8%, and for purposes of this illustration I've omitted the effects of taxes.

Answer to question at chapter opening: *A one-time investment of $3,000 in a tax-free account, left untouched to compound at 10% a year, would be worth $352,173 after 50 years.*

In a Nutshell

You can accomplish impressive things if you start investing early and keep investing.

- **Compounding adds up.** Your investments will earn interest and dividends, and those reinvested earnings in turn will generate additional earnings.

- **Time reduces risk.** While stocks are a very risky investment in any single year, the relative risk of a diversified stock portfolio is diluted over long periods of time.

- **It's never too late.** Don't be deterred if you're getting a late start on a retirement savings program—you can still put time to work on your behalf.

chapter sixteen

GIVE YOUR PORTFOLIO AN OCCASIONAL TUNE-UP

If you own a car, you understand the importance of maintaining it properly—or you should. A car that's maintained well will run more smoothly and be less likely to break down. To keep a car in good working order, you take it to the shop periodically for a checkup and routine service, and you have it tuned up when necessary.

Your investment portfolio will also benefit from a periodic checkup and a tune-up. And the good news is that with your portfolio—unlike your engine—you should be familiar with what's under the hood.

There are two reasons to make adjustments in your portfolio:

1. Your personal financial situation may change.
2. Market fluctuations will alter the mix of assets over time. To get the mix back to your target allocations, you'll need to rebalance your holdings.

In this chapter, we'll take a look at the simple truths behind rebalancing, and I'll discuss how to go about making changes when appropriate.

Your Personal Situation

No successful investor I know puts everything on autopilot. Personal financial situations do change. Your income will drop if you lose a job or retire. Your wealth could increase if you inherit money. Other events, such as marriage, the death of a spouse, or a child's departure from home, can cause fundamental changes in one's financial situation. Whenever you experience such a change, it's a good idea to reassess how you manage your financial affairs.

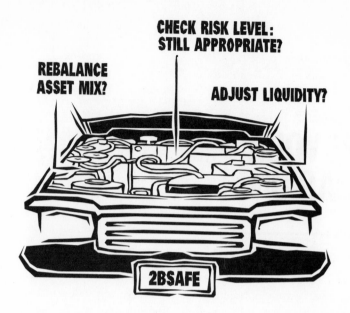

You might need to adjust your portfolio's risk level or take steps to increase its liquidity. For example, if you lose your job, you will likely need to draw on your emergency-fund savings and temporarily stop adding to other accounts. But if you switch jobs and move to a position that pays more but offers less job security, you may decide to increase your savings rate and put more into your emergency fund, just in case things don't work out.

You'll also likely want to make some changes in your portfolio as you get closer in time to your investment objective. For example, most investors shift to a more conservative asset mix as they approach retirement. And if you're saving for a child's education, it's best not to be depending on the stock market's benevolence when those first tuition payments get near.

Life events don't always dictate massive changes in your investment program. There are plenty of smart, successful investors who stick to the same program, month after month, year after year, making steady progress toward their goals. But even if you want to be one of them, you'll need to do periodic check-ups to make sure you're leaving things alone for good, solid reasons, and not just because of inertia.

Rebalancing a Portfolio

Even though most people don't need to change their investment programs very often, every long-term investor should rebalance his or her portfolio from time to time.

TABLE 16.1   How the Markets Can Tilt a 50%/50% Portfolio Off-Balance

Year	Beginning Value of Portfolio	Return on Stocks	Return on Bonds	Ending Value of Portfolio	% Stocks/Bonds
1996	$50,000	21.2%	3.6%	$56,211	54%/46%
1997	$56,203	31.3%	9.7%	$68,193	58%/42%
1998	$68,183	23.4%	8.7%	$79,983	61%/39%
1999	$79,973	23.6%	−0.8%	$92,299	66%/34%

Sources: Wilshire 5000 Index; Lehman Aggregate Bond Index.

Rebalancing—the equivalent of an engine tune-up—means getting your investments back into line with your target asset mix. If you initially decided to split your assets evenly between stocks and bonds, you'll discover sooner or later that they aren't evenly split any more; the different returns on the two asset classes will have changed the proportions. For example, if you began 1996 with a $50,000 retirement account divided evenly between stocks and bonds, you ended the year with a portfolio that was 54% stocks and 46% bonds. That's not a huge shift, but let's look at what the markets would have done to your allocation over the next three years if you didn't do any rebalancing.

As shown in Table 16.1, your half-and-half portfolio would have become a 66%/34% portfolio by the end of 1999. "Who cares?" you may be thinking. "Look how much money I made!" Yes, the value of the account would have nearly doubled over the four years, growing from $50,000 to $92,299. But there's a risk monster lurking in this portfolio.

Why Rebalance? To Fend Off the Risk Monster

People tend to think about investing only in terms of making money. Making money *is* why we invest, but the reality is that if you don't remember to manage risk along the way, you won't do well at making money. The point of rebalancing is to manage your risk, not to maximize your returns. But if you don't manage risk, you might end up minimizing your long-term returns.

Let's think about the impact of rebalancing on a portfolio held for a long time. Consider another hypothetical portfolio, evenly divided between stocks and bonds and rebalanced every six months from January 1960 through December 2001. That long span included some great periods and some bad periods in terms of performance. According to calculations we did at Vanguard, the portfolio that was rebalanced twice a year would have generated an average annualized return of 9.3% over four decades, which is marginally lower than the 9.5% return it would have earned if never rebalanced. Does that mean that rebalancing lost the race? Not unless you have nerves of steel.

The rebalancing substantially reduced the portfolio's volatility. Without rebalancing, the portfolio would have suffered declines of 5% or more during more than 11% of those six-month periods. With rebalancing, the portfolio declined to that degree in only about 6% of the periods. Which portfolio would have produced more anxious, sleepless nights? And which would have helped you to keep your equilibrium when the markets lost theirs?

There are times when rebalancing can actually add value to your returns. From the end of 1996 through December 2001, a portfolio of half stocks/half bonds that was rebalanced semiannually had a total cumulative gain of 46.9%, about 2 percentage points higher than the return of a portfolio that started out with the same mix but was never rebalanced. In investing, minimizing declines is as desirable a goal as increasing returns. Over the two years following March 2000, the rebalanced portfolio declined 3.4%, or about one-half of the 6.7% decline of the never-rebalanced portfolio. You can't count on rebalancing to produce better returns and lower risk, but it's nice to know that both can occur.

Pitfall: Don't Forget Those Buckets When You Tune Up Your Portfolio

Remember our discussion in Chapter 3 about the buckets that represent your financial objectives? You'll want to keep those separate buckets in mind when you are giving your portfolio its checkup. Suppose your portfolio includes retirement investments as well as savings earmarked for your children's college costs. If you are using the bucket approach, you've probably designated different asset mixes for each of those investment programs, so you should review them separately rather than as parts of an overall portfolio.

And when you're looking at asset weightings, take a global view of everything that belongs in your retirement savings bucket. I've noticed that investors often mentally segregate their retirement savings by account type. For example, they think of their IRA and 401(k) accounts as two separate stashes, instead of as parts of the same nest egg. (It's especially easy to compartmentalize like that if you're dealing with different providers on the accounts.) And don't overlook your pension assets if you are fortunate enough to have them—even a small monthly pension is equivalent to earnings on a substantial lump sum of savings.

To make sure you are seeing things clearly, it's not a bad idea to take inventory of all your financial resources when you give your portfolio its periodic checkup. Put everything down on paper. Add up all of your assets bucket by bucket. Laying it all out in front of you will provide a scorecard, so that over time you can easily see whether you are progressing toward your objectives as you intended.

When to Rebalance

When you rebalance and how you go about it will depend a lot on your personal circumstances—your age, how much money you have, and your tax bracket—and you may even want to discuss some of the decisions with your financial adviser or accountant. But here are some general rules of thumb:

- **Rebalance on a regular schedule—quarterly, semiannually, or annually.** Our research shows that the frequency of rebalancing is not a big deal; in other words, results don't vary much according to whether you're rebalancing quarterly, semiannually, or annually. What's important is that you do it. For most people, an annual rebalancing is adequate. Choose your birthday, anniversary, or some other fixed date, such as April 15, the tax-filing deadline. This will impose some discipline on the process. Otherwise, you might allow external events, short market swings, or emotions to sway your decision about when to rebalance.

- **Rebalance only if your asset mix has strayed from its target by more than 5 percentage points.** If the variation is less, the benefit of rebalancing probably isn't worth the bother.

- **Don't get too carried away with "micro" issues.** Some investors try to establish precise weightings for specific market segments in their portfolios. For example, they try to maintain certain proportions of U.S. and international stocks, growth and value stocks, large-cap and small-cap stocks, or bonds of particular types and maturities. These micro "slice and dice" matters aren't the most pressing rebalancing issues. Worry about them only after you have made sure you are on target with your overall asset mix. And here also, rebalance only if your asset mix has strayed from its target by more than 5 percentage points.

The Tax Monster Joins the Risk Monster

If all your assets were in tax-deferred retirement accounts, rebalancing would be relatively simple. You could move money around within your IRA and your

401(k) without triggering any capital gains liabilities. But sooner or later, you will probably have to rebalance your taxable accounts, and that could lead to a tax consequence. Let's say you need to adjust the stock component of your $100,000 portfolio from 80% to 75%. You decide the best way to do that is to move $5,000 from a stock fund into a bond fund—but you'll have a capital gain on the exchange, which will mean taxes. In such a case, you'll generally do best to just bite the bullet, exchange the shares, and pay the tax. It can be penny-wise and pound-foolish to let tax considerations drive your overall investment strategy.

One way to minimize tax liabilities when rebalancing is to change your investment pattern instead of moving existing assets around. You can redirect new investments to the part of your portfolio that you want to beef up. Or, since your dividend and capital gains distributions are already being taxed anyway, you could redirect those distributions from the asset that has performed well and have them invested in the one that has fallen below your target weighting.

Rebalancing Takes Discipline

The biggest challenge of rebalancing is finding the discipline to do it. First of all, rebalancing *feels* unreasonable. If stocks are booming and bonds are hurting, you're apt to ask yourself why you would want to move money from stocks to the bond portion of your portfolio. It's hard to see the wisdom in shuffling the cards when it looks like you're holding a winning hand.

Remember the importance of your asset mix in determining your investment returns. You originally decided on your asset-allocation plan for specific reasons, one of which was managing risk. Trust your own good judgment and force yourself to rebalance periodically. If you don't, you could very well wind up with a portfolio that's far riskier than you intended.

You can always learn lessons as an investor, and the value of rebalancing is one of the key things that I've learned by seeing it firsthand over 20 years. What drove it home was watching fund managers pursue their own rebalancing chores. I've talked about the challenge of this discipline for an individual investor; fund managers face the same thing on a much larger scale.

The event that most underscored for me the value of disciplined rebalancing occurred on October 20, 1987. It was the day after the largest one-day percentage drop in stock market history: The market fell 22.6% on Monday, October 19. Professionals and nonprofessionals alike felt very panicky about stocks that day. But the managers of Vanguard Wellington Fund had to buy millions of dollars' worth of stocks to restore the 65% stock/35% bond mix required by the fund's investment policy. The managers had no choice. The plunging stock market and surging bond market had taken their stock allocation well below their target, so they had to sell bonds and add stocks to rebalance. Had they let emotions rather than discipline dictate their actions, they would have missed the sharp rally that began later that day. Discipline pays.

In a Nutshell

Your investment portfolio needs a periodic checkup to make sure it's still serving your needs. There are two reasons to make adjustments:

- **Life events may dictate some changes.** You may need to adjust your portfolio if your financial situation has changed or if you are getting closer in time to your investment objective.

- **Market fluctuations can knock your portfolio's asset mix off kilter over time.** It's a good idea to check your portfolio once a year or so and rebalance it if it has drifted by 5 percentage points or more from the target asset allocation.

chapter seventeen
STUPID MATH TRICKS FOR SMART INVESTORS

One of the trademarks of comic David Letterman's *Late Show* on TV is "Stupid Pet Tricks," in which pet owners show off the antics of their animals. Believe it or not, there are quite a few "stupid math tricks" in investing. They're not really stupid at all, of course—just fun and useful to know, and to me more interesting than a jump-roping dog. Understanding the math tricks of investing will help you to become a sharp-eyed consumer of financial products and services.

1. **Dollars, not percent signs, are what you carry in your wallet.** The investment industry measures costs and performance in percentage terms, but for practical decision-making it can help to translate those percentages into dollars. For example, suppose you're considering making a $10,000 investment through a broker who charges a 5% sales commission. You may not mind paying the broker 5%, but how do you feel about paying him *$500*?

2. **Make estimates in a flash with the Rule of 72.** Want to know how fast your money will double? You don't need a calculator. Estimate your yearly rate of return and divide it into the number 72. The result is the number of years it will take for your investment to roughly double in value. The rule works with any amount of money (See Table 17.1).

   The Rule of 72 is a nifty trick, but it can do more for you than impress your friends. Suppose you're mulling what to do with a long-term investment of $10,000. If you put the sum in a money market fund and earn an average of 3% a year, you will double your money in about 24 years (72 ÷ 3 = 24). But if you invest the same sum in a stock fund that returns 9% a

year on average, you'll get to $20,000 after about eight years ($72 \div 9 = 8$). (For simplicity, I'm ignoring taxes in these examples.)

The Rule of 72 also gives a powerful demonstration of the impact of small differences in return over time. Consider two mutual funds that have the same gross returns—that is, performance before costs are subtracted—but different expense ratios, which result in average net returns of 8% and 7%, respectively. The Rule of 72 tells us that an investment in the 8% fund will double after nine years, while money in the 7% fund will take more than a decade to double. Keeping costs low can help you boost your returns and double your money more quickly.

3. **Even in the bargain basement, some stocks are overpriced.** Someone gave me a T-shirt bearing the name of a once-legendary dot-com company. Now that the company's stock has fallen from around $180 a share to less than 50 cents, I calculate that my T-shirt is worth ten shares of stock. When I made this observation to a friend outside the financial industry, he

TABLE 17.1 Growth of an Investment at Different Rates of Return (Pre-Tax)

	Annual Return			
	3%	*6%*	*9%*	*12%*
Years until investment doubles	24	12	8	6

said earnestly: "Maybe I should buy that stock. At 50 cents a share, how much money could I lose?"

The answer is, "All of it." If an investment is risky, it doesn't matter whether you pay 50 cents a share or $50 a share—you are still at risk of losing all of it.

Investors sometimes get suckered into thinking that a stock whose price has fallen a long way must therefore offer good value. They forget that maybe it hasn't yet fallen *far enough*. This attitude was especially noticeable after the collapse of the dot-com bubble in 2000. Although the prices of many stocks fell at that point, market prices overall were still quite high in relation to traditional yardsticks. Few investors seemed to realize how much risk was embedded in those prices.

4. **Up 100% and down 50% means you've gone nowhere.** Suppose you invest in a stock whose share price falls from $50 to $25, a decline of 50%. If you hope to get back to your starting point, you need a 50% gain, right? Wrong—you need a 100% gain. Here's the same math, but starting from the other end: A stock that goes from $25 to $50 a share is up 100%. If it falls by 50%, you're back where you started.

This is important to keep in mind, especially during periods of stock market euphoria. Percentages seem particularly perplexing for investors at such times—perhaps the market's rapid rise goes to people's heads. Stupid Math Trick #4 will stand you in good stead if anyone tries to sell you a volatile investment by emphasizing its upward moves more than its declines. Remember that a stock that soars by 100% in a short time may be capable of falling 50% just as fast, putting you right back at zero.

5. **The bigger the fall, the longer the recovery.** When a stock or a fund declines by a lot, it generally takes a very long time to recover. This stupid math trick is something that conservative investors understand intuitively. Suppose a stock falls by 60%—declining from $100 a share to $40. That's a large decline (and if it's your money, you might even call it cataclysmic). As Table 17.2 shows, even at a hearty recovery rate of 10% a year the stock would need a decade to regain its value. At a 9% rate, the stock would take a year longer.

An understanding of the mathematics of declines and recoveries will give you a new perspective on the financial news. For example, after the Nasdaq Composite Index plunged from its high of 5,048.62 on March 10, 2000, to a (then) low of 1,423.19 on September 21, 2001, the pundits were all wondering whether the Nasdaq would get back to 5,000 again anytime soon. That would be mathematically challenging, to say the least. Although it took the Nasdaq Composite just 2¾ years during the euphoric 1990s to zoom from 1,423 to 5,048, the index would need 13 years to

TABLE 17.2   Recoveries Can Take a Long Time

Year	Value at Beginning	% Change	Value at End
0	$100	−60%	$40
1	40	+10	44
2	44	+10	48
3	48	+10	53
4	53	+10	59
5	59	+10	64
6	64	+10	71
7	71	+10	78
8	78	+10	86
9	86	+10	94
10	94	+10	104

regain that peak at a more reasonable growth rate of 10% a year. The fall took just a bit more than 18 months.

The math of declines and recoveries also demonstrates the folly in waiting to "get back to even." Just like gamblers on losing streaks, some investors feel that they absolutely have to stick with a volatile investment until they get back to their break-even point. But it's extremely difficult to get back to even on an investment that has lost a significant chunk of its value. Some investors never get there. I'll talk more about dealing with losses in a future chapter, but I want to make the point here that optimism is emotion, and you should never let emotion override mathematics.

6. **Cumulative returns can be misleading.** When a fund reports cumulative returns, it is giving only starting and ending values, with no indication about what happened along the way. Would you be attracted to a stock fund that had earned a cumulative return of 250% over 20 years? Sounds great, doesn't it? But if you do the math, you'll find out that the fund was earning an average of 6% a year—nothing spectacular. When you're evaluating a fund's performance, focus on average annual returns, not cumulative returns. An investment that averages about 11% annually over 20 years produces a cumulative return of 706%.

Cumulative returns can be useful for calculating how much an initial lump-sum investment would be worth at the end of a given period. A $1,000 investment with a 706% cumulative return would be worth $8,060 at the end of the period (leaving aside taxes).

7. **Sometimes a falling share price is good news.** When interest rates rise, a bond fund's share price falls. This can look like bad news when you get your account statement. But if you're a long-term investor, it's actually something to cheer about.

   As Figure 17.1 illustrates, over long periods most of the return on a bond fund comes from interest payments, not from increases in bond prices. Let's assume that your bond fund's share price falls from $10 to $9 as interest rates rise from 5% to 6.5%. Since you're there for the long term, the share price shouldn't matter to you, but the higher level of interest income does. It means that there will be more money going into your account as the fund reinvests assets at the new prevailing interest rates. The bottom line: If you are a long-term investor in a bond fund, don't worry about declines in your funds' share price caused by interest rate fluctuations.

   The converse of this stupid math trick: When a decline in interest rates drives up the share prices of bond funds, don't join in the stampede of investors who suddenly want to own bonds. The decline in interest rates means that the funds' income is about to decline.

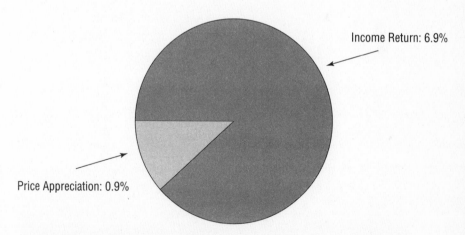

Income Return: 6.9%

Price Appreciation: 0.9%

FIGURE 17.1   Average Annual Return on a Broad Bond Market Index Fund: 1991–2000

Most of a bond fund's long-term return comes from reinvested income dividends. A bond index fund tracking the Lehman Aggregate Bond Index returned 7.8% a year on average for the 1991–2000 period. Of that return, 6.9 percentage points came from reinvested dividends, while 0.9 percentage point resulted from price appreciation.

In a Nutshell

You don't need to keep a calculator at your side whenever you are thinking about investing, but as a consumer of investments, you do need to be aware of some mathematical peculiarities that can be a little counterintuitive:

- **Use the Rule of 72 to make quick projections.** Divide your rate of return into 72 and the result is roughly the number of years that it will take an investment to double.

- **Don't get flummoxed by percentages.** Paying a 5% sales commission on a $10,000 investment may not sound like much, but it's $500 of your hard-earned money.

- **Look past the cumulative return.** When you are evaluating a fund's performance, focus on average annual returns, not cumulative returns.

PART FOUR

Stay on Course

chapter eighteen
"IT'S A MAD, MAD, MAD, MAD WORLD"

At the outset of this book, I asserted that the key to successful investing is to get a few important things right and avoid making dangerous mistakes. I've already discussed the good habits that investors need to develop—saving money, investing regularly, being a buy-and-hold investor, and minimizing costs, among others. Now we'll turn our attention to the distractions and temptations that can undermine your investment program.

As we've witnessed in the last two years, the financial markets can present difficult challenges to investors. But those aren't the only tests that you will face as an investor. You'll encounter information that can lead you astray. You'll be buffeted at times by your own emotions or psychological factors that can hamper your judgment. In this section of the book, I aim to examine all those issues in an effort to provide you with some defensive tools before you embark on your journey as an investor.

In the hope that a little knowledge will help to inoculate you against temptations, I'm devoting this chapter to past fads and bubbles. There's no question that it is a "mad, mad, mad, mad world" out there, to borrow a famous old movie title. As an investor, you're sure to encounter conspiratorial rumors, multiply-your-money tips, invitations to seminars on "secrets even the pros don't know," maybe even solicitations for illegal pyramid schemes. I hope you're equipped by now to resist all these. But from time to time, you'll be tempted by something much more seductive—a speculative fever over some sector of the market that really seems to offer great promise. You'll try to stay clearheaded about it, but before long you'll feel like a fool because it seems that everybody else is getting rich while you cling to your old-fogey investment "wisdom" about balance and

SEPTEMBER   **FEBRUARY**
1636   **1637**

diversification. Maybe they're right and you're wrong, you'll think—maybe you should alter your investment plan to take advantage of this new thing everyone else is into. Beware of the bubble! Here's why.

Speculative Bubbles

A speculative bubble is a kind of social epidemic. Euphoria over stocks or some other asset seems to spread through the population. In a bubble, it is the enthusiasm itself, not the fundamental value of the investment, that drives prices higher and higher. Afterward, the reality becomes abundantly clear. Once a speculative bubble bursts and prices collapse—and they always do, eventually—it suddenly seems absolutely incredible that people could have been so foolish.

There have been many epidemics of speculation in history. Bubbles have swelled around many different commodities, including stocks, real estate, gold, oil—even tulip bulbs. It's important for every investor to know something about the history of these bubbles. If you're familiar with some of the crazy things that led our forebears to part with their savings, you may be better able to resist the crazes you're likely to encounter in the future.

Tulipmania

In Holland during the early seventeenth century, investors went bonkers over tulip bulbs. The frenzy erupted after it was discovered that some bulbs produced flowers with special colorations. (Nobody knew at the time, but the bulbs were infected with a nonfatal virus called mosaic.) People bid up the prices of those diseased tulip bulbs to unbelievable levels—some sold for as much as a house of the time. People from all walks of life were trading in tulip bulbs at the peak of the mania. My friend and colleague Burt Malkiel provides this account of the end of Tulipmania in his investment classic, *A Random Walk Down Wall Street*:

> Apparently, as happens in all speculative crazes, prices eventually got so high that some people decided they would be prudent and sell their bulbs. Soon others followed suit. Like a snowball rolling downhill, bulb deflation grew at an increasingly rapid pace, and in no time at all panic reigned.
>
> [Despite government attempts to halt the panic] prices continued to decline. Down and down they went until most bulbs became almost worthless—selling for no more than the price of a common onion.[1]

The South Sea Bubble

Less than a century later, in 1720, England experienced its first stock market crash as the result of a speculative frenzy over a firm called the South Sea Company. The company, formed in 1711, held a monopoly over all trade to Central and South America. It had obtained those monopoly rights from the British government in return for taking on a large share of the debt the government had incurred in its war with Spain.

The early eighteenth century was a time of great public enthusiasm about the profits to be made from trade with the New World. Once the war was over, British merchants hoped to gain great wealth by trading with Spain's rich colonies in South America. In fact, the South Sea Company's prospects were nowhere near as promising as its stock price implied. The people running the company had no experience in trade, but they were masters at hoodwinking the public with complex financial schemes. Many Englishmen who owned government securities exchanged them for shares in the South Sea Company, and the company gave additional shares of stock to prominent officials in the government. As word spread about the fortunes to be made, people from every social class clamored for shares, driving prices up eightfold in six months' time. Many borrowed the money to buy shares.

As the speculative fever grew, more new companies appeared on the scene with ridiculous business proposals aimed at separating investors from their money. One company even advertised a proposal "for carrying on an undertaking

---

[1]Burton G. Malkiel, *A Random Walk Down Wall Street* (New York: W.W. Norton & Company), 1996, pages 37–38.

of great advantage but no one to know what it is."[2] In his book, *Devil Take the Hindmost: A History of Financial Speculation*, Edward Chancellor writes:[3] "Speculators did not buy bubble company shares as long-term investments; they bought them with the intention of selling them on to greater fools. In a very short time, however, they were to discover that there were no greater fools in the market than themselves."

Thousands of fortunes, both large and small, were ruined in the collapse of the South Sea Bubble. Some banks failed because they had lent money to people to invest. There were riots. Facing public demands for punishment of those responsible, the government confiscated the estates of some of the South Sea Company directors, and Parliament passed legislation outlawing unincorporated joint stock enterprises.

The Roaring Twenties

Until the 1990s, the biggest and most notorious bubble in the history of the U.S. stock market was the one that led to the market crash of 1929. During the Roaring Twenties, investing became the national pastime. People were enthusiastic about the new technologies of the time—automobiles, radio, television, and the young aircraft industry. Many people invested with borrowed money.

The conventional wisdom was that America had entered a new era of limitless prosperity. For a long time, the stock market made it all seem true. The Dow Jones Industrial Average began 1921 at 71.95 and peaked at 381.17 on September 3, 1929—an increase of 430%. A Yale economist named Irving Fisher entered the ranks of history's famously wrong by declaring, just before the market's crash in October 1929, that stock prices had reached "a permanently high plateau." In the plunge, the Dow lost more than 96 points, nearly 30% of its value, over the course of six days, setting the stage for the Great Depression. The Dow reached a low point of 41.22 in 1932, with the Depression still deepening. It didn't top 300 again until 1954.

Never Again? That's What They Said When . . .

So we learned our lesson in the Depression, right? I wish the answer were yes. Unfortunately, the twentieth century was full of smaller-scale fads and bubbles, surfacing every several years right up to the dot-com obsession of the 1990s. In

---

[2]Charles MacKay, *Extraordinary Popular Delusions & the Madness of Crowds* (New York: Farrar, Straus and Giroux, 1932), page 60.
[3]Edward Chancellor, *Devil Take the Hindmost: A History of Financial Speculation* (New York: Farrar, Straus and Giroux, 1999), pages 72–73.

the 1950s, uranium mining stocks were aglow with promise. In the 1960s, stock investors were hypnotized by companies with "tronics" in their names. In the 1970s, the "Nifty Fifty" stocks were all the rage, and in the 1980s, junk bonds were one of the hot investments. And stocks and bonds weren't the only investments that triggered speculative interest.

Oil Futures

In 1980, when energy stocks were leading the market, many ordinary investors were seduced by the idea of trading in oil futures contracts. A futures contract is an agreement to take or make delivery of a specific commodity at a set price on a future date. Futures contracts are essential risk-management tools in many businesses, but they also attract speculators who want to bet on price movements. And you can lose a lot of money in futures if you bet wrong. Many of the investors who decided to dabble in oil futures in 1980 knew nothing about futures and nothing about oil, but they couldn't resist what they thought was a sure thing. According to one of my colleagues, who worked in the oil industry back then, many knowledgeable people truly believed that oil prices would reach $150 a barrel by 2002. In fact, at this writing, oil is selling for under $25 a barrel.

A Modern Gold Rush

Precious metals have also seen their share of speculative bubbles over the years. In times of crisis—when the stock market tumbles, or inflation climbs, or the dollar weakens—gold and other precious metals are seen by some as a safe haven. One of the biggest gold booms in recent history occurred in the late 1970s, when inflation was high and the dollar was declining. Gold prices shot up to $850 an ounce on the London market in January 1980. Then they fell sharply. As Peter L. Bernstein says in his book *The Power of Gold*:

> Few people who bought at $35, or even under $100, held on to sell at $850. Most of the early buyers undoubtedly took their profits and bailed out long before the peak, for the path to $850 was volatile all the way. The likelihood is that many more people were sucked into the gold market as it approached $850—and shortly afterward—than those who were farsighted enough to go in when the price was fussing around $40.[4]

Except for a brief spike after the 1987 stock market crash, 1980 was as good as it got for goldbugs. In mid-2002, an ounce of gold was selling for about $320.

---

[4]Peter L. Bernstein, *The Power of Gold: The History of an Obsession* (John Wiley & Sons: New York, 2000), page 359.

Silver Fever

Even sophisticated investors can blow up in speculative bubbles, as the Hunt brothers proved. In an effort to corner the global silver market, Texas billionaires Nelson Bunker Hunt and William Herbert Hunt started amassing silver in the late 1970s, using borrowed money to finance some of the purchases. The Hunt brothers bought up more than 200 million ounces of silver—more than half the world's deliverable silver—pushing the price from $10 an ounce in 1979 to $50 an ounce a year later. But the brothers overlooked a basic economic truth—higher prices stimulate more supply. People began melting down their jewelry and their tea sets to cash in on the boom. In doing so, they helped to flood the market with "new" silver. The price fell back to $10 an ounce in March 1980. The Hunt brothers had to sell their holdings to make good on margin loans and were forced into bankruptcy. The silver market crashed and has never quite recovered.

You didn't have to be a silver speculator to be affected by those events, as people who got married in 1979 or 1980 can attest. My wife and I were married at the height of the silver bubble, and I well remember writing thank-you notes for many wedding gifts of crystal. Few brides and grooms received gifts of silver back then because prices were so high. (We also felt the effect of the runup in gold prices. We paid twice as much for our wedding rings as they would cost today.)

The Dot-Com Bubble

One of my all-time favorite movies is *King of Hearts*, a 1966 film about a Scottish soldier in World War I who is sent into a French village to defuse some explosives that the Germans have set to detonate at midnight. The village has been abandoned by its residents and now is populated by the inmates of a nearby insane asylum who were set free after their caretakers fled. The soldier, played by Alan Bates, doesn't realize why the shopkeepers and other residents are behaving so oddly. (For example, the proprietor of the crowded barbershop explains that he has many customers because he pays *them*. The zookeeper leaves the door of the lion's cage open, saying that the beast is too used to captivity to want to escape.) Surrounded by crazy behavior in the face of danger, the soldier wonders whether *he* has lost his mind.

Many of us felt like the Bates character in *King of Hearts* during the 1990s frenzy over the Internet. No matter how sure we felt about our investment principles, after a while we couldn't help wondering whether our allegiance to "old-fashioned" ideas like diversification meant we had lost our senses. In fact, it was the people around us who had abandoned rational thinking. Companies with no profits or revenues were suddenly seen as smart investments just because they were involved in e-business. CEOs would say with straight faces that their companies' revenues and profits would grow at 15% a year for the foreseeable future—a highly implausible prognosis, if you do the math, because as a company gets larger, each percentage point of growth requires ever-larger amounts of revenue. Both sophisticated and unsophisticated investors seemed to have abandoned all skepticism, blinded to risk by the prospect of riches.

Trillions of dollars of wealth evaporated when the dot-com bubble burst, earning it a spot in the record books as history's worst speculative bubble. Fortunately, although the collapse affected just about all investors, it appears that most ordinary people had not sunk their retirement savings into Internet stocks. And now, having experienced a bubble first-hand, they may feel better equipped to resist future ones.

How to Recognize a Bubble

When you read about Tulipmania or South Sea stocks, it's tempting to think of these as quaint tales of long ago when people were much more gullible and foolish than they are now. But as the 1990s showed, the progress of civilization hasn't changed some aspects of human nature. Here are traits common to all bubbles.

- **A valid reason for some investor optimism.** There's typically some real basis for the excitement that starts a bubble—whether it's the strong demand for rare and beautiful tulip bulbs, the prospect of new markets for trade, or the potential of a technological breakthrough like the Internet. But as buyers pour in, stock prices begin rising on their own momentum.

- **Bubbles feed on greed.** Once a bubble starts growing, many people jump in purely as speculators. They're not interested in the underlying investment; they just believe they can make a killing by buying something and then selling it to someone else at a higher price. This is called *the greater fool theory*—the notion that although prices may seem high, a buyer can always find some bigger fool who is willing to pay even more. It's a prime inflator for a bubble.

- **"It's different this time."** In a bubble, the believers dismiss naysayers as hopelessly out of step with the times. At the height of the dot-com bubble, we heard endless talk about the "new economy" in which old notions about stock price valuation no longer applied. Things certainly were changing— 15 years earlier, would most of us have imagined anything like the Internet? More prosaically, who would have predicted the peaceful collapse of the Soviet Union or the rise of global commerce? But changing circumstances don't imply changing principles of investing. That's why "It's different this time" are said to be the four most dangerous words in investing.

- **"What risk?"** Although the old adage is that Wall Street knows only two emotions—fear and greed—during a bubble it knows just one. People lose their fear of risk; all they see is that caution does not make you rich. One young investor, quoted in *The Wall Street Journal* near the peak of the Nasdaq, said, "What's scarier is not to be in the market now than to worry about a downturn."

- **Bubbles are tough to resist.** In a bubble, large numbers of people become swept up in the euphoria over investing. In the 1990s, it seemed that investing was the new national pastime. Companies that had been obscure suddenly became household names. Wall Street analysts and financial journalists were celebrities. Ordinary people followed the financial markets as closely as they once followed sports.

  The market mania was pervasive. One evening in the early spring of 2000, I stopped at a Burger King on the Massachusetts Turnpike while returning to Philadelphia from a trip with my family to Boston. My wife and I happened to strike up a conversation with two retired couples who were sipping coffee at a table as they watched the financial news on the restaurant's television. They told us that they met there every night to catch the financial news on CNN because they didn't have cable at home. It was astonishing to me—and more than a little frightening—that these senior citizens were so actively engaged in following the daily movements of the stock market.

  Some people who join in a bubble are confident that they will be able to get out before it bursts. That's a dangerous delusion. In the 1990s, some very smart people who had studied the markets for many years were sure they were seeing a bubble, but none of them could predict how or when it would end. Booms can go bust because of broad economic factors or unexpected bad news from one of the companies at the center of the boom. But neither the bubble—nor the pin that pops it—is apparent until afterward.

How to Protect Yourself from Speculative Bubbles

You'll know there's a speculative bubble in the making when the friends and acquaintances who usually talk to you about sports or other interests start chatting instead about how much they have made in oil futures, aerospace stocks, one-decision stocks, Japanese real estate, Internet stocks—or whatever.

If they tell you that this is a sure-fire technology that's certain to produce great wealth, don't believe it. Just because a new technology offers great promise doesn't mean every company will profit from it. Railroads and commercial aviation revolutionized transportation, but they have not, over time, produced huge profits for investors. Exciting new technologies often attract a lot of competition, and many of the companies that supposedly have first-mover advantages don't survive. In the aftermath of the dot-com blow-up, many of the companies that were seen as sure wins went under.

Yes, some people will make money on a speculative bubble. But most won't. Most people who try either get there too late to profit in a big way or stay too long at the party and get caught in the stampede out. Remember reading about the California Gold Rush of 1849? One of the most famous success stories of the period was Levi Strauss, but he made his money selling denim clothing to miners instead of panning for gold himself.

Here's some concrete data to help you fend off people who say there's money to be made on a hot sector of the market. In the stock market, it's a reality that some sectors will outperform the others at any given moment. But history shows that the top performer in a given year rarely stays at the top of the heap. As shown in Table 18.1, there have been only three times since 1980 when a sector managed to stay on top two years running. And in no case did one sector lead the market for three years in a row.

I've made it pretty plain that I think most investors would be wise to use broad market index funds as the core of their portfolios. So now you may be wondering: If you're invested in a broad index fund, how can you escape collateral damage from fads and bubbles? After all, your fund will by definition be exposed to whatever sector of the market is exciting so many investors.

I'll be frank: If you are broadly invested in the markets when a major speculative bubble occurs, it's impossible to escape the effects entirely. But here again, diversification proves its benefits. If your portfolio is broadly diversified, you're likely to suffer less damage than someone with a portfolio concentrated in the hot investment. And if you are a long-term investor, you will have time to recover from the bubble's collateral effects. In any case, don't be deterred from participating in the markets because prices look, well, bubblicious. If you sit on the sidelines debating when to get in, you're making no progress toward your financial goals.

What can you do if you have lost a lot of money by allowing yourself to become swept up in the dot-com bubble? That's a tough situation, particularly if your investment time horizon is limited. Don't roll the dice again by betting on another hot trend. The only thing you can reasonably do is to dust yourself off, make an honest assessment of your investment program, and decide on a sensible course of action going forward. If you find you are uncomfortable owning growth stocks because you now realize they are too risky, get rid of them. You must be able to say, "I made a mistake, but that's in the past. Now I'll go forward based on my best assessment of what I need to do for the future." But recognize that, once you make such a decision, a time is sure to come when growth stocks have a great two-year run. You can't let yourself say, "If only I hadn't sold those growth stocks!" and buy them all over again.

"If only . . ." may be the *two* worst words in investing.

TABLE 18.1   Top-Performing Stock Market Sectors, 1980–2001

Year	Top-Ranked Sector for Performance	Rank in Subsequent Year (Among 11 Sectors)
1980	Energy	11
1981	Communication Services	9
1982	Consumer Cyclicals	4
1983	Capital Goods	8
1984	Communication Services	4
1985	Consumer Staples	2
1986	Health Care	5
1987	Basic Materials	10
1988	Transportation	9
1989	Communication Services	8
1990	Health Care	1
1991	Health Care	11
1992	Financials	9
1993	Transportation	11
1994	Technology	3
1995	Health Care	8
1996	Financials	1
1997	Financials	8
1998	Technology	1
1999	Technology	10
2000	Utilities	11
2001	Consumer Cyclicals	Time will tell . . .

Source: Wilshire 5000 Index.

In a Nutshell

Don't let seductive factors like market fads and speculative bubbles derail your investment program. You can protect yourself if you:

- **Don't follow the crowd.** Speculative fevers have occurred from time to time throughout history—and we haven't seen the last of them with the bursting of the dot-com bubble.

- **Remain grateful, not greedy, when the markets are bountiful.** During periods of euphoria about the markets, greed blinds investors to the dangers in investing. Never forget that risk is always present.

- **Tune out anyone who claims that a particular company, industry sector, or new technology is a surefire, risk-free way to achieve great wealth.** Where the potential rewards are great, so are the risks.

- **Stay broadly invested and aren't tempted to jump into top-performing market sectors.** Chances are, you'll be joining the party just as it's ending.

chapter nineteen
WHY YOU MAY BE YOUR OWN WORST ENEMY

The comic strip character Pogo observed many years ago, "We have met the enemy, and he is us." Although Pogo was talking about pollution, he could as easily have been talking about the behavior of investors. The fact is that investors often act irrationally and in ways that are contrary to their own interests.

In recent years, an entire academic discipline has sprung up on this topic— *behavioral finance*, the study of investor behavior and psychology. Scholars have written dissertations on how people make investment choices, and a few universities have established endowed professorships in the field. Students of behavioral finance apply scientific methods to analyze behavior that has been described anecdotally for a long time.

Although we investors like to think we always carefully weigh our options and sensibly choose the ones that offer the most benefits, in fact we often don't. It turns out that real people aren't very good at even identifying options, let alone choosing the right one. We tend to misinterpret information and miscalculate simple statistical probabilities. And we react to events in emotional and often contradictory ways.

Although *I* haven't formally studied investor psychology, I have had the opportunity over the years to observe many investors, both successful and not-so-successful ones. My experience bears out some of what the behavioral-finance experts have begun telling us. On the basis of how real people react to real events in the markets, here's a brief list of some of the pitfalls to watch for and how to avoid them.

Being Overconfident about Your Own Abilities

Remember humorist Garrison Keillor's mythical town of Lake Wobegon, where "all the women are strong, all the men are good-looking, and all the children are above-average"? I have no data about strength and looks, but it turns out to be pretty common for people to think they are above-average in many ways. Numerous surveys have found that large majorities of people believe that they are better drivers than most other people, that they are less likely to lose their jobs than their coworkers are, and that they have a better chance than their friends of avoiding a heart attack.

If you are overconfident about your abilities as an investor, you are likely to underestimate risk. Such thinking could lead you to dismiss time-tested principles of investing—balance and diversification, for example—in the belief that you can win big by picking one or two superbly performing funds or securities.

Allowing the Current Environment to Blind You to the Larger Context

People have a tendency to assume that current conditions will continue—whatever those conditions may be. As a result, when markets are very good, investors tend to be overly optimistic, and when markets are bad, investors tend to be overly pessimistic.

I've observed this tendency again and again at the conferences we hold with clients all over the country. We customarily open these sessions by asking everyone to jot down a forecast for stock market and bond market returns for the next 12 months. At the end of the meeting, we announce the results of our informal poll. Almost invariably, the returns that the clients predict are very close to the actual returns that the markets produced in the most recent past.

It's uncanny how this tendency repeats itself, even though the market conditions change. During the roaring bull market of the 1990s, when stocks were compounding at 18% or 20% a year, the attendees at our client meetings would project stock market returns of 18% to 20% for the next 12 months. Once the markets headed downward in 2000, our clients grew much more pessimistic in their forecasts.

There's a real danger in the tendency to base expectations on current market conditions. Investors who lose sight of the big picture can end up constantly revising their strategies. In essence, they're always buying firewood just in time for the heat wave, or throwing away their umbrellas just as the heavy clouds move in.

Thinking You See a Pattern Where None Exists

Human beings like patterns and tend to believe they exist even when events are totally random. People also think they can use those patterns to their advantage. Indeed, one of the first things every baby learns is a kind of cause-and-effect pattern—he throws his spoon on the floor, you pick it up, and he throws it down again.

Statisticians explain the mirage of patterns in terms of coin tosses. If you toss a coin five times, the probability of getting heads (or tails) remains 50/50 each time, no matter what the sequence of previous tosses. Each toss of the coin is what statisticians call an *independent event*. That's a difficult concept for many people to internalize. They expect a sequence of coin tosses to result in heads–tails–heads–tails–heads more often than in some other mix of results.

Given this general human tendency, it's no surprise that investors also believe they've spotted patterns in the financial markets even if none exist. During the 1990s, investors noticed that each sharp drop in the stock market was followed by a sharp recovery. They concluded that quick rebounds were the rule and they started telling each other to "buy on the dips." In fact, the markets don't always rebound quickly, as investors were reminded by the prolonged decline that began in 2000.

Patterns also inspire investment gimmicks, such as the "Dogs of the Dow" strategy. Pursuing the Dogs of the Dow involved looking at the 30 stocks tracked by the Dow Jones Industrial Average and buying whichever 10 had the highest dividend yields (dividend divided by price). Each year, you were supposed to replace your old "dogs" with the new list of the Dow's 10 highest-yielding stocks. The strategy became popular in the mid 1990s, and stopped working shortly thereafter.

Focusing Too Much on Short-Term Losses

People tend to feel losses more acutely than gains. Suppose I invite you to bet on a coin toss in which you'll lose $100 if tails comes up or win $100 if heads does. Would you make that bet? Probably not, even for the chance of getting $100 from me. Well, how about if I offer to ante up more on my end—how much would I have to agree to pay in order for you to feel it's worth the risk of losing $100? If you think like most people, you'd insist on receiving at least $200, according to experiments conducted by two leading academic experts on investor psychology, Daniel Kahneman and Amos Tversky. In other words, it takes the potential pleasure of winning $200 to balance out the potential pain of losing $100.

Because losses are so painful, investors sometimes do peculiar things to avoid incurring even a short-term loss. They might hold on to losing funds or securities far longer than they should, waiting to "get back to even" before they sell. Or they may sell investments that are rising because they're fearful of future losses. If you are a long-term investor, you shouldn't allow this instinctive aversion to loss to cloud your judgment.

Feeling Compelled to Do Something—Anything

Even investors who understand the wisdom of the buy-and-hold philosophy sometimes feel uncomfortable doing nothing, especially when so many environmental forces are enticing us to trade investments, switch financial firms, try new investment strategies, and so on. Thanks to the Internet, it's easier than ever to give in to that impulse to tinker.

Online account management is a great convenience, but it has the drawback of providing increased opportunity to meddle with your investment program. Some people check on their account balances obsessively. At Vanguard, we've noticed that the most active traders in the 401(k) plans we administer tend to be the ones with online account access. In just a few minutes online, you can switch from one fund to another or redirect where your payroll deductions are going. And you can do it all over again tomorrow. But in most cases, you won't be doing yourself any favors. Research has shown repeatedly that the active traders underperform the buy-and-holders. If you possibly can, resist the temptation to look at your account balance more than once a quarter.

Letting False Reference Points Distort Your View of Value

Ever wonder why car dealers like to quote you such high prices initially, when you and they are fully aware that they're going to allow you to negotiate a lower one? It's because of *anchoring*—the tendency of buyers to relate their estimates of value to some previously established benchmark. Without always realizing it, people tend to form opinions based on a reference point that may or may not be meaningful. Once a car's sticker price is lodged in your mind, you are likely to think that anything lower is a good deal.

In investing, anchoring can cause you to judge the performance of a particular investment in light of factors that aren't truly relevant—the price you paid for it long ago, its all-time high or low price, or an analyst's estimate of what its future price will be. It's difficult to shake an anchor once it's in your consciousness. For example, if you learn that a prominent financial analyst predicts a stock's price will rise from $100 to $250 a share, you are likely to conclude that it's a good value at $150 a share, even if the company's fundamentals don't support that valuation.

Remembering Things Selectively

Unfortunately, people's memories are very uneven. We tend to remember our triumphs and forget our failures. You've probably noticed that people who regularly go to casinos tend to talk about the times they won, not the trips when they lost. Similarly, lottery players remember the stories about winners of multimillion-dollar jackpots, not the stories that mention the multimillion-to-one odds against winning. We also tend to remember the tales we've heard about people who made a pile in the financial markets by following some scheme or other. We don't think much about the blowups—the people who took big risks and lost.

How to Foil Your Own Worst Enemy

Have I depressed you enough? At this stage, you may be wondering why you should even bother to try to invest successfully, given that we are all so likely to sabotage ourselves. But don't let these examples of investor foibles leave you in despair. The reason the study of behavioral finance is so useful is that it can help us to recognize self-thwarting behavior. Then we have a chance to take preventive measures.

By now, you know which ones I recommend: Make conscious, deliberate decisions about risk and reward when you construct your portfolio. Be a buy-and-hold investor. Keep an eye on costs. Let time be your ally. Stick to your investment program in good times and bad. If you do all of these things, the emotion and irrationality that affect us all won't have free rein.

A Cautionary Tale

Investors in commercial real estate have discovered how easy it is to get tripped up by emotional thinking. Commercial real estate is an asset class notorious for its booms and busts. Many fortunes have been made there and lost over the years, most recently during the boom–bust cycle of the 1980s.

A highly educated friend of mine who owned an office park complex found out that a similar property in his community had just sold for $195 per square foot—a big increase over its previous sale price of $145 per foot. Shortly thereafter, some foreign investors offered my friend $220 per foot for his property. In the belief that the market would drive prices still higher, my friend turned them down.

Not long afterward, the real estate market collapsed. My friend was forced to sell his property to pay off loans, and he realized only about $130 per foot. Years later, he said to me: "You know, something that I learned in this whole episode was that when I didn't *sell* it at $220 a foot, I *bought* it at $220 a foot."

My friend's experience was a great lesson in the pain of a missed opportunity. By not being a seller, he was, in a very real sense, a buyer. His mistake was in thinking that he knew where the market was headed. Had someone offered him $190 a foot for that property a year earlier, he probably would have accepted it gladly. But he thought he recognized a pattern—the market was clearly headed higher, or so it seemed. He assumed that the momentum would keep going. I've never forgotten that line, "When I wasn't a seller, I was a buyer."

What's the Lesson?

Understanding our human tendency toward irrational behavior won't protect you from doing dumb things sometimes. But if you can develop a bit of skepticism about your own motivations, you'll have a better chance of maintaining a disciplined approach to investing. Feelings are intangible things, but they can have very tangible effects on your investment program.

In a Nutshell

It's human nature to do some pretty irrational things. Self-awareness cannot prevent all of these mistakes, but you may be able to keep yourself in check if you:

- **Remain humble about your ability to pick winning investments.** Instead of trying to trade your way to wealth, design a sound portfolio and then follow a buy-and-hold strategy.

- **Recognize in both good markets and bad ones that "This too shall pass."** Don't pay attention to short-term fluctuations that are meaningless to your long-term plan.

- **Don't believe investment gurus who claim to have spotted patterns in the market that can be turned to financial advantage.** If they exist at all, those patterns probably are short-lived. In the long run, balance and diversification are the only reliable investment strategies.

chapter twenty
BEAR MARKETS WILL TEST YOUR RESOLVE

Can you advise me of the action to take regarding this fund? I have lost $50,000 in this fund (I want to throw up as I write this) and am curious about the reason for the losses and, more importantly, the prediction for the future performance.

I usually stay the course but am now questioning that course of non-action and seek your advice.

—Letter from a Vanguard shareholder

Bear markets are a regular part of investing. But that's small consolation when you're stuck in the middle of one. Even the most seasoned investors find bear markets difficult to endure.

As I put the finishing touches on this book in July 2002, we were mired in a deep and prolonged bear market. As of July 31, it was the longest bear market for U.S. stocks since World War II. Over 28 months, stocks have fallen 38.5% from their peak even with reinvested dividends, rivaling the 48% decline in the 1973–1974 bear market. I hope the environment is better as you read this; as I write it, many investors are feeling as if the bad news will never end.

The current bear market began unofficially in March 2000 with the bursting of the speculative bubble in technology and Internet stocks. Although the tech stocks in the Nasdaq Composite Index were hit hardest, they pulled many other stocks down with them. As measured by the Wilshire 5000 Index, the overall

stock market fell 10.9% in 2000, 11% in 2001, and 11.8% in the first half of 2002.

Obviously, market slumps are no fun. Still, they offer some lessons that can help you to be a better investor. In this chapter, I'll discuss those lessons and offer some advice on how to get through the emotional and financial challenges that are posed by a bear market.

Some Background on Bear Markets

Since the terminology can be confusing, let's begin with some definitions. A bear market in stocks is often defined as a price decline of 20% or more over at least a two-month period. A brief downturn is a *market correction*, usually defined as a sudden, sharp decline in stock prices that lasts only a few days or weeks. We experienced a correction in October 1997, when the S&P 500 Index lost about 10% of its value in a one-week period.

Don't get too hung up on these definitions. The news media typically note with great fanfare when the S&P or the Dow or the Nasdaq passes into bear or bull territory. But if you're a long-term investor, it's irrelevant to you whether the market is officially in bear territory or just down 19%. In neither case should you necessarily make changes in your investment program. Worrying about whether we're in a bear market or "only" a correction is like worrying about whether a spell of hot weather began when the temperature hit 98 degrees or 100 degrees.

Most corrections and mild bear markets result from normal business-cycle fluctuations. But stock market declines don't always predict economic recessions, nor are they always caused by recessions. The severe bear markets in United States history have typically been related to wars, the bursting of speculative bubbles, or exogenous economic factors.

No one can predict the length or magnitude of a bear market, but history reveals some interesting facts. Over the last 50 years, bear markets in stocks have occurred once every five years on average (see Table 20.1). They have lasted about a year, again on average—the shortest was three months. Of course, the worst bear market in the nation's history was the one that lasted from September 1929 through July 1932, when stock prices fell 86%. Regulatory changes and economic policy changes in response to the Great Depression make it unlikely that we'll experience another decline of such magnitude, but I'm of the school that says you should always keep in mind that anything is possible in the financial markets.

Bear markets strike bonds as well as stocks (see Table 20.2). For bonds, the most recent one started in December 1998 and continued into January 2000, a period when surging interest rates sent bond prices tumbling 14.6% (as measured by the 10-year U.S. Treasury bond).

TABLE 20.1 Bear Markets in Stocks: August 1956–July 2002

Start of Bear Market	*Length (in Months)*	*Percent Price Decline*
August 1956	15	–21.6%
December 1961	6	–28.0
February 1966	8	–22.2
November 1968	18	–36.1
January 1973	21	–48.2
September 1976	17	–19.4
January 1981	19	–25.8
August 1987	3	–33.5
July 1990	3	–19.9
*March 2000	28*	–40.3*

Source: Standard & Poor's Corporation.

*As of July 31, 2002.

TABLE 20.2   Bear Markets in Bonds: March 1967–July 2002

Start of Bear Market	*Length (in months)*	*Percent Price Decline (10-year maturity)*
March 1967	38	–23.0%
March 1971	54	–18.2
December 1976	39	–32.7
June 1980	15	–27.9
May 1983	13	–17.1
January 1987	9	–15.5
October 1993	13	–17.9
December 1998	13	–14.6

Source: Vanguard Fixed Income Group.

How Does a Bear Market Feel? Very Scary

You should view bear markets as a regular part of investing and prepare for them by being prudent in the ways I've already discussed—holding a balanced and diversified portfolio that is appropriate for your investment time horizon. But even if you are doing the right things financially, I assure you that you will feel some anguish. You may experience emotional and physical symptoms—for instance, you may have trouble sleeping, or you may walk around all day with a sick feeling in your stomach or a feeling of panic.

Imagine what it was like to be an investor caught in the bear market that lasted from January 1973 until October 1974. The U.S. stock market declined a stunning 48% over a 21-month period. In dollar terms, an investor who had $10,000 invested in the broad stock market lost $4,800—nearly half the value of the portfolio. In addition, because inflation jumped significantly at the same time, the loss in terms of purchasing power was even worse. Someone who was investing at that time had no way of knowing how long the bear market would last or how bad it would get. I was in my late teens, and my recollection is that the evening newspaper was always full of bad news about the markets and the economy. There was plenty of other unsettling news to go with it—the period saw the resignations of both the vice president and the president of the United States, the drawn-out ending of the war in Vietnam, and continuing conflict in the Middle East.

Many of today's investors have been at it only a relatively short time. Until 2000, they had known only bull markets. Now here comes a statement that may surprise you: I think anyone who has been investing for just the last 5 to 10 years ought to count himself fortunate to have experienced both a great bull market *and* a scary bear market in such a brief period. Believe me, these things were going to happen to you at some point. It's better to experience them at the beginning of your investing career than at the end, when your portfolio is likely to be much larger and you won't have as much time to recover.

The Lesson of Balance and Diversification (Again)

Bear markets are the times when well-designed portfolios show their strength. A balanced portfolio of stocks and bonds fared much better during the 1973–1974 bear market than one invested entirely in stocks. The investor with 60% in stocks and 40% in bonds lost "only" $29,000 of a $100,000 portfolio, compared with the $48,000 loss of a hypothetical investor with an all-stock portfolio.

Holding a balanced, diversified portfolio will reduce the pain of a bear market, but it won't protect you completely. Your specific holdings will determine how severely your portfolio is affected. For instance, growth funds are likely to see sharper declines than more conservative, value-oriented funds. If interest rates are rising and you hold bond funds, you should be prepared to see prices fall farthest for the funds with longer maturities.

The 2000–2002 bear market has demonstrated anew the benefits of diversification. Here's an e-mail we received from a shareholder who was very concerned, but had learned to take the long view and adhere to his investment program.

> How much further can the market drop? At one period in my investing life, I would really worry about any market decline. All my waking hours were dominated by the same dismal thoughts—I was losing money and I was sorry I ever invested. But since I changed my investments I don't give the market much thought. Oh, I keep abreast, but I know everything that can be done has been done properly. With proper diversification, low expenses, looking at the long term, and expecting inevitable losses and downturns, I know my final returns (in ten years) will be very pleasing.

The market has always eventually recovered from its declines, but here again, there is no reliable pattern. The recovery can take quite a while, as with the six years that the stock market spent getting back to its precollapse peak after the 1973–1974 slump. Or the recovery can occur within a few months, as it did following the brief 1990 bear market.

What Not to Do in a Bear Market

There are two main risks when your investments sour. One, you may panic and want to get out, particularly if the decline is severe. Two, you may think a decline spells good value and want to "buy on the dip."

Neither of those responses is the correct one. If you panic, you may end up selling at or near the bottom of the downturn and missing the rebound. Many investors did just that in the market decline of 1973–1974. Those who fled stocks missed an extraordinary climb in stock values. After reaching a low point in October 1974, the stock market became extremely generous. The S&P 500 Index returned 37.1% in 1975. As measured by the S&P 500, the market provided yearly returns that averaged 14.8% over the 10 years from 1975 to 1984, 16.6% over the 15 years from 1975 to 1989, 14.6% over the 20 years from 1975 to 1994, and 17.2% over the 25 years from 1975 to 1999.

As for buying on the dips, hindsight makes it obvious why that's not a good plan in a bear market. The problem is that you don't have hindsight in the beginning. There can be numerous interim rallies in a bear market, and if you are trying to dabble in market-timing you can get severely burned. The 1973–1974 slump featured several of these so-called *sucker's rallies*. People who bought on those dips merely deepened their losses. These facts prove the wisdom in a comment once made by economist John Maynard Keynes: "Markets can remain irrational longer than you can remain solvent."

Tips for Enduring Bear Markets

If you had a sound plan in place before the bear market started, the main task is to keep your head. That can be harder than it sounds, once the financial press gets going with dire analyses, the politicians start weighing in, and your account balance seems to have gone on a crash diet. The following can help you get through the slump.

- **Continue investing regularly.** If you invest through an automatic investment plan or a payroll deduction, continue making contributions. Remember that what you are doing is *dollar-cost averaging*, and it can achieve the most for you when the markets are down. I won't repeat all that was said about dollar-cost averaging in Chapter 13, but I want to remind you about the two biggest benefits because they can help you endure a bear market. (1) Since prices are low, your regular investments will be buying you more shares, and (2) the discipline involved will fortify you against emotional decisions. Another point that bears repeating: You must stick with dollar-cost averaging in bad markets as well as good to reap the benefits.

- **Maintain perspective.** Your purpose as a long-term investor is to achieve your ultimate goals, not to avoid interim losses. When you originally set up your investment plan, you put your money where it offered the best prospects for long-term reward. That meant accepting some risk—and now you're seeing what the risk entails. But that doesn't mean your plan was a mistake. So your account is way down from where it was? "Where it was" may have been an unrealistic level. Remember—the bear market that started in 2000 wiped out a lot of wealth, but investors who had been in the stock market for many years were still far wealthier than when they started.

- **Make gradual shifts (*if* necessary).** Resist the temptation to make major changes in your investment strategy simply because one part of it is in trouble. Moving your money from stocks and bonds to more conservative investments in hopes of avoiding a loss or finding a gain is seldom successful. If you absolutely *must* make a change, do so gradually, selling or exchanging shares in small increments to prevent yourself from careening from one impulse to another.

- **Have realistic expectations.** I don't know what the stock market will do next year—or even next month. But over the next decade or so, I don't expect to see anything like the 17.1% average yearly gain measured by the all-market Wilshire 5000 Index from the end of 1979 through the end of 1999. I expect smaller returns because dividend yields are much lower and price/earnings ratios are much higher on stocks today than they were 20 years ago. That's another way of saying that stock prices remain fairly high. It means that investors are still, in the aggregate, enthusiastic about future stock market returns, whereas in 1980 investors as a group were still leery of stocks after the relatively poor returns of the 1970s.

A fair guesstimate of stock market returns over the next decade would be 7% to 9% annually. I get that figure by starting with the current dividend yield on stocks—about 1.5% as of mid-year 2002. To that yield I would add 6% to 7% a year—equivalent to the long-term average growth rate for corporate profits. Actual year-to-year returns will certainly vary from my estimate as the markets are buffeted both by economic events and changes in investor psychology. Also, let me be clear: I'm not about to take any bets that my guesstimate is right, even for the long-term average return. If investors become less enthusiastic about stocks and our economic prospects, price/earnings ratios could decline, and the average return over the next decade would be lower, too. If investors get substantially more enthusiastic about stocks—not an outcome I would expect—my guess could be too low.

Although my scenario isn't rosy, neither is it grim. After all, if inflation remains subdued, in the range of 2% or 3% annually, a return of 7% to 9% on stocks would be pretty good—not very far below the average inflation-adjusted return of 7.6% on stocks from 1926 through 2001. As I mentioned in Chapter 5 in the discussion on financial planning, I'd certainly rather use conservative assumptions and be pleasantly surprised than be overly optimistic and fall far short of my investment goals.

What You Should Do in a Bear Market

The correct response to a bear market is to take an objective look at the situation and reassess your own circumstances. What's your time horizon? What are your objectives? If your time horizon is long and your financial situation hasn't changed, you should probably choose to sit tight.

It may sound counterintuitive, but for people who are investing regularly for a long-term goal—*not* those who are drawing on their investments—bear markets are good things. If you are investing for retirement, and retirement is decades away, a decline in your account value is not a "real" loss. What matters is what your account will be worth in 30 years, not 30 days or even 30 weeks. If prices are depressed, your contributions are now buying more shares at a cheaper price, so that's more wealth for you in the future when the market has recovered.

In bond investing particularly, what seems like bad news can actually be good news. Yes, the share price falls when interest rates rise—but does that mean you should get out of the investment? On the contrary—if you are a long-term investor, you should congratulate yourself. That interest rate hike is going to mean that the income dividends you reinvest will be more productive as they are put to work at higher interest rates in new bonds. (I realize we've covered this point about bonds already, but it's so important and so widely misunderstood that it bears repeating.)

But—if you are near or in retirement, a bear market is a menace to your investment goals. You probably don't have the luxury of waiting for the markets to rebound, and you can't take comfort in the thought of making regular investments at lower prices. Perhaps you amassed a sizable nest egg by investing regularly and sensibly for more than 30 years, only to watch the bear market ravage your portfolio.

What do you do? Again, if your portfolio has an appropriate asset mix for your objectives, time horizon, and risk tolerance, your best move may be to sit tight. You can compound the damage if you react emotionally and make sweeping changes in your investment strategy. If you must change your mix of assets, make small changes and implement them gradually. It's possible that you may have to revise your expectations for retirement. In the aftermath of the dot-com meltdown, some investors who had been dreaming of early retirement said they were resigning themselves to saving more, spending less, and working longer.

It's to avert such situations that asset-allocation specialists recommend changing your portfolio to a more conservative balance as you near your retirement years. That can be hard, especially if no bears are in sight. You'll never feel joyous about moving your money into bonds while the stock market is on a roll. On the other hand, it's a lot more pleasant to buy a few bond funds than to be forced to keep working when you had planned to relax at last.

The Advantages of Buying "Hamburger" in a Sideways Market

I'm in the habit of running at lunchtime with some colleagues who are 15 years younger than I am, and for some time now they have been telling me how lucky I am to have been investing for retirement since the beginning of the bull market in 1982.

In my view, that's not something to envy. As a regular investor through payroll deductions, I was dollar-cost averaging into an upward market for 18 straight years. As the market climbed higher and higher, I was buying fund shares at steadily higher prices. In my view, these younger colleagues are on a much better footing. They are investing through sideways and declining markets as they accumulate wealth, so they are buying mutual fund shares at a much cheaper price than I was able to pay at their age.

For a regular investor with a long time horizon, a market whose performance is moving sideways or down is a good thing—even though it no doubt feels uncomfortable. Buying shares at a lower price improves your chances of making money over the course of your investing years.

Renowned investor Warren Buffett, the chairman of Berkshire Hathaway, talks about this investing trade-off in terms of buying hamburger. In a letter to his company's shareholders back in 1997, he wrote:

> A short quiz: If you plan to eat hamburgers throughout your life and are not a cattle producer, should you wish for higher or lower prices for beef? Likewise, if you are going to buy a car from time to time but are not an auto manufacturer, should you prefer higher or lower car prices? These questions, of course, answer themselves.
>
> But now for the final exam: If you expect to be a net saver during the next five years, should you hope for a higher or lower stock market during that period? Many investors get this one wrong. Even though they are going to be net buyers of stocks for many years to come, they are elated when stock prices rise and depressed when they fall. In effect, they rejoice because prices have risen for the "hamburgers" they will soon be buying. This reaction makes no sense. Only those who will be sellers of equities in the near future should be happy at seeing stocks rise. Prospective purchasers should much prefer sinking prices.[1]

As a retirement investor, I bought "hamburger" at continually more expensive prices from 1982 to 2000. Obviously, in the midst of a bear market, some of the hamburger that I paid top dollar for is now worth less. My younger colleagues are putting their money to work in a market that is moving sideways or down. Time is on their side, and the current market decline probably won't leave permanent scars on their investments.

---

[1]Warren Buffett, 1997 Annual Report to Shareholders of Berkshire Hathaway Inc., page 4.

In a Nutshell

Bear markets are a regular part of investing. You can endure the emotional and financial challenges if you:

- **Prepare for tough times by holding a balanced and diversified portfolio that is right for your needs.** Knowing that you have designed an appropriate portfolio can give you the confidence to endure a bear market.

- **Continue investing regularly.** Dollar-cost averaging can give you the discipline to endure tough times.

- **Make gradual changes *if* necessary.** If your long-term strategy is still sound, you will do best to avoid major changes during a bear market. Should a change be necessary, make it slowly.

- **Maintain perspective.** Your ultimate objective is to achieve your financial goals. If you have a time horizon of 10 years or more, you shouldn't be concerned about what you earn in any single year.

chapter twenty-one
"AIN'T GOT NO DISTRACTIONS, CAN'T HEAR THOSE BUZZERS AND BELLS"

The 1970s rock opera *Tommy*, by The Who, is about a "deaf, dumb, and blind kid" who "sure plays a mean pinball." As the song *Pinball Wizard* says, "He ain't got no distractions, can't hear those buzzers and bells." It's a great song, but Tommy's story is a sad one and I won't dwell on it here. Still, I can't help but remember Tommy when I think about investing in today's noisy world. The most successful investors are those who can tune out distractions.

Coping with the onslaught of financial information and news is one of the toughest challenges that today's investors face. We're all bombarded in print, on TV and radio, and online by information about investing and news coverage of the financial markets. Much of what's reported is either exaggerated, flat-out wrong, or simply not relevant to an ordinary investor. Even sophisticated investors can find it very tough to maintain perspective in the face of these distractions.

Every day, as I drive to work, I hear a 5:55 A.M. business report about what happened in overnight trading in S&P futures and on the Tokyo stock exchange. This information may be useful to traders, but it's not information that most listeners need in order to manage their day. If you're a long-term, buy-and-hold investor with a sensibly constructed portfolio, there's no good reason to pay attention to the short-term movements of the financial markets. What the market did yesterday and what people think it will do tomorrow don't affect your investment strategy.

I acknowledge that news can be useful and entertaining. And most thoughtful people enjoy being well-informed about current events. For these reasons, I'll

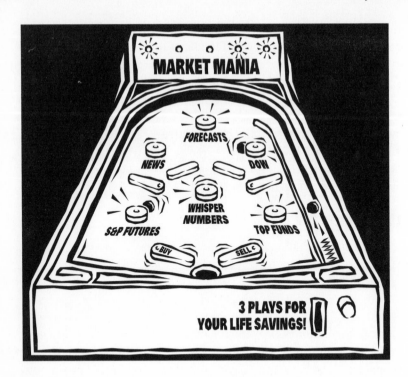

focus in this chapter on how to manage the distractions of our mass-media culture, absorbing the useful stuff and tuning out the rest.

Over the last 25 years, the news media have done a great deal of good by raising public awareness about investing. Ordinary people have become much more financially literate. Although the long bull market was a huge factor in attracting the general public to investing, the growth of news on the topic also played a big role. Many of the personal-finance columnists in the major newspapers and magazines perform a valuable service by providing sensible information that truly serves the needs of their readers. There are some very high-quality columnists whose work I often circulate.

Nevertheless, you have to exercise caution as a consumer of business and financial news. If you're new to investing, you may think you should subscribe to every finance publication and listen to every radio and TV program on the subject. Don't do it. You won't know how to distinguish useful information from what's worthless or wrong, and you will be overwhelmed. To get started as an investor, what you need is an understanding of the fundamentals of investing, not a blizzard of data about the current state of affairs in the financial markets.

Once you've set up your investment program and developed some confidence about investing, it is wise to remain selective about what you read and listen to.

Information overload isn't just annoying, it can be downright dangerous for someone who intends to be a buy-and-hold investor. Even if you aren't normally inclined to fret over your investments, the constant media chatter may make you think you *need* to check on them frequently. And once you start doing that, you may be tempted to begin second-guessing your decisions. The insidious danger of the noise is that if you pay attention to it, it can tempt you to act and make investment moves that aren't in your best long-term interests. If you hear that the stock market is down 100 points for the third day in a row, you may begin to wonder, "Should I shift from stocks to bonds?"

Trust the Truths You Already Know

This may seem odd, but the most valuable information you'll encounter in the media should be old news to you. Pay attention to stories that emphasize the value of holding a diversified portfolio, minimizing costs and taxes, and maintaining a long-term perspective. Those are the important and enduring principles in investing, and they are reaffirmed over and over again by events.

A former financial columnist who now works at Vanguard once shared with me a quote from the great American novelist Willa Cather. He carries it in his wallet, and here's what it says: "There are only two or three human stories, and they go on repeating themselves as fiercely as if they had never happened before." My colleague believes that something similar is true for financial writing, that there are only a handful of truly important themes for individual investors—save money for your future needs, invest in stocks for the long term, and so forth. And ever since he told me that, I've been struck by the wisdom in it.

The remainder of this chapter offers some tips to help you be a wise consumer of news about investing.

Recognize That Everyone Has an Agenda

It may sound cynical, but it's a fact of life. When politicians and government officials appear on TV to discuss the issues of the day, we're all aware that they are advocating a particular point of view. Whether we agree or not, we recognize that the arguments they make are part of a larger agenda. You should approach financial news with a similar awareness.

One of the major contributors to the dot-com bubble of the 1990s was that people failed to recognize the agendas of all those talking heads on TV financial news programs. News is supposed to be objective, but the information provided on the business news programs often was not objective at all. The journalists themselves tended to be overly bullish on the stock market. And no wonder;

enthusiasm about stocks would attract more viewers and get better ratings for their programs. The CEOs who made guest appearances also had agendas—talking up their companies would entice investors and pump up stock prices. And, as investors learned later, yet another set of agendas was being pursued by the Wall Street analysts who made all those rosy stock recommendations. Many of their brokerage firms were hoping to get or keep lucrative investment-banking deals with the very companies being evaluated.

I'm not saying that all commentators are self-interested or even that everyone with an agenda is nefarious and not to be trusted. But I am suggesting that you need to consider their biases before you buy what they're saying.

Never Believe Market Predictions

Today's wired investment world is full of pundits ready to make sound-bite-sized predictions about what the markets will do next. But despite all their computer models or impressive-sounding rationales, these "experts" don't have any certain knowledge of what is coming. Sure, some of them will be right sometimes, but that could just as easily be luck as brains.

Why do the financial news programs keep airing market predictions? Consider their agenda. Predictions are entertaining, and "infotainment" attracts audiences. The money managers and Wall Street analysts happily provide those predictions because it's the way they gain exposure. No one will call them for quotes if they're honest enough to say, "Beats me. I don't know what stocks are going to do next."

Or, as William Bernstein says in his book, *The Intelligent Asset Allocator*:

> There are two kinds of investors, be they large or small: those who don't know where the market is headed, and those who don't know that they don't know. Then again, there is actually a third type of investor—the investment professional, who indeed knows that he or she doesn't know, but whose livelihood depends on appearing to know.[1]

Be Skeptical of Hype about Hot Performance

Some financial publications claim to be champions of investment fundamentals, but then they splash headlines across their covers about fund rankings and

---

[1]William Bernstein, *The Intelligent Asset Allocator: How to Build Your Portfolio to Maximize Returns and Minimize Risk* (New York: McGraw-Hill, 2001), page 85.

"Which 'Safe' Stocks to Buy Now." I suppose headlines like those help to sell magazines, but they don't really do readers any service. The problem with rankings is that they focus on yesterday's high performers, regardless of long-term merits. As discussed in Chapter 9, fund rankings are meaningless when based primarily on past performance, as most are.

Other distortions occur when someone or something involved with investing is lionized or vilified. I've seen this happen many times with money managers, investment strategies and products, or even market sectors—they're acclaimed as infallible or condemned as worthless, when the reality is usually somewhere in between.

Be Suspicious of Experts

It's human nature to put far too much credence in the opinion of someone who's presented as an authority on a complex subject. Unfortunately, the fact that you read something in the press or hear it on television doesn't mean it is true. As you develop your knowledge about investing, you will come to recognize that there can be many different points of view about the meaning of a given financial or economic trend. That someone has a title and an air of authority does not make his or her interpretation correct. Sometimes the experts are dead wrong. Even if they are right, you should ask yourself whether the information is relevant to you. If it's not, tune it out.

Newscasters often report that on a down day in the markets there were "more sellers than buyers." Feel free to laugh out loud when you hear such statements. For a trade to happen at all, there must be a buyer *and* a seller. Indeed, the simple fact that there is always someone else on the other side of any transaction should give us pause when we are tempted to speculate in the markets. Maybe that other person knows something we don't.

What Makes Headlines Is Not Always New

The news media are in the business of reporting what's new, and that's a difficult job to do well day in and day out. In reality, many significant developments that are reported as news are already known to a lot of people.

A case in point is the coverage of the collapse of Enron in the fall of 2001. The media had written many glowing stories about the company over the years, but reporters were slow to learn of its problems. Talk about the company's troubles was filtering through investment circles during the summer of 2001, when CEO Jeffrey Skilling stepped down, citing personal reasons. But the full story of Enron's problems didn't become public until after the company filed for bankruptcy that

December, the biggest such filing in U.S. history until WorldCom's July 2002 bankruptcy filing. (To their credit, journalists themselves are often their most severe critics. The *American Journalism Review* called the profession's handling of the Enron story one of the biggest failures in financial journalism.[2])

There have been many other occasions when the news media were slow to report on positive trends, including the rise of the Internet. I mention this tendency to be late with the news as a warning to investors who think that the media are a good source of investment tips. If you are hearing about an investment with fabulous potential, recognize that lots of other people know about it, too. Chances are, that information is already reflected in stock prices.

Beware the New New Thing

The news media are very competitive with each other, and there is enormous, constant pressure to come up with fresh angles and new ideas. As a result, it's easy for journalists to become infatuated with fads—just like most folks.

Fads are part of our popular culture. New ones surface all the time. Fortunately, most fads are pretty innocuous things. Many people enjoy getting swept up in the latest craze, whether it's scooter mania among kids or the fitness regimens of adults. Sooner or later, every fad fizzles, but most of them do little damage. So what if you succumbed to the rage for bell-bottom jeans, and they quickly went out of fashion? You're out $35—no big deal.

Investment fads are a different matter. Allowing yourself to be carried away by an investment fad can endanger your financial well-being. You can lose serious money, and there's an extra hidden cost: When you detour from your investment program to indulge in a fad, you miss the opportunity to make money on worthwhile investments. And that means you have squandered not just money but also that very precious commodity, time.

In the 1980s, tax shelters became a big investment fad. Investors put billions of dollars into esoteric tax shelters based on investments in real estate and energy resources without having a clear understanding of the underlying economics and without thinking about how future changes in tax laws could affect the shelters. Many were later very sorry. In the late 1990s, there was a media infatuation with day trading. You saw a flurry of stories about people who believed they could get rich making frequent short-term bets on stocks. Attracted by low commissions offered by online-trading firms, some day traders quit their jobs to speculate.

---

[2]Kelly Heyboer, "The One That Got Away," *American Journalism Review*, March 2002, page 12.

Journalists who extolled those investment fads without examining the trade-offs in areas such as risk and cost did a grave disservice to their readers.

Lately, some in the media have become intrigued by the records of a few star hedge-fund managers and have suggested that such funds ought to be made available to ordinary investors. Hedge funds are unregistered, private investment pools that are currently available only to people with large amounts of money to invest. These funds make money—or try to—by relying on the savvy of their managers to spot subtle opportunities involving timing or pricing in the markets. The trade-off hedge funds offer is the potential for very big returns along with the potential for very big blowups—and that trade-off hasn't received as much coverage as it should have.

Hedge funds lack many of the important investor protections that are offered by mutual funds. Sophisticated investors may not think that they need those protections, but most people emphatically do. Hedge funds are not required to disclose information about their holdings and performance beyond what the sponsor voluntarily chooses to provide. There are no limits on the fees they can charge. Typically, the manager takes a fee of 1% or 2% of net assets, plus 20% of the annual returns. In other words, the managers are handsomely rewarded for taking extra risks with your money. If the risks don't pay off, the hedge fund manager isn't going to make up your losses.

In his book on investing, *Winning the Loser's Game*, my friend and colleague Charles Ellis has a pithy bit of advice about investment novelties:

> Don't invest in new or "interesting" investments. They are all too often designed to be *sold to* investors, not to be *owned* by investors. (When the novice fisherman expressed wonderment that fish would actually go for the gaudily decorated lures offered at the bait shop, the proprietor's laconic reply was, "We don't sell them lures to fish.")[3]

That's something that newspeople and news consumers would do well to remember. Beware of investment fads. Unless you're someone who equates success in life with joining in whatever is making headlines at the moment, fads are not worth the risk.

The bottom line for you as an investor in a mass-media environment is that the media are both your friend and your foe. Good information about investing will help you to become a better investor, but bad information can lead you to make big mistakes. You will need to assess which stuff to heed and which stuff to tune out.

---

[3]Charles Ellis, *Winning the Loser's Game: Timeless Strategies for Successful Investing*, Fourth Edition (New York: McGraw-Hill, 2002), page 142.

In speeches and in casual conversations with investors, I often emphasize the importance of tuning out distractions by sharing a story about "the three best investors I know." People always expect me to name current mutual fund stars or legendary financiers, but the three best investors I know are my children. Like Tommy the pinball wizard, my children participate in the markets with minimum distractions. My wife and I have put money aside for their college educations over the years. Frankly, the children have no idea that the accounts are set up for them.

As a result, they've never been subject to euphoria during bull runs, nor have they felt despair during bear markets. But the fact of the matter is that their college investment programs have been very successful anyway. I can assure you that their preferred newscast is ESPN Sports Center, and it will never be replaced by CNBC.

In a Nutshell

With so much news and information about the financial markets surrounding us, trying to be an informed investor is a bit like trying to drink from a fire hose. You probably can't tune out all the noise, so apply a few caveats:

- **Be selective about what you read and listen to.** You'll drive yourself crazy, and perhaps do some real damage to your financial program, if you pay too much attention to financial news.

- **Trust the truths you already know.** Diversification and balance pay off in the long run. Cost matters. Buy-and-hold works.

- **Tune out information and advice that is irrelevant to you.** Never believe market predictions. Recognize that many experts have agendas—and they may not be in sync with yours.

- **Beware of hype.** Whether the hoopla focuses on a money manager who seems to have a golden touch or on a "new new thing" in investing, it always pays to be skeptical.

chapter twenty-two
REGRETS? I'VE HAD A FEW

One of the toughest challenges in investing is dealing with our own mistakes. To prove the point that investors need to be able to acknowledge their missteps, I'll share a couple of mine with you.

Many years ago, my wife and her friends started an investment club. They were interested in assembling a portfolio of individual stocks, not mutual funds, and they sought some advice from me and another friend who is now a very successful fund manager.

The two of us recommended a stock called Dome Petroleum that was selling at $1 a share at the time. In our collective wisdom, we thought, how much can it lose? (If you don't remember that the answer to this question is "All of it," go back and read Chapter 17.) So the investment club bought Dome Petroleum as its pick for the month. And sure enough, the members lost all of their investment. Ugh!

The second mistake I'll share was more recent. My wife and I had established a donor-advised charitable endowment fund. Since we intended this as a very-long-term endeavor, we decided the fund's investments should be placed entirely in stocks instead of in a balanced fund with a mix of stocks and bonds. It was the fall of 2000, six months into the bear market.

Despite my personal misgivings about the high valuation of the stock market, my understanding of the principle of dollar-cost averaging, and my appreciation for prudence and planning, I ignored my own rules and moved a largish lump sum from a balanced fund into a stock fund at the end of September 2000.

If I had taken the sensible approach, I would have used dollar-cost averaging and moved the money into the stock fund gradually over the course of a year. In fact, I always employ dollar-cost averaging with my investments. But this time I didn't, because I was too distracted by other things. As a result, the account is worth thousands of dollars less today than it would have been otherwise. It was an expensive reminder about discipline.

If you've read this book from front to back, you can easily identify my regrets in these two instances. Here are the lessons I overlooked:

1. Just because something has a low price doesn't mean it's a good value.

2. Dollar-cost averaging is a wise strategy to use when you decide to move a sizable chunk of assets, because you won't worry that you picked the wrong day to make the transaction.

Investment mistakes can serve you well as long as you draw the right lessons from them. This concept may seem glaringly obvious, but believe it or not, many investors don't learn from their mistakes.

Ever since I was in high school, I have coached kids' sports as an avocation. One thing I've told the kids over and over through the years is: "That's why we practice." Somebody drops a pass—"That's why we practice." Somebody runs the wrong way on a play—"That's why we practice." Athletes practice to learn from their mistakes and to build a cumulative knowledge base. The hope is that they'll leave most of their mistakes on the practice field, reducing the errors that they make when it's time to keep score.

From an investment standpoint, mistakes—and regrets—serve the same purpose. You may find it hard to tune out that nagging little voice in the back of your head that calls you a fool for this investment decision or that one. In fact, there's little you can do about the mistakes from the past except take lessons from them. Learn to think of your investment mistakes as *sunk costs*—losses that cannot be altered by current or future actions. You can't change history.

Here's an example. When something that you bought for $20 a share is selling for $10, the market is telling you that, as of today, the market's best assessment of the value of that asset is $10 a share. The fact that the price used to be $20 is irrelevant. There may be tax benefits in your loss, but from an investment standpoint, the $10 decline is a sunk cost. Your challenge is to decide whether you want to continue to own that asset at the new price of $10 a share. The answer may well be yes if you believe that, relative to other opportunities, this is still a good investment. But don't hang on to it simply to get back to even. And don't pick on yourself about it—call it "practice" and look to the future.

Always remember, too, that short-term losses—or gains, for that matter—are irrelevant if you are investing for the long term. Interim changes in your portfolio aren't real—they exist only on paper until you sell out. If you're not planning to tap into those assets soon, a decline isn't a loss. Neither is a gain on paper an actual gain.

During the past year or so—a very difficult time in the stock market—I've talked with many, many investors about lessons they learned from the bear market that commenced in March 2000. Interestingly, investors in very similar circumstances sometimes have entirely different reactions.

For example, some folks who were heavily invested in stocks say they've learned they can't tolerate downturns as well as they'd thought. I'd say that is a valuable lesson, which ought to serve them well in the years ahead. But others in the same situation say that their painful losses have taught them not to own stocks at all—that stocks are just too risky. In my opinion, these investors are likely to have a new set of regrets down the road a few years.

Others who are ruing the damage to their account balances say they've learned to monitor the news so that "next time, I'll get out of stocks when the market starts to drop." I wish that they were right about market-timing, and that it were possible to know when to get in and out of the markets. But the markets are just not that easy to figure out, I'm afraid.

Still other folks say they've learned, or re-learned, the value of balance and diversification—how these simple strategies make it easier to endure the tough times. That lesson is a keeper, a lesson to hold on to for life.

My own belief is that you should accept your mistakes and learn from them, then get over them. Move on with a sense of optimism and confidence.

I hope that this book has helped you to build a sense of trust in your ability to invest wisely and fruitfully, and to recover from those occasional but inevitable mistakes. I wish you the very best success with your investment program, and I hope you accomplish your objectives and then some, with only a few regrets along the way.

In a Nutshell

You're sure to make some mistakes at some point in your career as an investor. Accept them and move on. Once you've internalized the fundamental principles that we've discussed throughout this book, you'll understand how to invest confidently and successfully. I've boiled them down into this 10-point list:

1. **Develop a financial game plan.** Identify your financial objectives and design an investment program that will enable you to reach those objectives. Be conservative when you project how fast your money will grow.

2. **Become a disciplined saver.** Learn to live below your means and make a habit of putting money away. If you aren't naturally disposed toward saving money, find ways to trick yourself into doing it.

3. **Start investing early, and keep it up.** Make time your ally, and start setting aside money for your goals as soon as possible. Keep plugging away toward

your objectives, contributing fixed amounts on a regular schedule in good markets and in bad.

4. **Invest with balance and diversification.** For balance, invest across at least two of the three major asset classes: stocks, bonds, and cash investments. For diversification, make sure you are not overly concentrated in any single company, industry, or category of issuer. For an individual, mutual funds are the simplest, most effective vehicle for accomplishing both of these strategies.

5. **Control your costs.** Choose no-load funds that have low expense ratios. The average mutual fund expense ratio was 1.34% in 2001, but there are funds that charge much less. While you watch your costs, don't forget to minimize the tax bite.

6. **Manage risk prudently.** Create a portfolio that will allow you to sleep at night. If you design it to suit your objectives, time horizon, risk tolerance, and financial situation, you should be able to endure volatile times in the markets without feeling that you have to make drastic changes in your investments.

7. **Be a buy-and-hold investor.** Investors who frequently buy and sell securities or mutual funds rarely succeed over the long term. A surer path to long-term success is to set up a sensible portfolio and stick to it through thick and thin.

8. **Avoid fads and "can't-miss" opportunities.** You're sure to encounter people promoting alluring new investment opportunities in individual securities or narrow market sectors. Don't be tempted to abandon your diversified strategy— you can undo all the good things you've accomplished if you make mistakes like these.

9. **Tune out distractions.** Resist the barrage of news and information about the daily movements of the markets. Much of this information is irrelevant to your investment objectives as a long-term, buy-and-hold investor. The danger is that it can tempt you to make investment moves that aren't in your best long-term interests.

10. **Maintain a long-term perspective.** There will be good times and challenging times during your investment career. When times are good, be grateful, not greedy. When times are bad, be patient. Remaining focused on your long-term objectives is a winning strategy for all seasons.

A GUIDE TO STOCK AND BOND FUNDS

There are many different kinds of stock and bond funds. You don't need to hold all of them in your portfolio to be successful. But because you're likely to encounter the terms as you learn more about investing, I've included information here to supplement the discussion of funds in Chapter 9.

Stock Funds—When Your Goal Is to Grow Your Capital

The discussion of stock funds in Chapter 9 took a high-level look at how U.S. stock funds can be classified according to the size of the companies they invest in and whether they are growth- or value-oriented. Here, I'll amplify on growth and value a little more, and then offer some guidance on other types of stock funds.

The U.S. stock market consists of roughly 5,800 individual stocks—representing 5,800 different companies that, as a group, are involved in just about every type of business imaginable. Yet just three labels—*growth*, *value*, and *blend*—are used to categorize the vast majority of these stocks and the thousands of funds that invest in them. But just as three labels could never adequately describe 5,800 individual human beings, the three stock labels have their limitations in describing mutual funds and individual securities.

For mutual fund investors, the key thing to know about growth and value stocks is that you want exposure to both types. Their long-term results have been similar, but there can be long stretches when one group dominates and the other lags far behind. In the late 1990s, for example, growth stocks ruled. Since then, value stocks have done much better than growth issues. If you lean heavily toward either category, you'll risk badly underperforming the overall market from time to time.

Growth and Value Are in the Eyes of the Beholder

The terms *growth* and *value* can be confusing in this context because, obviously, *all* investors—amateur and professional alike—want to own stocks that will grow and that represent good value. Another difficulty is that there is no single measure that determines whether a stock or mutual fund should have a growth or value label. (Indeed, the term *blend* is used to describe mutual funds that hold stocks with both growth and value characteristics.)

The classic value investor is a bargain-hunter who is leery of paying high prices for growth potential. A great example was John Neff, who retired in 1995 after more than 30 distinguished years as manager of Vanguard Windsor Fund. John liked to look for "woebegone" stocks that had, for one reason or another, fallen out of favor among many investors. Of course, some of these stocks had low prices for a good reason—they were crummy companies. But other stocks, Neff believed, were beaten down because the market was overreacting to problems that would prove to be temporary. Those were the stocks he wanted to buy. Value investors also often look for relatively high dividend yields—it is nice to be able to collect some cash while you wait for a company or stock to rebound.

Growth investors, on the other hand, typically are looking for companies with prospects for rapid growth in sales or earnings. Classic growth stocks generally have some special edge over competitors—patents, or processes, or a brand with unique appeal—that allow them to boost sales volumes or prices to generate higher profits. Some growth stocks are clustered in industries that depend on new technologies or new products. Others are in traditional businesses, like retailing or restaurants, but are generating fast growth from a new concept. Because fast-growing companies usually need to reinvest all the earnings they generate, growth stocks tend to pay little or nothing in dividends.

How can you distinguish a growth stock from a value stock? The stock price alone won't tell you—it's meaningless without a yardstick. One common method, as I mentioned in Chapter 9, is simply to compare the stock price to various basic business measures (or *fundamentals*, as the lingo goes). Growth stocks are those whose prices are high compared with these measures, and value stocks are those whose prices are low in the same regard. Some commonly used measures are earnings, book value, dividends, cash flow, and sales or revenue.

In general, the higher the ratio of prices to earnings, book value, or other measures, the higher are the market expectations for a company's future prospects.

Lower ratios usually indicate that the market does not expect rapid growth from a company. Mutual funds are categorized as growth, value, or blend depending on the average valuations of the stocks they hold at a point in time.

For those who want to delve further, a brief description of the key measures follows.

- **Earnings.** Companies are in business to make money, of course. Each share of stock represents part ownership in a company's net profits, or earnings. So a key measure of a stock's valuation is the price/earnings (P/E) ratio—the price of a share of stock divided by the earnings per share. A stock with a share price of $10 and annual earnings of 50 cents a share has a P/E of 20 ($10 divided by $0.50). As an investor, you know the price for certain. But earnings are a trickier concept, even when there's no question about the accuracy of a company's accounting. The P/E ratio can be based on the profits reported for the past 12 months (known as *trailing earnings*) or on the expected earnings for the next year (known as *forward earnings*). Obviously, forecasts of future earnings have to be taken with a grain of salt. The key thing is to make sure, when comparing the P/E ratios of stocks or the average P/E ratios of stock funds, that you're using the same period and the same basis (trailing or forward) for earnings. When a company has losses instead of earnings, investors may use estimates of future earnings or a base level of past earnings to conjure up a P/E.

- **Book value.** This is a company's net worth—what is left when you subtract a company's debts, or liabilities, from its assets. The stock price is compared with the per-share book value to create the price/book (P/B) ratio. The P/B ratio can be useful in comparing companies within the same industry, but it is not as useful in comparing, say, a computer software company with an auto manufacturer.

- **Dividends.** There is such a thing as a price/dividend ratio, but that's not what investors usually focus on when comparing stocks. Instead, they look at the *dividend yield*—the annualized rate of dividends paid by a stock, divided by its price. A stock priced at $10 a share and paying 20 cents a share in dividends over a year would have a dividend yield of 2% ($0.20 divided by $10). You can flip this ratio around to come up with a price/dividend ratio (it would be 50 in our example—the $10 stock price divided by the $0.20 dividend). As a valuation measure, dividends have the virtue of being real money that an investor gets from her stock—not just an accounting measure. But don't focus solely on dividend yields; a high yield may simply mean that the stock price has fallen because investors believe that the company's future earnings are in doubt.

- **Cash flow.** *Cash flow* is another accounting term. Definitions vary, but the idea is to reflect the actual cash flowing into and out of a company. So expenses such as depreciation, which does not represent actual dollars being paid out, are added back into net income to obtain a figure for cash flow. Measures of cash flow can be helpful in analyzing the value of a fast-growing company. But they also can be misused to justify overly high prices for stocks.

- **Sales per share.** This is simply a company's sales, or revenue, divided by the number of shares outstanding. It can be useful in comparing companies within the same industry. However, high sales/share figures by themselves don't mean a company will earn high profits.

Other Kinds of Stock Funds

There are special kinds of stock funds that may make sense for your portfolio, but you should consider their different characteristics and risks before investing your money.

International Funds.   These funds invest in the stocks of markets outside the United States, allowing you to gain exposure to the money-making opportunities in the rest of the world. Categories of international funds include:

- **Emerging-markets funds**, which invest in companies based in developing nations or in countries that have switched to a capitalist economic system from a socialist system.

- **Regional funds**, which emphasize stocks from one part of the world, such as Southeast Asia, Latin America, Africa, or Europe.

- **Single-country funds**, which invest in securities of only one country. Frankly, investing in a single foreign market is generally far too risky for most people.

- **Global funds**, which invest both in the U.S. stock market and in international markets.

International stocks carry additional risks, including political risk and currency risk. Therefore, I'd suggest that you limit your holdings of international stock funds to 10% or 20% of your long-term allocation to stocks.

Sector Funds.   These funds invest in a single industry or economic sector, such as real estate, utilities, health care, technology, or precious metals. Because they are so concentrated, their returns tend to be especially volatile, and therefore they're not suitable as core holdings in a long-term portfolio. Use sector funds only in moderation, and only if you have carefully researched the risks.

Bear in mind that there are always one or two sectors doing much better than the stock market as a whole. You probably will feel tempted to invest in these, because when a particular sector is in favor, its returns will be excellent. But industry sectors invariably cool off—and, unfortunately, it's usually soon after investors begin to pour large sums into sector funds!

Convertible Securities Funds. These funds invest in hybrid corporate securities that have aspects of both bonds and stocks. Convertibles are like bonds in that they pay a stated interest rate, but they can be swapped, or *converted*, into the company's common stock at a certain share price. If the issuing company's stock price rises substantially, the holder of a convertible can decide to exchange it for shares of stock, sell them, and make a profit. Yes, there is a trade-off for this opportunity—the interest paid on the convertible bond is lower than the issuing company would pay on a regular bond. Convertibles often perform like a cross between stocks and bonds—with volatility and long-term returns somewhere in between those of stocks and bonds.

Bond Funds—A Source of Income and a Way to Achieve Balance

Bond funds invest in the debt securities issued by the U.S. government, government agencies, corporations, or municipalities. You can choose among funds that focus on one, several, or most of these issuers. You'll get the widest diversification by investing in a broad bond index fund, but there can be good reasons to devote a part of your bond portfolio to a specific type of issue. In Chapter 9, I focused primarily on funds that invest in Treasury bonds or high-quality corporate bonds. There are three other types of bond funds that are definitely worth knowing about:

GNMA ("Ginnie Mae") Funds. Ginnie Mae certificates, a type of mortgage-backed security, are named for the company that issues them: the Government National Mortgage Association, or GNMA. A Ginnie Mae certificate represents part ownership in a pool of mortgage loans. Earnings come from the monthly payments that homeowners make on their mortgages. These payments (as most of us homeowners know) include both interest on the mortgage loan and some repayment of principal.

What if somebody defaults on one of the mortgage loans in the pool? It's no problem for Ginnie Mae investors, because the U.S. government guarantees the loan payments. That's why these securities are popular: They offer both unimpeachable credit quality and higher interest income than comparable U.S. Treasury securities.

Of course, there is a trade-off: Ginnie Maes pay higher interest because they're subject to one risk you don't have with Treasury bonds. That is *prepayment risk*—the chance that homeowners will pay off their mortgage loans early and return principal to the mortgage pool faster than expected. When interest rates fall substantially, millions of people refinance their old home loans with new loans at lower interest rates (you may well have done this yourself). As the old loans are paid off, Ginnie Mae pools get their principal back and can reinvest it only at the new, lower prevailing interest rates.

The upshot is that Ginnie Mae securities and Ginnie Mae funds tend not to perform as well as other bond funds when interest rates are falling. Yet that's just when many investors have tended to flock to GNMA funds, attracted by their relatively high stated yields. Here's what to watch out for: Falling interest rates bring the prepayment risk to life; GNMA yields will drop as soon as people start refinancing their home loans.

Prepayment risk doesn't make Ginnie Maes a bad investment. They pay higher yields specifically to compensate for that risk over the long term. It's just important to understand the trade-off.

High-Yield ("Junk") Bonds.   To understand junk bonds, you need to remember that bond issuers and bond investors have conflicting motives. The issuer wants to pay the lowest interest rate possible (just as you do when you borrow money for a house). The investor, of course, wants to earn the highest rate, which is why high-yield bonds get people's attention. But there is a reason the issuers of these bonds have to pay higher yields: The companies (or municipalities) issuing them are believed to have financial weaknesses that make these bonds extra-risky.

These weaknesses are flagged by agencies like Moody's and Standard & Poor's that conduct research to evaluate the creditworthiness of bond issuers. The agencies give "below investment-grade" credit ratings to the risky issuers, alerting prospective investors that there is some danger of a default that would make the bonds worth little or nothing. This is why they are called junk bonds. Low credit ratings can be issued to companies because they are unprofitable or because they face big payments from lawsuits or because they have so much debt that their future profitability is in question. There are a variety of junk ratings to identify degrees of risk, ranging from companies whose problems seem relatively mild to those skirting bankruptcy.

High-yield bonds tend to be much more volatile than investment-grade bonds. In fact, at times high-yield issues trade more like stocks than like bonds. For example, when the economy is headed into a recession, the prices of the highest-quality bonds typically rise and interest rates fall, because investors are worrying less about inflation and starting to prize the guaranteed income offered by high-quality bonds. But a recession often means trouble for the prices of stocks and high-yield bonds, because investors figure that a shrinking economy will result in shrinking corporate profits—making it harder for companies to meet the interest payments on their bonds.

When you evaluate high-yield bonds, it is best to assume that some of those bonds will default and their prices will plummet or even go to zero. Default rates on high-yield bonds vary widely from year to year. Although default rates have averaged just under 4% a year for the past 20 years, in 2001 the default rate exceeded 9%, according to Moody's. When you look at a bond fund's yield, mentally adjust it to account for that risk.

If you want to invest in high-yield bonds, use a well-diversified mutual fund. Don't buy individual high-yield bonds—the loss you could suffer if one of them defaulted is simply too great to be worth the risk. You're really better off using a fund and letting an experienced professional select the bonds. Just make sure the fund is very broadly diversified, so problems with a few companies or a single industry sector don't cause you huge losses. Consider the risks when deciding how big a place junk bonds should have in your portfolio.

Inflation-Protected Bonds. In 1997, the U.S. Treasury began to issue inflation-indexed bonds and notes. These securities (nicknamed *TIPS*, for "Treasury inflation-protected securities") are like regular bonds in some respects—they pay a stated interest rate on the principal of the bond, and the bond matures on a particular date in the future.

But there's a big difference: The Treasury adjusts the principal value of these bonds for inflation. Suppose, for example, that the Treasury has issued a $10,000 inflation-indexed bond with a coupon rate of 3%. The interest payment would be $300. But if consumer prices rose by 4% in the year after the bond was issued, the Treasury would increase the value of the bond's principal by 4% to $10,400. Then the 3% coupon rate, applied to the new, larger principal, would generate $312 in income.

TIPS can be bought directly from the Treasury, through brokerage firms, or in mutual funds that hold the securities. When evaluating TIPS, or funds holding them, you'll see that their stated yields are lower than yields on regular bonds. That's because TIPS yields don't reflect any assumptions about inflation, whereas the yields of other bonds do. (If that's not clear, imagine that somebody wants to sell you a 20-year bond paying 2.5% interest. Not very inviting, is it? Part of the reason is that you intuitively fear that your earnings on the bond would be outrun by inflation over two decades. The bond issuer is going to have to offer you more—enough to make you feel that you'll come out ahead of inflation—or no sale.)

The difference between yields on TIPS and those on conventional Treasury bonds of the same maturity can be considered the "break-even" inflation rate. If future inflation is higher than the break-even rate, the inflation-adjusted securities should perform better than the conventional bonds. And vice versa.

TIPS, or a low-cost mutual fund investing in TIPS, can be a sensible addition to your retirement portfolio—as much as 25% to 50% of your allocation to bonds. Think of them as insurance against the damage that inflation can do to your portfolio. However, TIPS are probably better held in a tax-sheltered account, such as an IRA or 401(k) plan. The reason is the peculiar way in which these bonds are taxed. When inflation-protected bonds are held in regular, taxable accounts, the IRS considers the inflation adjustment to principal as current taxable income—even though the Treasury doesn't pay that adjustment until the bond matures.

appendix b
SOME INDUSTRY JARGON

As you embark on your investment program, you are sure to encounter some unfamiliar terminology. I've provided definitions of the most common industry jargon to ease your way.

Active management

An investment strategy that tries to beat the returns of the financial markets. Active managers rely on research, market forecasts, and their own judgment and experience in making investment decisions. You choose active managers in the hopes of outpacing the market. The opposite of active management is passive management.

Aggressive growth fund

A mutual fund that seeks to provide maximum long-term capital growth by investing primarily in the stocks of smaller companies or narrow market segments. Dividend income is incidental. In investing, *aggressive* is a code word for risky.

Asset allocation

The process of deciding how your investment dollars will be split among various classes of financial assets, such as stocks, bonds, and cash investments. Spend a lot of time on this decision—it is the most important one you will make.

Asset allocation fund

A type of balanced mutual fund whose investment adviser might change the fund's mix of stocks, bonds, or cash investments in an effort to find the best combination of risk and potential return. With this type of fund, you are relying on a professional to choose your mix. Recognize that at any given time, the fund's mix may not suit your needs.

Asset classes

Major categories of financial assets, or securities. The three primary classes are common stocks, bonds, and cash investments. There are other, more exotic asset classes, but most folks can do just fine with a mix of these.

Back-end load

A sales commission paid when the investor sells mutual fund shares. May also be called a *contingent deferred sales charge*. Some funds gradually phase out back-end loads for investors who stay in a fund for several years. Avoid back-end loads like the plague.

Balanced fund

A mutual fund that invests in more than one type of financial asset (stocks, bonds, and, in some cases, cash investments). These might not be sexy, but they have demonstrated their value over time.

Bonds

An IOU issued by corporations, governments, or government agencies. The issuer makes regular interest payments on the bond and promises to pay back your "loan" at a specified point in the future, called the maturity date. The regular interest payments from bonds make them a key part of retirees' portfolios and can be comforting to any investor when the stock market is in a slump.

Capital gains distribution

A fund's payment to mutual fund shareholders of gains (profits) realized on the sale of securities. Capital gains are distributed on a "net" basis, after the fund subtracts any capital losses for the year. When gains exceed losses, you—the fund investor—owe taxes on your share of the gain, unless those shares are held in a tax-sheltered account such as an IRA or 401(k) plan. (Yes, you owe taxes even if you didn't sell *your* shares.) When losses exceed gains for a year, the fund carries the difference forward to offset future gains.

Cash investments

Investments in interest-bearing bank deposits, money market instruments, and U.S. Treasury bills or notes. These are conservative short-term investments, typically with maturities of 90 days or less. They are terrific for near-term needs but won't do much to advance you toward your long-term goals, such as retirement.

Compounding

The growth that you get if you reinvest your investment income and capital gains instead of taking the cash. You earn money on your investment, then you earn money on your original investment plus the amount you earned. It might be the most powerful force in investing. Take advantage of it.

Contingent deferred sales charge

See *back-end load*. (Pay special attention to the part about avoiding them like the plague.)

Credit risk

The chance that the issuer of a bond fails to pay interest or to repay the original principal on time—or at all. Every bond is subject to credit risk, but some issuers are extremely safe (U.S. Treasury and government agencies), some are safe (large, financially sound companies with good track records), and some can be downright dangerous (small, young companies with shaky finances). The greater the credit risk, the higher the interest rate, or yield, a bond should pay.

Diversification

Spreading your money among different classes of financial assets and among the securities of many issuers. It's an investor's best friend. Diversifying your investments helps to smooth out volatility in your portfolio so you can sleep better.

Dividend

A mutual fund's payment of income to shareholders from interest or dividends generated by the fund's investments. Also, cash payments to owners of common stock, paid out of a company's profits.

Dollar-cost averaging

Investing equal amounts of money at regular intervals on an ongoing basis. This technique reduces risk of loss from a sudden market downturn and reduces the average cost of shares over time, since you acquire more shares when prices are lower and fewer shares when prices are higher. It also requires a strong stomach because for dollar-cost averaging to work, you must continue to invest money when it's no fun at all. The reward for your diligence, though, can be significant.

Duration

A way to gauge how much the price of a bond or bond fund will go up or down when interest rates fluctuate. A fund with an average duration of 10 years will see its price drop about 10% with every 1 percentage point increase in market interest rates; the price would rise 10% if interest rates fell 1 percentage point. A bond fund with a duration of 2 years would see its share price rise or fall by about 2% in response to a 1 percentage point decrease or increase in interest rates. In short, the longer the duration, the bigger the price change for a bond fund or bond when interest rates rise or fall.

Education Savings Account

A tax-deferred investment for helping pay education costs. Contributions are taxed but earnings are not, as long as they're used for education expenses. Annual contributions to an ESA are capped at a fairly low level—a maximum of $2,000—but these accounts can help build up a child's education savings.

Expense ratio

The percentage of a fund's average net assets—*your* money—used to pay annual fund expenses. The expense ratio takes into account costs such as management fees, legal and administrative outlays, and any 12b-1 marketing fees. You should care about expenses because they directly reduce the return you receive. It's as simple as that.

Front-end load

A sales commission, or load, that you pay when you buy shares of a mutual fund. For example, if you invest $3,000 in a fund with a front-end load of 4%, you'll start off with an account balance of $2,880. Think hard before you pay a load to buy a fund. There are plenty of no-load funds to choose from.

Growth fund

A mutual fund that emphasizes stocks of companies that are believed to offer above-average prospects for appreciation due to their strong potential for growth in earnings and sales. Growth stocks tend to offer relatively low dividend yields, because these companies prefer to reinvest earnings in research and development rather than paying them out to investors. Growth is one of the two main investing "styles." The other is *value*. A well-diversified investor has exposure to both.

High-yield bond

A bond (or an IOU) issued by a company or a government with a low credit rating. Also known as *junk bonds*. High-yield bonds exemplify a key trade-off in investing: Higher-risk investments offer the potential for greater reward. Companies with iffy prospects must pay higher rates of interest in order to entice investors to lend them money. It's up to you to decide whether the extra yield is worth the extra risk.

Income

Interest and dividends earned on securities held by a mutual fund. These earnings are paid to fund shareholders in the form of income dividends. The fund shareholders then owe taxes on this income unless the fund is held in a tax-sheltered account such as an IRA or 401(k).

Income risk

The possibility that the income stream you're receiving from a mutual fund or other investment will decline. This risk is most acute with money market funds and other short-term investments. Here's how it goes: Interest rates fall, short-term investments quickly reflect the new rates, and the income you were getting from your money market fund drops.

Index

A statistical benchmark that's used to measure the performance of the stock or bond markets—or particular parts of these markets. Indexes are standards against which investors can measure the performance of their investment portfolios. (Be sure to compare your fund's performance with a *relevant* index.)

Index fund

A mutual fund that seeks to track the performance of a market benchmark, or index. Indexing is a very cost-effective investment strategy, so index funds should have a place in your investment program.

Individual retirement account (IRA)

A tax-advantaged way to save for retirement. If you have earned income from a job, you can put money in these accounts for yourself and for your spouse, if the spouse does not work outside the home. Investment earnings within a *traditional IRA* are not taxed until withdrawn from the account, and the money you put into the account can be deducted from taxes, if you qualify under the rules. With a *Roth IRA*, you don't get an upfront tax deduction, but the earnings on the account may be withdrawn tax-free (under certain conditions, of course). Withdrawals from an IRA made before age 59-1/2 may be subject to a 10% federal penalty tax.

Inflation

A general rise in the prices of goods and services. This is a big concern for investors—especially those with long-term goals—because the amount you're investing and earning will lose purchasing power as inflation rises. The higher the rate of inflation, the more you'll have to invest or earn to stay ahead. Over decades, inflation can end up confiscating a significant chunk of your assets.

Inflation-protected securities

A special type of bonds whose principal value changes to reflect changes in the level of consumer prices. These sound more complex than they actually are. The key thing to know is that the principal value of the bonds goes up with inflation, so they can be a good addition to your investment program.

Interest rate risk

The risk that a bond or bond fund will decline in price because of a rise in market interest rates. Prices move in the opposite direction from interest rates. If you own a bond that pays 5% in annual interest and new bonds coming onto the market pay 6%, the market value of your bond would fall to reflect the fact that higher-yielding bonds are available.

Investment adviser

An individual or organization that manages a mutual fund portfolio and makes day-to-day decisions regarding what securities to buy or sell. Also called a *fund manager*.

Investment horizon

The length of time you expect to keep a sum of money invested. Many of your financial decisions will hinge on the answer to the question: When will you need the money?

Investment objective

A mutual fund's goal. Stock funds tend to pursue long-term capital appreciation, bond funds typically seek high current income or tax-exempt income, and money market funds aim to preserve your principal while earning you some money along the way. Make sure that you know the objective of each fund that you own and that you've thought about how it can help you reach *your* goal.

Load fund

A mutual fund that charges a sales commission, or load. These commissions can be as high as 8.5% of the amount you invest. Why would you invest in a load fund? Good question.

Low-load fund

A mutual fund that charges a sales commission equal to 3% or less of the amount invested. A low load is still a load. And it still doesn't make sense to pay it.

Management fee

The fee paid by a mutual fund to its investment adviser. The fee is based on a percentage of assets, and it may vary depending on how the fund performs relative to a market benchmark. This fee is part of a fund's expenses, which are taken out before you earn anything from the fund.

Market capitalization

What a company is worth in the stock market. Market capitalization equals a stock's share price multiplied by the number of shares outstanding. For a stock mutual fund, market capitalization is determined by the market caps of the securities it owns. It's important to know whether a fund focuses on large-, mid-, or small-caps—or on companies of all sizes—so that you can build a diversified portfolio and so that you can be sure that you're comparing your fund's performance against a relevant benchmark or competitive group.

Market risk

The possibility that an investment will fall in value because of a general decline in financial markets. This is one risk you can't avoid, no matter how much you diversify. When the broad stock market slumps, so will a well-diversified stock portfolio.

Money market fund

A mutual fund that seeks to maintain a stable share price and to earn current income by investing in interest-bearing instruments with short-term maturities (usually 90 days or less). Money funds are not insured by the federal government, but if you put $1 into the fund, you can reasonably expect to get $1 out, plus interest. Money funds are boring, but they are ideal for short-term investment goals and for the conservative portion of a long-term investment program.

Municipal bonds

See *tax-exempt bonds*.

Mutual fund

An investment company that pools money from investors and uses it to buy securities such as stocks, bonds, and money market instruments.

Net asset value (NAV)

The market value of a mutual fund's total assets, less its liabilities, divided by the number of shares outstanding. It is commonly known as a fund's share price.

No-load fund

A mutual fund that does not charge a commission on purchases or sales. Even a no-load fund has expenses, but there is no intermediary trying to make a profit when you buy or sell your shares.

Portfolio

For you, it's all the investments you own; for a fund, it's all the securities it holds. So, a fund's portfolio may be part of your portfolio (but not the other way around).

Principal

The amount of money you put into an investment. This term also refers to the face value of a bond and the amount still owed on a loan, like your home mortgage loan.

Prospectus

A legal document that provides detailed information about a mutual fund, including discussions of the fund's investment objectives and policies, risks, costs, past performance, and other useful information. See Chapter 9 for suggestions on what to look for in a prospectus. It's important to read the prospectus. Really.

Redemption fee

A fee that you may be charged for selling shares in certain funds. Some redemption fees are actually good for long-term investors—they're paid to the fund, not the management company, to compensate all fund shareholders for the costs of buying and selling securities and to discourage short-term traders. Don't confuse these with loads. (See *load fund*.)

Stocks

Securities that represent part ownership in a company. Each share of stock is a claim on a portion of the corporation's assets and profits, some of which may be paid out as dividends.

Tax-exempt bonds

Also known as municipal bonds. Typically, you won't pay federal income tax on interest you receive from an investment in bonds issued by municipal, county, and state governments and agencies. If you buy bonds issued by municipalities in the state where you live, you're off the hook on state and local income taxes, too.

Total return

The percentage change, over a given period, in the value of an investment, including any income paid on it. For a mutual fund, the total return consists of income dividends plus changes in the fund's net asset value, which fluctuates as the prices of the fund's holdings rise and fall. Total returns reported for a mutual fund take into account the effect of fund expenses and assume that income dividends or capital gains distributions are reinvested. This is the best measure of mutual fund performance over time.

Turnover rate

A measure of a mutual fund's trading activity, the turnover rate can affect a fund's tax efficiency. A turnover rate of 50% means that, during a year, a fund has sold and replaced securities with a value equal to 50% of its average net assets. Generally, the higher the turnover, the more likely it is that a fund will have capital gains to be paid out in distributions. And if you hold the fund in a regular, taxable account, you pay the tax bill on those profits. A fund's prospectus and its annual and semiannual reports will tell you its turnover rate, and you often can find out from the fund company's website as well.

Value fund

A mutual fund that emphasizes stocks of companies from which the market does not expect rapid growth in profits. Although value, like beauty, is in the eye of the beholder, value stocks typically have below-average prices when compared with such factors as earnings, book value, revenue, and dividends. Value is one of two main investing styles. The other is *growth*. A well-diversified investor has exposure to both.

Variable annuity

A tax-deferred investment that is much like a mutual fund, but with an insurance "wrapper." Investors in variable annuities typically are guaranteed that they'll receive at least the amount they invested, thanks to a contract that insures their initial investment. Money you make on variable annuities is not taxed until you take it out. However, because of the added cost of the insurance feature and because withdrawals are taxed as regular income, variable annuities aren't for everyone. But if you've made the maximum contributions to other types of tax-deferred investments, and you're in a high tax bracket, and you know you could hold the annuity for a long time, they can be worth a look.

Volatility

The fluctuations in market value or returns of a mutual fund or other security. The greater a fund's volatility, the wider the spread between its high and low prices. As an investor, you'll face volatility in stocks *and* bonds. As you develop your investment plan, consider your ability to ride it out without overreacting. Balance and diversification can help to mitigate volatility.

Yield

The rate at which an investment earns income, expressed as a percentage of the investment's current price. Yield is what you get paid for owning a fixed income investment such as a money market fund, a bond fund, or a bank certificate of deposit. Stocks that pay dividends to investors also have yields—the annual amount of the dividend, divided by the stock's price.

12b-1 fee

An annual fee that some mutual funds charge you to pay for their marketing and distribution activities. In other words, the fund company takes money from you to attract other investors. Not all funds charge 12b-1 fees; those that do must disclose them.

529 College Savings Plan

A state-sponsored, tax-free way to save for a child's education. These plans, which are typically administered by investment firms, allow people to invest money that can later be taken out to pay for tuition and other education expenses. As long as the investor follows certain rules, investments in a 529 Plan are free of federal taxes both while they are growing and when the money is withdrawn. (Contributions generally aren't tax-deductible.)

recommended reading
FOR BACKGROUND AND FOR FUN

As you learn more about investing, you may want to dip into some investment-related literature to broaden your perspective. Here are some titles that are among my favorites.

Barbarians at the Gate: The Fall of RJR Nabisco by Bryan Burrough and John Helyar.

> The story of greed and mismanagement in the leveraged buyout of RJR Nabisco, the biggest corporate takeover of the 1980s. This book will give you a good picture of Wall Street behind the scenes.

Buffett: The Making of an American Capitalist by Roger Lowenstein.

> A biography of Warren Buffett, the man who's been called America's greatest investor.

Devil Take the Hindmost: A History of Financial Speculation by Edward Chancellor.

> A very readable history of stock market speculation from the seventeenth century to the present day.

Extraordinary Popular Delusions & the Madness of Crowds by Charles MacKay.

> An investment classic, first published in 1841. It examines market manias of the past such as Tulipmania and the South Sea Bubble.

The Great Crash: 1929 by John Kenneth Galbraith.

A vivid and readable account of the worst stock market crash in U.S. history—useful background for anyone who wants to compare the speculative excesses of the 1990s with those of the 1920s.

Liar's Poker: Rising Through the Wreckage on Wall Street by Michael Lewis.

An insider's view of bond trading in the mid-1980s, written by a former bond salesman in the New York and London offices of Salomon Brothers. This is another great behind-the-scenes account—one that should make you leery of Wall Street sales pitches.

The Millionaire Next Door by Thomas J. Stanley and William D. Danko.

The real story on how to become wealthy in America. The authors discuss the seven common traits of those who have accumulated wealth. Surprise! One of the seven traits is living below your means.

The New New Thing: A Silicon Valley Story by Michael Lewis.

The story of entrepreneurism in the New Economy of the late 1990s, focusing on Jim Clark, the founder of Silicon Graphics and Netscape, who planned to revolutionize health care with an online business venture. This book will help you develop a healthy sense of skepticism about investment fads.

The Tipping Point: How Little Things Can Make a Big Difference by Malcolm Gladwell.

A fascinating book about social epidemics—how ideas, fads, and messages often spread like outbreaks of infectious disease once they reach a tipping point. This book will give you some insights about the spread of investment fads.

When Genius Failed: The Rise and Fall of Long-Term Capital Management by Roger Lowenstein.

The incredible story of the rise and fall of a famous hedge fund that was brought down by the hubris of the people behind it, including two Nobel Prize winners. The collapse of this one fund nearly brought down the global financial system in the 1990s.

The Winner's Curse: Paradoxes and Anomalies of Economic Life by Richard H. Thaler.

A look at the irrational things that people do when it comes to money—such as the sports fans who refuse to pay more than $200 for a Super Bowl ticket but won't sell the one they own for less than $400.

INDEX